The Birth of the Bill of Rights, 1776-1791

The Institute of
Early American History and Culture

IS SPONSORED JOINTLY BY THE
COLLEGE OF WILLIAM AND MARY
AND
COLONIAL WILLIAMSBURG
INCORPORATED

The Birth
of the
Bill of Rights
1776-1791

By ROBERT ALLEN RUTLAND

PUBLISHED FOR THE
Institute of Early American History and Culture
BY
THE UNIVERSITY OF NORTH CAROLINA PRESS
CHAPEL HILL

PREFACE

This book represents an effort to draw together in one volume the story of how Americans came to rely on legal guarantees for their personal freedom. The English common law, colonial charters, legislative enactments, and a variety of events in the thirteen colonies were the chief elements contributing to the rationale for a bill of rights. Throughout the research and writing it was obvious that no single man, no single occurrence, could be set apart for special distinction. The facts show that the Federal Bill of Rights and the antecedent state declarations of rights represented, more than anything else, the sum total of American experience and experimentation with civil liberty up to their adoption. It is worth noting that the Salem witchcraft trials and the adoption of the Federal Bill of Rights virtually opened and closed the 18th century; and these historical incidents indicate the tremendous American intellectual advancement during that stirring span of time.

While this is not a book "with a message," the author nevertheless hopes that the work will aid Americans in understanding the background of their Bill of Rights, and that they will thus regard more dearly the hard-earned rights bequeathed to them by the Revolutionary generation.

The assistance and encouragement of teachers and friends has been the sustaining force behind the book. Special acknowledgment must go to Robert E. Cushman of Cornell University and Aubrey C. Land of Vanderbilt University. Others who have generously offered advice and criticism include Paul Hardacre, Vanderbilt University; Mildred Throne, State Historical Society of Iowa; Stow Persons, State University of

Iowa; and Joseph A. Brandt and David G. Farrelly, University of California, Los Angeles.

The editors of the Institute of Early American History and Culture also deserve mention for their encouragement and assistance throughout the several revisions of the original manuscript. To all these, for their patience and their help, the author offers his deepest gratitude.

Robert Allen Rutland

Los Angeles
April 25, 1955

CONTENTS

The Birth of the Bill of Rights, 1776-1791

CHAPTER I

THE ENGLISH BEGINNINGS

REVOLTS HAVE distant repercussions. Ordinarily they are conceived to be efforts to effect sweeping changes in the existing social or political order. Nevertheless the American Revolution—certainly a revolt of huge significance in modern history—was promulgated as an attempt to give the people not something new, but that which they had formerly possessed. Thus the American Revolution had its seeds in the Puritan Revolt of English forebears, with the avowed goal of giving citizens the freedoms won a century earlier in the mother country.

Indeed, the Puritan Revolt furnished a philosophical basis for the American events of 1765 onward, and when the bills of rights were drafted during the American Revolution, the language and perhaps some of the spirit were borrowed from that earlier period.[1] Among their other accomplishments, the managers of the American Revolution were well-read in English constitutional history, and they therefore knew the historical background of their desired rights. When it came to the matter of personal freedom, there was general agreement as to what they wanted.

Long before the Revolution took place, however, those events were in motion which would make the bill of rights an integral part of the revolt. The English settlers on the Atlantic frontier in the seventeenth century brought with them the legal institutions of their homeland. Here they planted firmly, too, economic and religious ideas that gave them suffi-

---

[1] See Herbert W. Schneider, "Philosophical Differences Between the Constitution and the Bill of Rights," in Conyers Read, ed., *The Constitution Reconsidered* (New York, 1938), 147, 155.

cient zeal and tenacity to overcome the rigors of life in the new world. But it was the law which carried the promise of personal liberty—law dating before Magna Carta—"that palladium of our liberties," as the colonists themselves liked to say.

In the field of personal liberty the allusion to the Magna Carta of 1215 was on solid ground. That document, coupled with the common law, furnished the principal tenets for personal rights until the Puritan Revolution reinforced and somewhat enlarged the substantive rights of English freeholders. Significantly, the written guarantees in each case were produced in an effort to curb arbitrary power. Prior to the American Revolution they were set down by the colonists as reminders to their royal governors, or granted by proprietary interests, so that the freeborn rights of Englishmen were generally considered as applicable in America as they had been in England. In time, the English courts were called upon to make this clear, and Chief Justice Holt in 1694 declared that in the settlements overseas "all the laws in force in England are in force there." Attorney General West also attempted to make the laws of England follow the flag in 1720 with an opinion stating that the common law of England was carried to the colonies unless there was "some private Act to the contrary."[2] The point was by no means settled, however, and it became abundantly clear that when the American colonists cited Holt and West prior to 1775 they were thinking of those English laws which protected personal rights.

Certainly the laws of England included many safeguards for the private citizen of pre-revolutionary America. Every freeholder was guaranteed the sacred English right of the protection of his life, his liberty, and his property from arbitrary action. Foremost among these safeguards stood the writ of habeas corpus and trial by jury. Both had roots planted

[2] Quoted in St. George L. Sioussat, "The Theory of the Extension of English Statutes to the Plantations," in *Select Essays in Anglo-American Legal History* (Boston, 1907), I, 420.

earlier than 1215. Originally the writ of habeas corpus had been used by courts to bring persons whose presence or testimony was needed before the bench. For a time it was employed by judges of the King's Bench and Common Pleas in their attempts to establish supremacy over rival courts.[3] Under Charles I sheriffs, jailers, and other officials continued certain tactics of delay and evasion used in earlier reigns, thus causing Parliament to pass the first of several acts to delineate the power of the writ. Meant to serve as an effective check on arbitrary power, the writ was clearly established by Parliament in the late seventeenth century as a means of releasing a person unlawfully imprisoned.

Perhaps even further imbedded in the English consciousness of liberty under the law was the idea of trial by jury. The criminal jury is first mentioned in 1166 in the Assize of Clarendon, but the use of civil juries a century earlier has been established. In periods of crisis Englishmen were assured that "this great Jewel of Liberty, Trials by Juries . . . [has] no less than fifty-eight several times since the *Norman* Conquest, been established and confirmed by the legislative Power. . . ."[4] Most colonial lawyers were eager to believe such a statement and, in their lack of accurate historical knowledge, were unaware that it stretched the truth. Gradually the modern system of jury trial evolved and was refined to prevent the arbitrary confiscation of property, and to establish justice for the accused.

The right of an accused person to have the aid of learned counsel was recognized by the twelfth century. When brought to trial the person involved was permitted, as early as the reign of Henry I, to have friends counsel him; and the Statute of Merton (1236) conceded to every freeman the right to be

---

[3] William S. Holdsworth, *A History of English Law* (London, 1922-1952), I, 227-28.

[4] Henry Care, comp., *English Liberties, or the Free-born Subject's Inheritance* (Boston, 1721), 203. This work first appeared in England in 1680, went through four editions there before 1719, and was one of the handbooks of radical colonists.

represented by an attorney unless he was charged with a felony or treason.[5]

The English also highly regarded the prohibition against excessive fines and bails. In 1275 a clause in the first Statute of Westminster warned officers against extortion from prisoners. Another enactment in 1444 compelled sheriffs to release readily prisoners on bail unless their crime was of an extremely serious nature. When royal judges attempted to circumvent the writ of habeas corpus by fixing unusually large bails in Charles II's reign, Parliament soon sent up a protest that could not be disregarded.[6]

The exaltation of the prerogative by Charles II and James II eventually produced a reaction which undercut royal authority. Crown claims of the right to suspend laws, prosecution of petitioners, and martial law with all its attendant evils had been distressing signs that brought Parliament to submit the Petition of Right to Charles I in 1628. He had reluctantly agreed to the proposition that no freeman might lose his life, liberty, or property without due process of law; to end the illegal exactions and arbitrary commitments, and to halt the obnoxious practice of quartering troops and sailors on the populace. However, the Stuarts learned little and conveniently forgot what seemed bothersome. In 1672 Charles II suspended certain penal laws against nonconformists and recusants, and allowed Catholics to hold private services, before he was forced to acknowledge his error.[7] James II imitated his brother in 1687, and by his royal prerogative suspended penal laws "in matters ecclesiastical."[8] This was regarded as a direct blow at Protestantism and the rights of Englishmen which Parliament could not permit, and the Bill of Rights which soon

[5] Felix Rackow, "The Right to Counsel: English and American Precedents," *William and Mary Quarterly*, 3d ser., 11 (1954), 3-5.

[6] Statute of Westminster I, Chap. XXX; Holdsworth, *History of English Law*, IV, 526-27; *ibid.*, VI, 214, 232.

[7] Mark A. Thomson, *A Constitutional History of England, 1642-1801* (London, 1938), 91-92.

[8] Frederic W. Maitland, *The Constitutional History of England* (Cambridge, 1931), 305.

followed made the objection concrete: "The pretended power of suspending of laws, or the execution of laws by regal authority, without consent of parliament, is illegal."

Arbitrary power was the constant foe of freedom. A spirit of intolerance bred out of religious issues was the basis for press censorship in England long before the colonies were settled. When the printing industry was in its infancy, practically all books were religious works. Without complete freedom of religion, therefore, it was impossible to have a free press. Thus during the reign of Henry VIII a proclamation made the publishers and possessors of certain religious works with "divers heresies and erroneous opinions" liable to punishment.[9] Once the crown had established the right to censor one segment of the press, the whole field was open to official suppression. From the Star Chamber came a decree in 1586 which, in effect, limited printers to the publications of only the most innocuous sort of material. Noting the perverse spirit of the times in 1644, John Milton wrote his classic defense of a free press in the *Areopagitica,* which failed to win official tolerance despite his warning that "they who counsel ye to such a suppressing do as good as bid ye suppress yourselves." Surprisingly enough, Milton became an official censor himself in 1651. The Licensing Act of 1662 placed the English press under a strict code of control, creating a Surveyor of the Press who had the power to investigate and suppress unauthorized publications. Practical politics seem to have weaned Parliament away from press censorship, for attempts to renew the Act in 1695 were rejected. As the eighteenth century opened, newspapers were becoming more numerous, books on all sorts of subjects came from the presses, and arbitrary methods of suppression had been dropped.

John Lilburne ran afoul the authorities for his activities as a printer, but he is perhaps remembered more for his fight

[9] Carl Stephenson and Frederick G. Marcham, eds., *Sources of English Constitutional History* (New York, 1937), 387. See also Fredrick S. Siebert, *Freedom of the Press in England, 1476-1776* (Urbana, 1952), 48 *et seq.*

against self-incrimination than for a free press. He was taken before the Star Chamber in 1637, charged with printing and publishing seditious books. At his trial Lilburne said:

I am not willing to answer you to any more of these questions, because I see you go about by this Examination to ensnare me: for seeing the things for which I am imprisoned cannot be proved against me, you will get other matter out of my examination: and therefore if you will not ask me about the thing laid to my charge, I shall answer no more. . . . I think by the law of the land, that I may stand upon my just defence, and not answer to your interrogatories. . . .[10]

Indeed, the law of the land did favor Lilburne's argument, but the point had never been pressed too far for lack of solid evidence. In the sixteenth century, under Elizabeth and later under James, a holdover *ex officio* oath from the days of ecclesiastical courts permitted courts sometimes to "degenerate into a merely unlawful process of poking about in the speculation of finding something chargeable."[11] By the late 1500's there may have been a tendency to allow defendants a kind of privilege against self-incrimination, although Lilburne's case is the landmark. His defense was justified by an act of Parliament in 1641. By the end of Charles II's reign the point was beyond question.

These strides on behalf of personal freedom were made at a great turning point in English history. A long train of royal abuses was halted by the Puritan Revolution. The "radicals" of the period—the Levellers—wanted to make their liberties more secure by getting the constitution down on paper, where it had not been before, for all men to see. They failed in this attempt, but the English were at least ready to place considerable legislation in the statute books. By 1689 the crystallization of sentiment against arbitrary government brought the Toleration Act and Bill of Rights. As Lord

[10] 3 Cobbett's *State Trials* 1318. As the quotation indicates, Lilburne's assertion of the privilege against self-incrimination was not so sweeping as later interpretations of the principle.

[11] John H. Wigmore, "The Privilege Against Self-crimination: Its History," *Harvard Law Review*, 15 (1902), 617.

Macaulay noted, the Toleration Act solved a difficult problem by giving the people a large measure of religious concessions without creating further civil strife. Roman Catholics, of course, did not benefit from its provisions, which only legalized the worship of Protestant nonconformists. A wedge for further reform legislation had been entered, however, and the Bill of Rights shortly followed.

For Protestant England the Bill of Rights served to reinforce the common law and the statute law. This act of Parliament became the supreme law of the land, repeating and sanctifying the fundamental principles of English liberty as Englishmen then conceived them to be. Insofar as it condemned the arbitrary display of power of James II it was the forerunner of the Declaration of Independence. The Bill of Rights declared as unconstitutional the suspension of the acts of Parliament, the levying of taxes without the consent of Parliament, the maintenance of a standing army in time of peace, the interference with free elections, the infliction of cruel and unusual punishments, the exaction of excessive bails, and the denial of the right of petition. Protestants were assured of their right to bear arms.[12] When the American revolutionists came to draw up their own declarations of rights it was not the name of the English act alone which they borrowed. Some of the wording in the American bills of rights came from this enactment of 1689 *in toto*—as the clause "that excessive bail ought not to be required, nor excessive fines imposed, nor cruel and unusual punishments inflicted," which became so familiar to American drafting committees in the 1770's.

The Bill of Rights also dealt with the succession of English monarchs and declared William and Mary to be the lawful rulers of the realm. The sections on personal rights are the

[12] One able European scholar firmly maintained that this right, and the right of petition, were the only "individual rights" in the English Bill of Rights. See Georg Jellinek, *The Declaration of the Rights of Man and of Citizens*, Max Farrand, trans. (New York, 1901), 49.

real heart of the enactment, however, or at least that was the convenient view of the American revolutionaries.

Such were the statutory precedents for personal rights in England as her sons and daughters went about their business of building a thousand replicas of their homeland on the Atlantic seaboard in America. Added to these statutory laws, moreover, was the common law as interpreted by several great jurists. Sir Edward Coke had set down in his *Second Institutes* (1642) a series of common law rights that protected the freeman's life and liberty—due process of law, habeas corpus, and an admonition "that no man ought to be imprisoned, but for some certain cause: and . . . cause must be shewed; for otherwise how can the Court take order therein according to the Law?"[13] The common law also offered accused persons the expectation that they would readily be "tried in the county where the fact is committed."[14] Double jeopardy for the accused was forbidden, as Blackstone informed generations of English lawyers, for in common law courts "the pleas of *auterfoits acquit,* or a former acquittal, is grounded on this universal maxim . . . that no man is to be brought into jeopardy of his life, more than once, for the same offence."[15]

All of these safeguards for the individual, some of them effective before American settlement began and some after, were limited in scope. Freedom of speech, for example, was not guaranteed to the Englishman. Chief Justice Holt declared in 1704 that publication of criticism intended to disseminate an "ill opinion" of the government was seditious libel.[16] From here it was only a step to declare vocal criticisms of the crown or the government to be of a criminal nature. This narrow concept was not enlarged until the climate of opinion in

[13] Sir Edward Coke, *Second Part of the Institutes of the Laws of England* (London, 1671), I, 52-53.

[14] Sir William Blackstone, *Commentaries on the Laws of England* (Worcester, Mass., 1790), IV, 305.

[15] *Ibid.,* 335.

[16] Holdsworth, *History of English Law,* VI, 266. Cf. Sir James F. Stephen, *A History of the Criminal Law of England* (London, 1883), II, 365; James Paterson, *The Liberty of the Press, Speech, and Public Worship* (London, 1880), 77-81.

England was vastly altered toward the latter part of the same century. The same might be said of freedom of the press, which came about only by a series of judicial decisions and popular opposition to suppressive measures.

Revolutionary America was concerned over the use of general warrants, and her lawyers scurried to their bookshelves to find prohibitions against their use. Under the Navigation laws crown agents were empowered with the right to use writs of assistance and general warrants in an effort to stop smuggling, thus ending a long period of "salutary neglect" or winking at the law. These warrants gave royal officials a *carte blanche* which in many cases was abused. Colonists who spoke out against their use had no support from Lord Mansfield's decision in 1765 in which he recognized the right of Parliament to give broad authority to crown officers "to take up loose idle and disorderly people."[17] This pronouncement on the eve of the Revolution was, however, at odds with the contemporary precedent in England that was an outgrowth of the arrest of John Wilkes by a general warrant. The fiery Englishman was placed in the Tower of London for a week, then released as a privileged member of Parliament. The case was a notorious one, and the upshot of the affair was that the practice of issuing general warrants drew official disfavor. Blackstone's comment that a general warrant "to apprehend all persons suspected, without naming or particularly describing any person in special, is illegal and void for its uncertainty" was regarded by Americans as a correct view of the matter.[18]

Exactly what the prohibition of cruel and unusual punishments forbade was also a questionable point. In that handbook of the American revolutionary, Blackstone's *Commentaries*, readers found that the admissible punishment for crimes ran the gamut from "embowelling alive, beheading, and quartering" for treason, to branding, slitting the nostrils for minor crimes, and finally to the lowly ducking stool.[19] Although

[17] Quoted, *ibid.*, X, 668.   [18] Blackstone, *Commentaries*, IV, 291.
[19] *Ibid.*, 376-77.

some of these practices were followed in America, a more enlightened code was to be adopted as the limits of English law were abandoned in favor of the principles advocated by reformers such as Beccaria.

Had the Englishmen who migrated to America ignored the great body of statutes and common law it would have indeed been remarkable. The American colonists for a time had only "a rude, untechnical popular law, followed, as lawyers became numerous and the study of law prominent, by the gradual reception of most of the rules of the English common law."[20] Charters and the common law became the principal depositories of the citizen's rights, but as time elapsed a strikingly new concept of individual rights evolved in the American colonies. Jellinek pointed out long ago that the rights of conscience granted in America were no part of the inherited English law, and he maintained that the real movement for personal rights in America came after religious toleration was assured.[21] It certainly is a fact that the colonists went beyond their forebears when drafting laws and constitutions (after 1775)—notably in the fields of freedom of religion, speech, and the press.

The Americans of 1776 were thus drawing on a vast and rich background of legal knowledge accumulated in the mother country, but in going through their hands it was fused with their newer ideas and the results of their own experiences. Somehow the events in America breathed a new spirit into men in search of personal and collective freedom. The spirit of liberty was not an overnight creation, however. It was nurtured, almost accidentally, by men on the Atlantic frontier who believed in the supremacy of the law.

[20] Paul S. Reinsch, "The English Common Law in the Early American Colonies," in *Selected Essays in Anglo-American Legal History*, I, 370.

[21] Jellinek, *The Declaration of Rights*, 74-76. Another European said that in seeking religious freedom, certain sects stood up "against State omnipotence [and] they secured individual liberty in spite of themselves." John N. Figgis, *Studies in Political Thought from Gerson to Grotius* . . . (Cambridge, 1923), 180.

CHAPTER II

COLONIAL ACHIEVEMENT

THE ENGLISH settlers who came to the North Atlantic frontier early in the seventeenth century were not blind to the necessity of enacting laws which would afford them the same protection of life, liberty, and property in their new homes that they had enjoyed in their old. It would be a grave mistake to interpret the early actions of the English colonists as an attempt at something new—an innovation in legal safeguards for personal liberty. They too gloried in the English Constitution, but they also shared with their brethren at home an uncertainty as to precisely what the Constitution embraced. This was the age of Francis Bacon. They must have agreed with Sir Francis in his sentiment: "That law may be set down as good which is certain in meaning, just in precept, convenient in execution, agreeable to the form of government, and productive of virtue in those that live under it."[1] To assure certainty of meaning they chose to write down their laws from the earliest times. Once this practice was engrained, the Americans continued to insist on written laws, leaving nothing to uncertainty when other means were at hand.

In their search for a workable method of transferring the laws and liberties of the old realm, the various colonies tended to follow a pattern. The work of one colonial legislature was often imitated by another, partly because both had access to the common law and also because similar circumstances made the borrowing of ideas and laws inevitable. Certainly one result of the practice of adopting a neighbor's code of laws was

[1] *On the Dignity and Advancement of Learning*, bk. VIII, ch. 3, Aphorism vii.

the spread of ideas concerning personal freedom. Here were found the first seeds of the bills of rights of 1776.

Although the Virginia House of Burgesses passed a series of laws in 1624 which dealt with the individual freeman, these laws were enacted principally as a means of protecting the general welfare of the struggling colony at a time when the preservation of life itself transcended regard for personal rights. It was of necessity an arbitrary code, concerned with the obligations rather than the rights of free men. More deserving of the label "bill of rights"—despite its brevity—is the "Act for the liberties of the people" approved by the Maryland General Assembly in 1639. Reinforcing the 1632 charter, this enactment declared that all Christian inhabitants of the colony, slaves excepted, "Shall have and enjoy all such rights liberties immunities priviledges and free customs . . . as any naturall born subject of England hath or ought to have or enjoy." The common law was specifically mentioned as part of this heritage. Maryland freemen were further assured that they would "not be imprisoned nor disseissed or dispossessed of their freehold goods or Chattels or be out Lawed Exiled or otherwise destroyed fore judged or punished" without due process of law.[2] The spirit of the act apparently suited later assemblies, since it was repassed in varied form as late as 1722.

After surviving the early hardships of frontier life the first colonial groups turned to the organization of a society which would meet their needs. In New England, where the Puritans began their struggle for existence as a theocratic oligarchy, time wrought numerous changes in their views on government. By 1639 the people "had long desired a body of laws, and thought their condition very unsafe," Governor Winthrop reported, "while so much power rested in the discretion of magistrates." The nature of the Massachusetts Bay Colony made community welfare a foremost objective of government, but

[2] William H. Browne, and others, eds., *Archives of Maryland* (Baltimore, 1883-   ), I, 41.

the protection of personal rights was also essential. Thus the inhabitants sought a code of laws which would guarantee "such liberties Immunities and priveledges as humanitie, Civilitie, and Christianitie call for as due to every man in his place and proportion without impeachment and Infringement. . . ."[3] Their problem was to be solved by the promulgation in 1641 of the Body of Liberties.

Authorship of this first detailed American statement of personal rights under the law has been credited to the Reverend Nathaniel Ward of Ipswich. Ward, who had served as a minister in England and America, had studied law and had later practiced in the English common law courts.[4] His code was immediately styled the Body of Liberties with the expectation that it would be amended within the following three years, and then become perpetual.

Personal rights formed an integral part of the Body of Liberties. Various provisions prohibited authorities from depriving a citizen of life, liberty, or property without due process of law.[5] "Every person within this Jurisdiction, whether Inhabitant or forreiner" was entitled to the equal protection of the laws. Conscription for military service outside the colony was barred. The Body of Liberties guaranteed freemen the right of petition, forbade monopolies, and offered the free exercise of religion to refugees who professed adherence to the Congregational form of worship. A habeas corpus statute protected accused persons, and a declaration that for "bodilie punishments we allow amongst us none that are inhumane Barbarous or cruel" safeguarded persons already convicted of crime. In criminal cases involving the death penalty, the testimony of more than one witness was necessary for conviction. An accused person was permitted counsel "provided he give him noe fee or reward for his paines." Annual elections for

[3] James K. Hosmer, ed., *Winthrop's Journal "History of New England"* (New York, 1908), I, 323; F. C. Gray, "Early Laws of Massachusetts," Massachusetts Historical Society, *Collections*, 3d ser., 8 (1843), 216.
[4] Hosmer, ed., *Winthrop's Journal*, II, 49.   [5] Gray, "Early Laws," 216ff.

each township were stipulated. "Liberties of Woemen" included freedom "from bodilie correction or stripes by her husband, unlesse it be in his owne defence under her assalt." Apparently, the shrewish wife was not unknown to our forebears. The right of emigration, not always recognized in the old world, gave every citizen greater control over his own destiny.

Despite the several basic personal rights recognized, the code was only a breach in the arbitrary legal system transported from the old world to the new. The Puritans were not ready to grant "hereticks" these privileges, as laws were soon passed which excluded Anabaptists and Quakers from the colony.[6] Still, the Body of Liberties was for its time a fairly enlightened code of rights, particularly in those sections which dealt with penal provisions. Its antecedents were to be found in the fundamental teachings of Calvinism, in the common law of England (which Ward seemed to know quite well), and the brief but beneficial experience in self-government on the American seacoast frontier. Before a decade had passed, the Connecticut General Court chose to borrow liberally from the Body of Liberties in forming its own code of laws.[7] Its "grandchildren" constantly reappeared in colonial legislatures, in declarations of rights enacted during the Revolution, and on the western frontier in 1796 when Tennessee lawmakers fashioned a bill of rights.

During the ensuing decades, while the home government was pressed with matters closer to the seat of power, Massachusetts Bay maintained its code and even enlarged its scope with new enactments. At the General Court session of June, 1661, resolutions were approved which among other things asserted the rights of freemen "to choose annually a Governor, Deputy Governor, Asistants, & theire select representatives or

[6] Ebenezer Hazard, comp., *State Papers of the United States* (Philadelphia, 1792-94), I, 538, 630-31.

[7] J. Hammond Trumbull and Charles J. Hoadly, eds., *Public Records of the Colony of Connecticut* (Hartford, 1850-90), I, 509ff.

deputies."[8] The earlier Body of Liberties had provided for
the calling of annual elections. Now a list of the officials who
were subject to the voters' approval had been added. The
1661 resolutions warned future sessions of the General Court
that any enactments passed in defiance of the existing legal
code would "be an infringement of our right." Clearly, the
Massachusetts Bay legislators did not consider the rights they
had been delineating as ephemeral.

The advanced ideas of Roger Williams and his band were
embodied in the Rhode Island charter of 1663—the first broad
declaration of religious freedom in the colonial settlements.
Professor J. Franklin Jameson has shown how the Revolution
helped loosen the bonds of the established church, but the
important fact that Rhode Island had been practicing freedom
of conscience a century before 1776 deserves emphasis. Some
years before New Jersey and Pennsylvania citizens were privileged to share a comparable degree of freedom, the Rhode
Island example stood as a model which, however, found few
imitators for decades to come. From Charles II the Rhode
Island and Providence Plantations solicited and received the
guarantee

that noe person within the sayd colonye, at any time hereafter, shall
bee any wise molested, punished, disquieted, or called in question, for
any differences in opinione in matters of religion . . . but that all the
everye person and persons may, from tyme to tyme, and at all tymes
hereafter, freelye and fullye have and enjoye his and theire owne
judgments and consciences, in matters of religious concernments
throughout the tract of lande . . .[9]

Although Rhode Island carried on the statute books from 1719
to 1783 a clause that excluded Roman Catholics from public
office, serious doubts have been expressed as to whether this

[8] Nathaniel B. Shurtleff, ed., *Records of the Governor and Company of the
Massachusetts Bay in New England* (Boston, 1853-54), IV, part 2, 25.
[9] Benjamin P. Poore, comp., *The Federal and State Constitutions, Colonial
Charters, and Other Organic Laws of the United States* (Washington, 1878),
II, 1596-97.

incongruous exception was actually enforced.[10] Perhaps Williams considered the charter provision an opening wedge for other rights. At any rate, he did not limit his own vision to religious freedom, but rather he espoused a radical doctrine calling for broad liberties that would permit the widest latitude for personal freedom.[11]

A distinct change in the method of securing the charter provisions that recognized personal rights took place when the Carolina proprietors received their royal charter in 1663. Whereas the earlier provisions had come from the citizens themselves, or from their solicitations to the crown, the Carolina charter carried a grant of limited religious toleration from the English proprietors. Here was a break in the procedure of procuring guarantees for personal liberty that other proprietary colonies imitated. Under the terms of the Carolina charter, limited toleration was conditioned on a loyalty oath made by dissenters.[12] The Carolina charter also prohibited religious nonconformists from practicing their beliefs if the peace of the community was disturbed. John Locke's draft in 1669 of another Carolina charter provided that no man should molest or "persecute another for his speculative opinion in religion, or his way of worship."[13] Locke's charter, interesting only for its ideas because it was never actually in force, also included a provision for jury trials for freemen.

After the Rhode Island charter the next significant development of personal freedom was made at the instigation of the New Jersey proprietors. Their action resulted in the set of fundamental laws of West New Jersey in 1676, granted by the proprietors on the specific condition that they were "to be the foundation of the government . . . not to be altered by

[10] John R. Bartlett, ed., *Records of the Colony of Rhode Island and Providence Plantations, in New England* (Providence, 1856-65), II, 36-37.

[11] Samuel H. Brockunier, *The Irrepressible Democrat* (New York, 1940), 284-89. Brockunier says Williams has attained the stature of "a folk hero popularly associated with the great heritage of the Bill of Rights." See also Harvey Wish, *Society and Thought in Early America* (New York, 1950), 37.

[12] Poore, *Constitutions and Charters*, II, 1389.

[13] *Ibid.*, II, 1408.

the Legislative authority" under any circumstances. Thus these provisions of what amounted to a West New Jersey charter were more binding than ordinary laws, such as the Body of Liberties, and at the same time were more considerate of the rights of freemen.

In the fundamental laws the West New Jersey proprietors, who included Sir George Carteret and William Penn, agreed to a provision assuring broad religious freedom. The provision declared that no citizen could be "called in question, or in the least punished or hurt, either in person, estate, or priviledge, for the sake of his opinion, judgment, faith or worship towards God in matters of religion." No freeholder or inhabitant of the province could be deprived of life, liberty, or property "without a due tryal, and judgment passed by twelve good and lawful men of his neighborhood first." Accused persons were permitted to challenge thirty-five prospective jurors "without any reason rendered," and if a valid excuse existed, there was no limit to the number of challenges. The testimony of at least two witnesses was required to establish proof of guilt in all criminal trials. Jury trials were mandatory in all cases, and the citizen was given "free liberty to plead his own cause, if he please" without retaining legal advice. This provision of the New Jersey code was a guarantee that justice for all citizens would be administered in an open court.[14]

By their act the West New Jersey proprietors had granted to freeholders in the New World a definite bill of rights. "We have made concessions by ourselves, being such as friends here and there (we question not) will approve of," they informed one of their agents, adding that "there we lay a foundation for after ages to understand their liberty as men and christians, that they may not be brought in bondage, but by their own consent. . . ."[15] The widest public recognition of the laws was

[14] Francis Newton Thorpe, comp., *The Federal and State Constitutions, Colonial Charters, and Other Organic Laws* (Washington, 1909), V, 2548-51.
[15] Proprietors of West Jersey to Richard Hartshone, June 26, 1676, William A. Whitehead, and others, eds., *Documents Relating to the Colonial History of the State of New Jersey* (Newark, 1880-   ), 1st ser., I, 228.

guaranteed by the proprietors' order that "the great charter
of fundamentals, be recorded in a fair table . . . in every common hall of justice within this Province." Certainly the proprietors were contributing toward the solid foundation of personal freedom in the new colony, a factor which could scarcely
be overlooked by the venturesome immigrant when choosing
a place of abode on the new continent.

Two colonial charters issued in the decade of the 1680's
followed the West New Jersey pattern. The New Hampshire
Charter of 1680, though silent on other personal rights, did
grant liberty of conscience to all Protestants.[16] Pennsylvania
was the scene of a more forthright experiment in freedom,
for there the ideas which had worked so well in New Jersey
were applied by William Penn. Penn made individually the
same concessions he had joined in granting collectively as one
of the New Jersey proprietors. The Pennsylvania Frame of
Government of 1683, which was properly termed a "charter
of liberties," granted freemen extensive personal rights. They
were authorized to elect a General Assembly to make the laws,
and were permitted to plead their own cases in court with
"justice speedily administered" by a jury of twelve men.[17]
This charter limited religious toleration to those "who confess
and acknowledge the one Almighty and eternal God, to be the
Creator, Upholder and Ruler of the world." Despite its restrictive character, this and similar religious provisions of other
charters which made concession to the growing number of
sects represented a notable break from the narrow conception
of toleration prevailing in most of Europe. Toleration in
even this limited sense was a long stride beyond the religious
views held in most of New England after the Revolution.

For a season proprietary and royal grants had provided at
least minimum guarantees of personal freedom. When higher
authority failed to hand down these safeguards from above,

[16] Poore, *Constitutions and Charters*, II, 1277.
[17] *Ibid.*, II, 1523-27.

the freemen initiated them at the local level. In New York the General Assembly passed a "Charter of Libertyes and priviledges" in 1683 which, among other provisions, guaranteed to freeholders substantive personal rights. This "charter" declared

THAT Noe Freeman shall be taken and imprisoned or be disseized of his Freehold or Libertye or Free Customes or be outlawed or Exiled or any other wayes destroyed nor shall be padded upon adjudged or condemned But by the Lawfull Judgment of his peers and by the Law of this province. Justice nor Right shall be neither sold denyed or deferred to any man within this province.[18]

A jury trial was assured to accused persons, with "reasonable Challenges." Bail was allowed in all cases except those involving treason or a felony. The quartering of troops in private dwellings in peacetime was forbidden. Another provision made it illegal for crown commissioners to proceed "by Marshall Law against any of his Majestyes Subjects," who were civilians. Christians were assured the free exercise of their faith as long as they did "not actually disturb the Civill peace" of the colony. Within a short time the Duke of York, now turned king, refused to approve this legislation. Undaunted, the New York citizens continued to press for the personal protection already enjoyed by their sister colonies, and in 1691 the provincial Legislative Council approved a second declaration of rights which included liberty of conscience (except for "any persons of the Romish Religion"), and repeated the guarantees of personal rights in the enactment of 1683.[19] The Glorious Revolution having placed James II safely out of the way, this bill appears to have become law, although it lacked the permanent character of the charter rights granted elsewhere.

With the turn of the new century greater concessions to the individual colonist were at hand. The Pennsylvania Charter of Privileges, which continued in force from 1701

[18] *The Colonial Laws of New York* (Albany, 1894-96), I, 113.
[19] *Journal of the Legislative Council of the Colony of New York, 1691-1743* (Albany, 1861), I, 8.

until 1776, was the most articulate declaration of the rights of man laid down prior to the Revolution. The first article of the charter declared that mankind could not know true happiness "though under the greatest Enjoyment of Civil Liberties, if abridged of the Freedom of their Consciences, as to their Religious Profession and Worship."[20] Pennsylvania freemen were therefore guaranteed toleration provided they confessed or acknowledged the existence of God; and those freemen who also confessed a belief in Jesus Christ were granted the right to hold office (from which Jews, Deists, and other non-Christians were barred). Article V stated "THAT all Criminals shall have the same Privileges of Witnesses and Council as their Prosecutors." Furthermore, no person could be deprived of his property without due process of law, and the estates of suicides were specifically protected from governmental seizure.

One section of Article VIII in the Charter of Privileges deserves particular attention. It was a declaration that any future attempt to alter provisions of the section on liberty of conscience would be illegal. This provision was similar to the resolution of 1661 passed by the Massachusetts Bay General Court, and the principle involved was utilized by Thomas Jefferson many years later in his Virginia statute of religious liberty, wherein he sought a check on the power of future legislators to repeal laws which safeguarded a basic freedom.[21] A final section held that any infringement of the "Liberties in this Charter contained and expressed" would be of "no Force or Effect."

Less than a century after the first permanent English settlement had been founded in America a distinct pattern for obtaining the necessary safeguards for personal liberty had been established. In New England and New York the people

---

[20] Poore, *Constitutions and Charters*, II, 1536-40.

[21] William W. Hening, comp., *Statutes at Large . . . of Virginia* (Richmond, 1819-23), XII, 86. Also found in Samuel E. Morison, ed., *Sources and Documents Illustrating the American Revolution* (London, 1948), 208.

acting through elected representatives had adopted a code of laws which protected their rights and their property from arbitrary infringement. In the proprietary colonies grants had been made to the colonists through explicit charter provisions which guaranteed certain basic rights to all freemen. In each of the American colonies settled during the seventeenth century these written guarantees were a part of the written law by 1701. Religious toleration was the most frequently encountered provision. This spirit of tolerance grew, as an entry of Nathaniel Ames in his *Almanack for 1767* indicates: "To defend the christian religion is one thing, and to knock a man on the head for being of a different religion is another."[22] But other checks on oppressive governments had not been overlooked. Experience had taught colonial Americans the wisdom of placing definite assurances for their liberties either in a compact or in a statute book. Thus the colonists were determined to be "ruled by *laws*, which they themselves approve, not by *edicts of men* over whom they have no controul."[23]

[22] Samuel Briggs, comp., *The Essays, Humor & Poems of Nathaniel Ames, Father and Son . . . 1726-75* (Cleveland, 1891), 387.

[23] Worthington C. Ford, and others, eds., *Journals of the Continental Congress, 1774-1789* (Washington, 1904-37), I, 107.

CHAPTER III

MR. MASON'S PROPOSAL

BY THE END of the seventeenth century the colonial phase of charter making was almost completed. The next six decades were crowded with an extension of settlement, increased commercial activity, and the other activities associated with the growth of a healthy and vigorous people. Abstract political theory played only a minor role in the lives of the colonists as they awakened to the economic potentialities of the new world. Political theories are seldom born in tranquil periods.

A crisis in relations with England after 1760 broke the calm which had marked the early period of colonial development. Aroused by passage of the Revenue Act of 1764, the colonists found able spokesmen who made a plea for the rights of Englishmen—especially of transplanted Englishmen. James Otis had entered the list of pamphleteers two years earlier with his defense of the Massachusetts legislature against an arbitrary governor. Now Otis became foremost among those who attacked British taxation policies. Quoting Locke, Coke, Rousseau, and the English Bill of Rights (and other sources), Otis used *The Rights of the British Colonies Asserted and Proved* to make claim for the natural liberties of Englishmen.[1] After 1765 and passage of the Stamp Act the colonists sought a defense for their conduct by claiming the rights which they had long enjoyed under their charters and codes. Thus a unity of thought unobtainable a decade earlier appeared throughout the colonies, although it must fairly be said that the economic

[1] Benjamin F. Wright, *American Interpretations of Natural Law* (Cambridge, 1931), 64-71.

element entered the argument. Daniel Dulany, the polished
Maryland lawyer, wrote an outstanding defense of the col-
lonial rights in his *Considerations on the Propriety of imposing
Taxes in the British Colonies, for the purpose of Raising a
Revenue, by Act of Parliament.*[2] This 1765 tract was a defense
of colonial economic rights, but many of Dulany's contemporaries were not willing to stop with a cold exposition on the
pounds and pence involved. Accordingly, when the Stamp
Act Congress of 1765 spoke of "the most essential rights and
liberties of the colonists," it was making a case for Americans
with a common set of grievances, not for scattered grumblers
in Pennsylvania or Virginia. Among the Congress' resolutions
were articles demanding trial by jury, the right of petition
and a "full and free enjoyment of their rights and liberties."[3]

Boston, a center of the controversy, produced another
early pronouncement which, in negative wording, reiterated
certain ideas regarding personal freedom which had been enunciated in some form since 1641. "A List of Infringements and
Violations of Rights" drawn up by the Boston town meeting
late in 1772 alluded to a number of personal rights which had
allegedly been violated by agents of the crown. The list included complaints against the writs of assistance which had
been employed by royal officers in their searches for contraband.
The Bostonians complained that "our houses and even our
bed chambers are exposed to be ransacked, our boxes, chests,
and trunks broke open, ravaged and plundered by wretches,
whom no prudent man would venture to employ even as menial
servants." Another charge assailed the practice of quartering
troops "in a free country in times of peace without the consent
of the people." The right of trial by jury was in jeopardy,
they charged, from the power of the vice-admiralty courts.
The indictment also expressed fear of any plan to erect an

[2] Morison, ed., *Sources and Documents Illustrating the American Revolution*,
24-32.
[3] *Ibid.*, 32-34.

American episcopate as a threat to "that Liberty wherewith Christ has made us free."[4]

As the revolutionary movement spread from isolated pockets of resistance into a general undertaking its leaders recognized the utility of a declaration of rights as an expression of dissatisfaction. On the eve of the first meeting of the Continental Congress in 1774 Samuel Adams said a bill of rights drawn by the colonists would aid their cause. Adams wrote a Virginia delegate to the coming Congress:

Should America hold up her own Importance to the Body of the Nation and at the same Time agree in one general Bill of Rights, the Dispute might be settled on the Principles of Equity and Harmony restored between Britain and the Colonies.[5]

Adams found his colleagues in Philadelphia agreed that a statement of fundamental rights was necessary. On October 14, 1774, the Congress approved a "Declaration of Rights." After a lengthy preamble reciting royal and parliamentary wrongs, the resolutions were pronounced valid on the basis of "the immutable laws of nature, the principles of the English constitution, and the several charters or compacts" of the colonies.[6]

In its declaration of rights the Continental Congress expressed current notions of what free men were entitled to, and did so with near unanimity. Eight of the resolutions were adopted *nemine contradicente*, as the *Journal* records, while two were opposed by the conservative elements in the Congress.[7] The high value Congress set upon the bill of rights as a propaganda instrument appears in the "Letter to the Inhabitants of Quebec," approved two weeks later. The "Letter," which is a gloss of the abstract language of the "Declaration" for the Canadians who were untutored in the meaning of

[4] *Ibid.*, 91-96.
[5] Samuel Adams to Richard Henry Lee, July 15, 1774, Harry A. Cushing, ed., *The Writings of Samuel Adams* (New York, 1904-08), III, 139.
[6] *Extracts from the Proceedings of the Continental Congress* (Philadelphia, 1774), 3.
[7] Ford, ed., *Journals of the Continental Congress*, I, 63 n.

British liberty, puts the rights in concrete form. Congress regarded the "Letter" as important enough to justify recommending "the delegates of the province of Pensylvania [to] superintend the translating, printing, publishing & dispersing" of pamphlets based on its contents.[8]

The first resolution of the Declaration, an echo of John Locke, stated the basic propositions that all men are entitled to life, liberty, and property, and that they cannot be deprived of these rights without their consent. The nine following resolves elaborated these two themes and applied them practically to the crisis which had arisen. They set forth that the colonists retain all and severally the "rights, liberties, and immunities of free and natural born subjects, within the realm of England," none of which had been forfeited by emigration. The resolutions specified particulars: the right of assembly and petition, the right to "the common law of England, and more especially to the great and inestimable priviledge of being tried by their peers of the vicinage, according to the course of that law." Next was posited the "right in the people to participate in their legislative council." Then follows the article declaring standing armies "in time of peace . . . against law" unless by "the consent of the legislature of that colony, in which such army is kept." The last resolution was a pronouncement on polity: "It is indispensably necessary to good government, and rendered essential by the English constitution, that the constituent branches of the legislature be independent of each other."[9]

In October, 1774, the colonists hoped that the freeholders of Quebec would share their indignation over recent British measures. Forgetting cultural differences between Americans and Canadians, Congress applauded Canada's "gallant and glorious resistance" in the French and Indian War and undertook to explain to the Canadians their rights. "Educated under

[8] *Ibid.*, I, 113.
[9] *Extracts from the Proceedings of the Continental Congress*, 6.

another form of government, [you] have artfully been kept from discovering the unspeakable worth of *that* form you are now undoubtedly entitled to."[10] These rights had been mentioned at an earlier time by Beccaria and Montesquieu, the "Letter" said, and included the right of government "by *laws,* which they [the people] themselves approve, not by edicts of men over whom they have no controul."[11] "The next great right is that of trial by jury," which preserves life, liberty, and property against the arbitrary will of capricious laws and men. "Another right relates merely to the liberty of the person," and promised habeas corpus. The fourth in this catalog of the citizen's rights which Congress broadcast as an educational tract was an obvious appeal to the penurious *canadien.* This was a right to hold lands "by the tenure of easy rents, and not by rigorous and oppressive services."[12] The last of these rights "without which a people cannot be free and happy" was freedom of the press. The importance of a free press consists,

besides the advancement of truth, science, morality, and arts in general, in its diffusion of liberal sentiments on the administration of Government, its ready communication of thoughts between subjects, and its consequential promotion of union among them, whereby oppressive officers are shamed or intimidated, into more honourable and just modes of conducting affairs.

In addition to these rights, Congress could not avoid mention of religion despite the fact that the appeal was addressed to Roman Catholics at a time when the word "Rome" was anathema to many Americans, Puritan and Anglican alike. Did the Canadian possess liberty of conscience? "No," Congress answered. "God gave it to you," but Parliament denied this right by maintaining an established church.[13] Thus did Congress go further in recognizing the principle of religious free-

[10] Ford, ed., *Journals of Continental Congress,* I, 106.
[11] *Ibid.,* 107.
[12] *Ibid.,* 108.
[13] *Ibid.*

dom than many colonies had gone in their own charters and fundamental codes.

This appeal to the Canadians failed to gain support for the American cause in Quebec, but the address is no less significant even though it fell short of the desired goal of a Canadian delegation in the Second Continental Congress. Five of the six rights enumerated represented the hard core of civil liberty which most Americans considered essential in 1774. For the first time in America, a group of public men had openly and explicitly declared freedom of the press to be a fundamental tenet of civil liberty. Since 1690, when the Boston *Publick Occurrences* had been suppressed, a free press had been championed in various colonies. The inclusion of the right "of holding lands by the tenure of easy rents" was an expedient recognition of a land problem peculiar to Canadian experience. If we discount the propaganda element, the "Letter" is a further amplification of prescriptive rights for all men, a step toward the complete platform now distinctly emerging.

Six months after Congress had undertaken the missionary project to its northern neighbors a "cold war" between the mother country and provinces burst into flame at Lexington and Concord. This turn of events necessitated the erection of a new structure of government, or at least a replacement for the old forms. The Continental Congress and provincial governments together managed to maintain an army in the field, send agents abroad, emit bills of credit, and preserve order, although their management of these enterprises caused even Washington to feel many an anxious moment. As the contest became increasingly bitter the colonies gave up what Washington called "the dainty food of reconciliation," and though they refused to sever the ties with Great Britain they began to act independently.[14]

To an acquaintance in Massachusetts John Adams confided

[14] George Washington to John Augustine Washington, May 21, 1776, John C. Fitzpatrick, ed., *The Writings of George Washington from the Original Manuscript Sources* (Washington, 1931-44), V, 92.

his view of the independence movement in the spring of 1776. Adams was not surprised by the resistance to independence that he had encountered. "All great changes are irksome to the human mind," he observed, "especially those which are attended with great dangers and uncertain effects."[15] The incongruous situation that found men nominally owing allegiance to a government which they were seeking to defeat with arms was at length recognized. The Continental Congress furnished the impetus for an improvement of this condition when it recommended the formation of state governments in May, 1776.[16]

The course of events in Virginia in the same period was especially illustrative of a change in American attitudes. "Things have gone such Lengths, that it is a Matter of Moonshine to us, whether Independence was at first intended, or not," George Mason later wrote when he reviewed events which led to the break with England.[17] He went on to denounce attempts made by the British ministry to promote the false notion

that this great Revolution has been the work of a faction, of a junto of ambitious men against the sense of the people of America. On the contrary, nothing has been done without the approbation of the people, who have indeed outrun their leaders, so that no capital measure has been adopted until they called loudly for it. . . .

The facts bear out Mason's view. A general convention of delegates from the counties had been called to meet in Williamsburg on May 6, 1776. "In many counties there have been warm contests for seats in our approaching Convention," a correspondent informed Richard Henry Lee. "Many new ones are got in," and "Colonel Mason, with great difficulty [was] returned for Fairfax."[18] When all the returns were

[15] John Adams to James Warren, April 22, 1776, Morison, ed., *Sources and Documents*, 147.

[16] Ford, ed., *Journals of Continental Congress*, IV, 342.

[17] George Mason to John Mercer, October 2, 1778, Mason Papers, Emmett Collection, New York Public Library.

[18] Robert Brent to Richard Henry Lee, April 28, 1776, Kate Mason Rowland, *The Life of George Mason* (Philadelphia, 1892), I, 222.

in, however, Patrick Henry and Edmund Pendleton, along with Mason and other eminent men, were selected as delegates for the May meeting. Virginia was the largest of the colonies, and it was natural that leaders of the revolutionary movement in other colonies should regard her actions with interest. "Virginia has hitherto taken the lead in great affairs, and many now look to her with anxious expectation," Richard Henry Lee wrote from his post in Congress.[19] Lee thought submission or independence would be the paramount issue before the convention. There was a reactionary element which was still audible, too. When Carter Braxton's ultra-conservative pamphlet, *An Address to the Convention . . . of Virginia*, reached Lee, he promptly wrote a denunciation of the whole performance. "This Contemptible little Tract, betrays the little Knot or Junto from whence it proceeded," he exclaimed. "Confusion of ideas, aristocratic pride, contradictory reasoning, with evident ill design put it out of danger of doing harm, and therefore I quit it."[20] Lee was doubtless pleased to hear that on May 15 the convention approved a far-reaching measure. President Edmund Pendleton, Thomas Nelson, and Patrick Henry had a hand in drafting the resolution which boldly asked Congress "to declare the United Colonies free and independent states."[21] Insofar as independence was concerned, the fat was now in the fire. Virginians celebrated the event with fireworks and speeches, fully assured by their "committee of safety and public virtue" that anarchy was not at all contemplated by the step.

At the same time that the Virginia convention made this extraordinary maneuver it took measures to insure the maintenance of orderly government. A sister resolution to the independency instructions called for a committee to prepare a

---

[19] Richard Henry Lee to [Patrick Henry], April 20, 1776, James C. Ballagh, ed., *The Letters of Richard Henry Lee* (New York, 1911-14), I, 176.
[20] Richard Henry Lee to [Edmund Pendleton?], May 12, 1776, *ibid.*, I, 190.
[21] David John Mays, *Edmund Pendleton, 1721-1803* (Cambridge, Mass., 1952), II, 108-09.

declaration of rights and a plan of government. A committee
of twenty-eight delegates, headed by Archibald Cary, was
named to draft the declaration. This committee included Meri-
wether Smith, Patrick Henry, Edmund Randolph, and Thomas
Ludwell Lee. George Mason and James Madison were among
four additional members appointed before the week ended.[22]
One delegate thought "the great business will go on well, *as
I think there will be no great difference of opinion among
our best speakers, Henry, Mason, Mercer, Dandridge, Smith,*
and I am apt to think *the President* will concur with them in
sentiment."[23] This feeling was shared by Thomas Ludwell
Lee, who expected the formation of "a just and equal government would not perhaps be so very difficult."[24]

Although many delegates shared this enthusiasm, a cautious faction had to be reckoned with by the convention leadership. Mason, who arrived in Williamsburg after delay of
almost two weeks caused by illness, found the committee he
served on burdened with "useless members." "You know our
Convention," he lamented as he explained that before any
real business could be accomplished they would hear "a thousand ridiculous and impracticable proposals," and possibly end
their labors with a plan "formed of hetrogeneous, jarring, and
unintelligible ingredients."[25] Mason believed the only hope
of success for the militant party lay in the exertions of "a few
men of integrity and abilities . . . undertaking this business and
defending it ably through every stage of opposition." Patrick
Henry was particularly suspicious of the conservative faction
led by Robert Carter Nicholas.

Perhaps I'm mistaken [Henry wrote], but I fear too great a Byass

[22] "Journal of the Virginia Convention," in Peter Force, comp., *American Archives* (Washington, 1837-53), 4th ser., VI, 1524-29. See also Hugh Blair Grigsby, *The Virginia Convention of 1776* (Richmond, 1855), 19ff.
[23] John Augustine Washington [?] to Richard Henry Lee, May 18, 1776, *Southern Literary Messenger,* 27 (1858), 330.
[24] Thomas Ludwell Lee to Richard Henry Lee, May 18, 1776, Rowland, *Life of Mason,* I, 225.
[25] George Mason to Richard Henry Lee, May 18, 1776, *ibid.,* 226.

to Aristocracy prevails among the opulent. . . . Vigor, animation, and
all the powers of mind and body, must now be summon'd and collected
together into one grand effort. . . . And to see those who have so
fatally advised us, still guiding, or at least sharing our public counsels,
alarms me.[26]

The monotonous formal entries in the official journals of
the Convention make it difficult to determine what actually
occurred in the committee room where Cary presided. Edmund Randolph, the youngest delegate to the convention, left
a record of the proceedings but it is not a contemporary one.
Randolph probably did not write his "Essay on the Revolutionary History of Virginia" until some thirty years after the Convention adjourned. Still it remains, with a similar recollection
from James Madison's pen, the best account of the actual
workings of the convention. Randolph recalled that the committee received "many projects of a bill of rights and constitution . . . [which revealed] the ardor for political notice, rather
than a ripeness in political wisdom." In the midst of considerable disorder, one figure stepped forward with a positive
program. The declaration of rights and constitution proposed
by George Mason, Randolph emphasized, "swallowed up all
the rest, by fixing the grounds and plan, which after great
discussion and correction, were finally ratified."[27] Madison's
autobiography confirms Randolph's account.[28] Three days before the Virginia Declaration of Rights was presented to the
convention, Pendleton had expected the chief work to come
from Mason. "The Political Cooks are busy in preparing the
dish," he wrote Jefferson, "and as Colo Mason seems to have
the Ascendancy in the great work, I have Sanguine hopes it
will be framed so as to Answer it's end, [which is] Prosperity

[26] Patrick Henry to Richard Henry Lee, May 20, 1776, *Southern Literary Messenger*, 8 (1842), 260.
[27] "Edmund Randolph's Essay on the Revolutionary History of Virginia," *Virginia Magazine of History and Biography*, 44 (1936), 44.
[28] Douglass Adair, ed., "James Madison's Autobiography," *William and Mary Quarterly*, 3d ser., 2 (1945), 199.

to the Community and Security to Individuals, but I am yet a stranger to the Plan."[29]

George Mason's reputation has lapsed considerably over the years. The comparatively low rank given him by later historians is in sharp contrast to his prominence among his contemporaries, who held his abilities in high esteem. Seven years the senior of his neighbor at Mount Vernon, Mason brought to the convention a longer record as a partisan of colonial rights. After repeal of the Stamp Act he continued to sound a call for vigilance. In reply to an address from London merchants to the planters of Virginia, Mason had written "To the Committee of Merchants in London" in 1766 a letter which was printed in the London *Public Ledger* over the signature of "A Virginia Planter."[30] Englishmen need not fear that repeal of the obnoxious act had made the colonists overconfident, he wrote, for "there is yet no cause that our joy should exceed the bounds of moderation." Threats to the accepted practice of trial by jury and injustices perpetrated by the vice-admiralty courts had become points of issue between America and England. "These things did not altogether depend upon the stamp act, and therefore are not repealed with it." He warned the English that free people are "impatient of restraint," for those who have once known liberty will not submit to tyranny. He concluded that "such another experiment as the stamp-act would produce a general revolt in America."

Time confirmed and strengthened Mason's views. As a member of the House of Burgesses he had helped draft the Non-Importation Resolutions for Virginia in 1769.[31] While gathering evidence to fortify his claims to lands in Fincastle County, Mason repeatedly encountered the phrases dealing with the "Liberties, Franchises, and Immunities of free Denizens and natural subjects" in the Virginia Company's charters.[32]

[29] Edmund Pendleton to Thomas Jefferson, May 24, 1776, Julian P. Boyd, and others, eds., *The Papers of Thomas Jefferson* (Princeton, 1950-   ), I, 296.
[30] Rowland, *Life of Mason*, I, 381-89.
[31] *Ibid.*, 389-93.   [32] *Ibid.*, 393-414.

These studies prepared Mason for authorship of the Fairfax Resolves which Washington had carried to Williamsburg in 1774. In these Resolves Mason declared the claims of Parliament were "diametrically contrary" to the early charters and "totally incompatible with the privileges of a free people and the natural rights of mankind. . . ."[33] Mason also shared with Jefferson and Washington an aversion to the institution of slavery, and he wrote into the Fairfax Resolves a plea for the abolition of "such a wicked, cruel, and unnatural trade."[34]

As the prospect of an open break with England became imminent, Mason had continued to expound his view of human dignity and freedom. He also realized the necessity for a framework of ideas that would express the sentiments and aspirations of his countrymen. The influence of John Locke is discernible in Mason's writing in the years just prior to 1776. But Mason was able to apply those principles to local politics and to give them a new meaning in their American application. He believed in equality for freemen, free elections, annual rotation in office, and a free press. He saw the necessity for designating the people as the source of all political power. These were among the rights of a free people, and they were ideas which gave the Revolution character as an intellectual as well as a political and military upheaval. Randolph has described Mason as indifferent to distinction, a man who loathed pomp and ostentation.[35] Like many other Revolutionary leaders who were his associates, Mason did not seek a host of offices, but rather served when his health, his conscience, and his constituents permitted. His career as a public servant reached a pinnacle with the adoption of the Virginia Declaration of Rights.

A comparison of the Mason proposal with the final draft of this far-reaching document indicates the harmony between his thinking and that of the articulate leaders of Virginia in 1776.

[33] *Ibid.*, 421.
[34] *Ibid.*, 425.
[35] "Randolph's Essay," *Virginia Magazine of History*, 43 (1935), 133.

Mason's original draft contained fourteen articles; in the final plan only two were added, neither of which Mason himself considered "of a fundamental nature."[36] The preamble declared that this list of rights was set down for the people of Virginia "and their posterity, as the basis and foundation of government." All men are created equally free and independent, with certain inherent rights, "namely, the enjoyment of life and liberty, with the means of acquiring and possessing property, and pursuing and obtaining happiness and safety."[37] The idea was Locke's, but the felicitous expression was Mason's. A comparison of the statement with Jefferson's wording of the Declaration of Independence suggests that Mason exerted an influence upon the final phraseology of that document.[38]

The language of the Declaration of Rights, stating that "all men are by nature equally free," raised many protests. Acrimonious debate centered around this revolutionary principle for four days. Robert Carter Nicholas seems to have led the opposition, suggesting that since slavery was a part of their society, a statement of freedom and equality would be "the forerunner or pretext of civil convulsion."[39] This attack disturbed the militant elements in the convention who had voted for independence and were now prepared to erect a liberal government. Their immediate, and apparently satisfactory, answer to Nicholas was that slaves were not "constituent members" of their society and therefore a general maxim could not apply to Negroes.

After almost a week of debate on provisions in the Declaration of Rights some delegates were plainly disheartened. Thomas Ludwell Lee complained about the tactics resorted

[36] Rowland, *Life of Mason*, I, 433-36.
[37] Morison, ed., *Sources and Documents*, 149.
[38] Julian P. Boyd, *The Declaration of Independence* (Washington, 1943), 21-22. Author Edward Dumbauld, in his *The Declaration of Independence* (Norman, Okla., 1950), 21 n, does not accept this view.
[39] "Randolph's Essay," *Virginia Magazine of History*, 44 (1936), 45.

to by the conservatives from the outset which had kept the convention

stumbling at the threshold. . . . we find such difficulty in laying the foundation stone, that I very much fear for that Temple to Liberty which was proposed to be erected thereon. . . . a certain set of Aristocrats,—for we have such monsters here,—finding that their execrable system cannot be reared on such foundations, have to this time kept us at Bay on the first line, which declares all men to be born equally free and independent.

Lee was convinced that the majority had favored an early vote on the proposals *in toto*. "The truth is we are quite overpowered by manoeuvre," he dolefully reported.[40]

A spirit of caution, unheeded by a man of Lee's temperament, probably held some of the delegates back from precipitous action. The reason for this cautious approach is suggested in General Washington's letter to his brother, John Augustine Washington, who was serving as a delegate. The Virginia declaration calling for independence had naturally pleased the General, but for the next step of constitution-making he urged "infinite care, and unbounded attention." Washington cautioned his brother (and, as letters from distinguished men were usually circulated among the receiver's friends, possibly other delegates as well) to remember that their work would "render Million's happy, or Miserable, and that a matter of such moment cannot be the Work of a day."[41] John Adams gave essentially the same advice. "Your intimation that the session of your representative body would be long, gave me great pleasure," Adams wrote Patrick Henry, "because we all look up to Virginia for examples."[42]

During the debates Henry joined the opposition to attack a proposed ban on ex post facto laws which stated that "all

[40] Thomas Ludwell Lee to Richard Henry Lee, June 1, 1776, *Southern Literary Messenger*, 27 (1858), 325.

[41] George Washington to John Augustine Washington, May 31, 1776, Fitzpatrick, ed., *Writings of Washington*, V, 92.

[42] John Adams to Patrick Henry, June 3, 1776, Charles F. Adams, ed., *The Works of John Adams* (Boston, 1850-56), IX, 387.

laws having a retrospect to crimes . . . ought to be avoided."
According to an eyewitness, Henry drew "a terrifying picture
of some towering public offender, against whom ordinary laws
would be impotent" and thus turned the convention against
the article.[43] When the Declaration of Rights came to a vote
on June 12, the opposition dropped its protest and joined in
adopting the measure unanimously.

The Virginia Declaration of Rights contained sixteen articles. Nine of them were regarded as the basic principles of a
free republic. The seven remaining articles enumerated the
rights of citizens.[44] The basic pronouncements of government
were human equality, the assertion that the people are the
source of all power, the right of revolution, majority rule,
the "separation of powers," the necessary subordination of military to civil power, and an admonition calling for a "frequent
recurrence to fundamental principles." The power of suspending laws was denounced as injurious to the rights of a free
people. All of these are positively declared in the Mason
draft. To them the committee had added Article XIV, which
stated that any movement to erect another government separate from Virginia would be illegal. Mason apparently did not
believe this latter provision was germane either to a statement
of principles or to an enumeration of the people's liberties and
seems to have regarded its inclusion as a mistake.[45]

The list of rights of the individual citizen in the Virginia
Declaration of Rights was impressive. Every man who could
give evidence of an interest and attachment to the community
was entitled to the right of suffrage. An accused citizen was
not to be compelled to give evidence against himself, was entitled to know the nature and cause of his arrest, and to a speedy
trial "by an impartial jury of his vicinage." Excessive bails
and fines as well as cruel and unusual punishments were pro-

---

[43] "Randolph's Essay," *Virginia Magazine of History*, 44 (1936), 47.
[44] See Appendix A.
[45] George Mason to [Colonel George Mercer ?], October 2, 1778, Mason
Papers, Emmett Collection, New York Public Library.

hibited. General warrants of search and seizure were held "grievous and oppressive," hence not to be granted. Lawsuits "between man and man" should be settled by a jury. Freedom of the press, as "one of the great bulwarks of liberty," was promised. Finally, the sixteenth article declared that "all men are equally entitled to the free exercise of religion, according to the dictates of conscience." James Madison, "young & in the midst of distinguished and experienced members," had suggested that Mason's wording in the original draft, which had called for toleration, should be broadened into a statement asserting freedom of conscience.[46] Except for this change, several less important alterations, and the committee additions, the Virginia Declaration of Rights was Mason's work. Before the month ended a constitution had been adopted to complete the work of the convention in erecting a government for the new state.

As the most powerful of the American colonies, Virginia willingly had taken a leading role in guiding the passive resistance to England until the abandonment of that strategy for an active rebellion. Virginia then had given her foremost citizens to the army and to the Continental Congress. Fully cognizant of the example expected of them by sister states, her leaders moved forward with vigor and boldness. Thus Virginia was the first state to adopt a declaration of rights and a permanent constitution. Edmund Randolph, after a long career of public service, looked back on the events of 1776 and declared:

In the formation of this bill of rights two objects were contemplated: one, that the legislature should not in their acts violate any of those cannons; the other, that in all the revolutions of time, of human opinion, and of government, a perpetual standard should be erected, around which the people might rally, and by a notorious record be forever admonished to be watchful, firm and virtuous.[47]

[46] Douglass Adair, ed., "James Madison's Autobiography," 199. See also Irving Brant, *James Madison, the Virginia Revolutionist* (Indianapolis, 1941), 245-50.
[47] "Randolph's Essay," *Virginia Magazine of History*, 44 (1936), 47.

A written constitution, Randolph explained, was "a standing ark, to which first principles can be brought on to a test."[48] The Virginia Declaration of Rights expanded the conception of the personal rights of citizens as no other document before its adoption had done. George Mason had drawn upon the whole of American experience prior to the Revolution in fashioning his draft. When he reviewed the events of 1776 and their outcome, he could write with satisfaction—"taking a retrospective view of what is passed, we seem to have been treading upon enchanted ground."[49]

[48] *Ibid.*, 45.
[49] George Mason to [Colonel George Mercer ?], October 2, 1778.

CHAPTER IV

THE NEW REPUBLIC ACTS

THE VIRGINIA convention speedily formulated and adopted a bill of rights and constitution, but this alacrity was not emulated by all her sister states, even after the Williamsburg assembly had furnished a bold example. Certain delegates in the Continental Congress had long seen the need for a Declaration of Independence, and pamphleteer Thomas Paine had done his best to persuade the common man that to remain within the British Empire meant abject slavery. By early summer the impatient radicals in Congress could wait no longer. With Jefferson as their main spokesman they took one of the most decisive steps in recorded history.

The Fourth of July manifesto pronounced the ties with England broken, but it did not accord with the usual conception of what constituted a declaration of rights. The Declaration of Independence was an indictment of England's misdeeds, an instrument of propaganda, and the clearest statement of the philosophy behind the American Revolution. It was not, however, a bill of rights, since it provided not a single legal assurance of personal freedom.

After the final break with England, most of the new commonwealths gradually fell into line with the Virginia example. By 1784 the sweep of constitution-making had covered every section of the Republic. In the spring of that year the New Hampshire convention finally proclaimed its bill of rights adopted. With the single exception of New Hampshire, the process had been completed with the Massachusetts Declaration of Rights in 1780.[1] Citizens of the Bay State, who had been in the front ranks of the revolutionary movement, deemed it wise to guarantee civil rights for freemen before endowing state lawmakers with the powers of government. John Adams thought the precaution necessary.

Significantly, most of the political leaders who launched the states on their new course did not want the citizen's personal rights dependent upon the common law alone. From the earliest times each colony only borrowed from common law those parts which suited its peculiar circumstances.[2] Even if a casual predilection toward usage of the common law had existed, there probably would have been a dozen separate views of what that law encompassed or left untouched. Prior to the Revolution, most of the colonies relied on the common law to supplement charter provisions and statutes. The habeas corpus had been regarded as the citizen's right in every colony, but what was the common law regarding a free press? Did the common law protect a defendant from self-incrimination?[3] Did common law protect a householder from an unwarranted search and seizure? Without bothering to examine the niceties of law, the Revolutionary legislators swept aside doubt by giving full expression to guarantees of civil liberty. Indeed, the whole catalog of human rights which colonists reviewed during the years preceding Lexington-Concord had been regarded not as common law rights, but as natural rights. As Alexander Hamilton had declared, "Civil liberty is only natural liberty, modified and secured by the sanctions of civil

[1] Connecticut and Rhode Island continued to operate under their colonial charters which contained substantial guarantees of personal rights. Georgia, South Carolina, New Jersey, and New York did not adopt separate bills of rights but incorporated the ordinary provisions of such bills in their state constitutions.

[2] Edward Channing, *A History of the United States* (New York, 1905-25), I, 529; Richard B. Morris, *Studies in the History of American Law* (New York, 1930), 12.

[3] "We think that the existence before the Revolution of a privilege of defendants is an illusion." Julius Goebel, Jr., and T. Raymond Naughton, *Law Enforcement in Colonial New York* (New York, 1944), 656.

society."[4] In working out a legal system that encompassed these ideas, the "natural rights" became civil rights, and these civil rights in turn received a constitutional sanction.[5]

Standing in the middle ground on the question of the common law versus explicit statements was the New Jersey Provincial Congress. Acting a few days after the Virginia convention had finished its work, the New Jersey representatives adopted a constitution which was both a bill of rights and a plan of government.[6] The rights of accused persons were protected, criminals were granted the right to counsel, and both common law and statute law "as have been heretofore practised in this Colony" were to remain in force. The same Article XXII went on to state that the right of trial by jury "shall remain confirmed as part of the law of this Colony, without repeal, forever." Here was a sweeping effort to weld together common law and constitution, and thus guard the individual citizen from arbitrary arrest and prosecution. Another article granted to every person the right to worship "Almighty God in a manner agreeable to the dictates of his own conscience," and the established church was repudiated. Full religious freedom was confined to Protestants, however, but the language of the New Jersey articles on religion moved the Reverend Ezra Stiles to compare them with the Virginia provision. "The Constitution of New Jersey surpasses it in the Catholic Establishment of Universal, equal religious, protestant Liberty," he surmised.[7]

Assuredly, the Virginia Declaration of Rights was not greeted with universal approbation, but the state lawmakers who prefaced their constitutions with bills of rights doubtless found it a handy model that might be altered or amplified to suit local conditions. These were years when the rights of

[4] Henry Cabot Lodge, ed., *The Works of Alexander Hamilton* (New York, 1904), I, 87.
[5] Clinton Rossiter, *Seedtime of the Republic* (New York, 1953), 383.
[6] Poore, comp., *Constitutions and Charters*, II, 1310-14.
[7] Franklin B. Dexter, ed., *The Literary Diary of Ezra Stiles* . . . (New York, 1901), II, 49.

man formed a lively topic of public discussion, in the course
of which a certain amount of agreement was reached regarding the nature of these rights. It is possible, even probable, that
without a model the principles already "on every man's lips"
would have been formulated in similar language everywhere.[8]

The fact remains that the Virginia Declaration of Rights
was broadcast throughout the colonies in private letters and
public print. Samuel Adams acknowledged a copy sent from
Richard Henry Lee and added that while he had "not yet
had time to peruse it . . . I dare say it will be a feast to our little
circle."[9] The constitutions "of *Virginia* and *New-York* are in
this city," Josiah Bartlett of New Hampshire wrote from Philadelphia. "I shall send them forward, and the Constitutions
of the other Colonies as they are formed, as possibly something
may be taken from them to amend our own."[10] Making some
allowance for the bad roads and other hazards that delayed
communications during this period, it still seems likely that
by the harvest time of 1776 there were copies of the Virginia
Declaration of Rights in law offices and printing shops from
New Hampshire to Georgia. Its form and phraseology must
have made a deep impression, as had the action of the Virginians in adopting a bill of rights separate from the constitution.
Therefore it is hardly remarkable that in the bills of rights
adopted in Pennsylvania, Delaware, Maryland, North Carolina, Vermont, Massachusetts, and New Hampshire, there are
provisions that carry either the import or the verbatim language of articles in the Virginia declaration.

In Pennsylvania the impatience of the ultra-Whig faction,
coupled with the May resolution from Congress, led to a
hurried constitutional movement in which the radicals seized
the initiative and held it.[11] The radicals gained control and

[8] Charles R. Lingley, *The Transition in Virginia from Colony to Common-wealth* (New York, 1910), 166.
[9] Samuel Adams to Richard Henry Lee, July 15, 1776, Force, comp., *American Archives*, 5th ser., I, 347.
[10] Josiah Bartlett to John Langdon, July 15, 1776, *ibid.*, 348.
[11] J. Paul Selsam, *The Pennsylvania Constitution of 1776* (Philadelphia, 1936), 136.

were willing to push the experiment in self government far beyond the point considered safe by the ousted conservatives. "The spirit of liberty reigns triumphant in Pennsylvania," Benjamin Rush noted. "The proprietary gentry have retired to their country seats, and honest men have taken the seats they abused so much in the government of our state."[12] Among the delegates were several outstanding figures whose roles in the making of the Pennsylvania Declaration of Rights are unknown because of the paucity of detailed information in the convention journal. The venerable Franklin was president of the convention but apparently took little part in drafting the articles. The actual framing was reportedly in the hands of such radical spirits as Thomas Paine, Dr. Thomas Young, James Cannon, George Bryan, and Timothy Matlack.[13]

Certainly the men now at the revolutionary helm were symbolic of the change in the political complexion of Pennsylvania. Landed gentry who held power in the Proprietary days were deposed by a class of men the landowners contemptuously alluded to as the "numsculs."[14] "The new Assembly," Professor Selsam declared, ". . . was the people's—the people were supreme." Dr. Young was a transplanted New Englander, a hotspur who had barely escaped the King's justice in Rhode Island during the first days of the war. Judge George Bryan was head of the Presbyterian element that was at odds with conservatism. Thomas Paine was readily admitted to this company for he was a known enemy of the aristocracy and revelled in his fearless trust of the common man. Only the Philadelphians—Cannon and Matlack—were actually delegates to the Assembly. Cannon was a schoolmaster turned politician, while Matlack was an unsuccessful business man who chose to cast his lot with the patriots' party.

[12] Benjamin Rush to Charles Lee, July 22, 1776, Lyman H. Butterfield, ed., *Letters of Benjamin Rush* (Princeton, 1951), I, 103.
[13] Selsam, *Pennsylvania Constitution*, 151; John Adams to Samuel Perley, June 19, 1809, Adams, ed., *Works of John Adams*, IX, 623.
[14] Selsam, *Pennsylvania Constitution*, 149.

Wasting precious little time, the Pennsylvania delegates and their friends were discussing a new frame of government less than two weeks after the Continental Congress formally dissolved the bonds with Great Britain. On July 18 a committee was appointed "to make an essay for a Declaration of Rights for this State."[15] When an urgent call from the Congress for militia demanded immediate action, the matter was nevertheless delayed because "so many of the Members had gone upon the Committee of the Declaration of Rights, that a quorum was not then in the House."[16] Within seven days the committee had furnished a first draft of this declaration, which after two readings and some debate was sent back to the committee for slight modifications. Hurriedly a new draft was prepared overnight. More time was consumed in further debate, however, before the new draft was sent to the printer with an order that ninety-six copies be prepared "for the further consideration of the Members of this House."[17]

When the convention sat as a committee of the whole the declaration and the proposed changes made up the main order of business. On August 16 the convention accepted a final draft. The whole process had consumed less than a month's time. "A Declaration of the Rights of the Inhabitants of the Commonwealth or State of Pennsylvania" was the result.

An examination of this document indicates the effect of reprints in the *Pennsylvania Evening Post* on June 6, and in the *Pennsylvania Gazette* on June 12, of Mason's Virginia declaration.[18] John Adams noted the similarities and deduced that the Pennsylvania declaration was "taken almost verbatim" from the Virginia Bill of Rights.[19] The two documents were on the same ground regarding the right of an accused person

[15] "Proceedings of the Pennsylvania Convention of 1776," Force, comp., *American Archives*, 5th ser., II, 5.

[16] *Ibid.*, 7.

[17] *Ibid.*, 12.

[18] Edmund C. Burnett, ed., *Letters and Correspondence of Members of the Continental Congress* (Washington, 1921-36), I, 480 n.

[19] Adams' Diary, Adams, ed., *Works of John Adams*, III, 220.

to a speedy and public jury trial, freedom from warrants of search and seizure, freedom of the press, the right to bear arms, and the subordination of the military to the civil powers. But in a few particulars the Pennsylvania Declaration of Rights either worked important changes in the Virginia plan or added to the list of rights reserved for the citizen. The Pennsylvania article on religion read, "All men have a natural and unalienable right to worship Almighty God according to the dictates of their own consciences and understanding." Conscientious dissenters were exempted from military service upon payment of a fee. While Virginia discouraged emigration, Section XV of the Pennsylvania declaration stated that emigration was a "natural inherent right," and it gave Pennsylvanians the right "to form a new State whenever they think that thereby they may promote their own happiness."

Although the French observer, Brissot de Warville, called the Pennsylvania Constitution of 1776 the closest approach to political perfection ever devised by mankind, the frame of government which the convention adopted on September 28 was headed for dark days.[20] Benjamin Rush, who had hailed the early assembly, decided within a brief span that the constitution was "absurd in its principles and incapable of execution without the most alarming influence upon liberty."[21] However, the Pennsylvania Declaration of Rights was spared the criticism directed at the constitution. Indeed, other states soon took note of the Pennsylvania declaration, which in time had its own influence on future conventions, particularly in Vermont. Several of the articles reappeared in the state constitutions which followed, including that which forbade the imprisonment of debtors—hardly an inalienable right, but a welcome relief to men who knew the oppressive power of the mortgage holders.

[20] J. Paul Selsam, "Brissot de Warville on the Pennsylvania Constitution of 1776," *Pennsylvania Magazine of History and Biography*, 72 (1948), 43.
[21] Benjamin Rush to Anthony Wayne, April 2, 1777, Butterfield, ed., *Letters of Benjamin Rush*, I, 137.

The scene of constitution-making then shifted to Maryland and Delaware. Both colonies had followed their neighbors and divorced themselves totally and completely from the British Empire. Some confusion in the chronology of events in both states has been cleared away only since the 1930's with the publication of relevant documents. It is now plain that although the Delaware Declaration of Rights reached the general public before the Maryland declaration, both stemmed from the work of the Annapolis convention.

Early in August, 1776, the Maryland delegates gathered at Annapolis to begin their deliberations. Their numbers included Charles Carroll of Carrollton, the planter who had signed the Declaration of Independence. Charles Carroll of Annapolis, the brilliant lawyer who went down in history as "the barrister" to avoid a confusion of names, was there. So were Samuel Chase, an office-trained lawyer who was something of a firebrand; Robert Goldsborough, a wealthy lawyer and former attorney general; and still another attorney, William Paca. Lawyers probably predominated in this group as in no earlier meeting to form a Revolutionary constitution. Indeed, the debates must have resounded with choice examples of courtroom oratory from the splendid array of legal talent thus assembled.

Even before the convention had met the question of individual rights had been forced to the delegates' attention. In the "Instructions of Anne Arundel county to delegates" 885 freemen of the county petitioned for male suffrage for all natives and freemen over 21 years of age, requested "that all elections be free . . . that the trial by Jury be held and kept sacred," and called for guarantees that the writ of habeas corpus would be preserved.[22] Their three elected delegates, Charles Carroll (the barrister), Brice T. B. Worthington, and Samuel Chase, replied with candor that "several of your last instructions, if carried into execution, [would be] destructive of a free

[22] Force, comp., *American Archives*, 5th ser., I, 1054.

Government." The delegates thereupon resigned from their seats because they could not conscientiously follow their instructions, although Worthington and Chase later reconsidered their resignations and consented to serve.[23] The freemen of Anne Arundel County clearly went much further in their demands for personal rights than did the men chosen to act on their behalf.[24]

The Maryland convention had hardly begun when Chase moved for the appointment of a committee to prepare "a Declaration and Charter of Rights, and a plan of Government . . . [which would] most effectually secure happiness and liberty to the people of this State." On the same day a committee, which included Matthew Tilghman, the convention president, Robert Goldsborough, Carroll (the barrister), and Chase, was appointed to draft a declaration. Within ten days the committee prepared a declaration and presented it to the convention on August 27.

Other business of a more urgent nature prevented consideration of the report.[25] Supply of men and munitions took precedence until September 17, when William Fitzhugh told his fellow delegates "the establishing a Bill of Rights and the formation of a new Government . . . are matters of the utmost importance to the good people of this State, and their posterity." Fitzhugh proposed, and the convention agreed to, the immediate publication of the declaration and constitution for distribution to the people, with twelve copies earmarked for each county.[26] After a brief adjournment, the problems of wartime government, plus the ordinary run of legislative business, continued to overshadow the declaration. Charles Carroll of Carrollton wrote his father on October 4:

[23] Kate Mason Rowland, *The Life of Charles Carroll of Carrollton* (New York, 1898), I, 187.

[24] See Philip A. Crowl, *Maryland during and after the Revolution* (Baltimore, 1943), 31.

[25] The conventions often carried on other business as a part of the regular legislative functions of the state assembly. The journal is reprinted in Force, comp., *American Archives*, 5th ser., III, 83ff.

[26] *Ibid.*, 112.

Our affairs are in a very critical situation: whether we shall go into the consideration of our bill of rights & form of govt I know not: to judge from the temper of the house I think we shall tho' I think that matter had better be postponed till there is greater certainty, than we have at present, of possessing a country & People to govern.[27]

Carroll's anxiety was shared by many of his colleagues, who were disheartened by recent British victories at Long Island and Fort Washington which had forced Washington's army into a southward retreat.

Despite temporary reverses on the battlefield the business of conducting government and laying the foundations for a permanent state could not be postponed indefinitely. On October 10, the convention in a committee of the whole began considering the declaration of rights and constitution. Delegate John Parnham became impatient when other business continued to interrupt deliberations. He asked that delegates "enter on no new business (except from evident necessity) until they have finished the consideration of the Declaration of Rights and form of Government."[28] The members even consented to stick to the problem "while that business is transacting, every evening till eight o'clock" if necessary.

The convention journal does not record the ensuing debates, nor does it give the changes made in the original committee report for a bill of rights. It is apparent, however, that these changes were significant. On October 30, Fitzhugh arose to say that "the Bill of Rights formerly printed for the consideration of the Members of the Convention has been materially altered by a Committee of the Whole House."[29] He therefore suggested that the revised declaration of rights should be printed for the use of members. Perhaps to avoid further delays the convention rejected Fitzhugh's resolution. Next day the committee of the whole heard a reading of the

[27] Letter dated October 4, 1776. Quoted in Ellen Hart Smith, *Charles Carroll of Carrollton* (Cambridge, Mass., 1942), 161.
[28] Force, comp., *American Archives*, 5th ser., III, 123.
[29] *Ibid.*, 134.

forty-two articles of the proposed declaration of rights, and for the first time ordered them entered in the journal.[30]

Attempts to change the final report were roughly handled, but the efforts were not completely in vain. During the debate the important third article, which specifically retained the common law of England and trial by jury, was approved. An amendment which sought to prevent lawyers from "being suffered to take, receive, or demand exorbitant fees for their services" mustered only six supporters.[31] An eleventh-hour attempt to permit either the eastern or western shore, if the inhabitants "judge it for their interest and happiness to separate from the other," was voted down.[32] Aside from a slight modification in the article on religion, the most significant alteration added the thirty-sixth article, which permitted "the people called Quakers, those called Dunkers, and those called Menonists," to make a solemn affirmation rather than take an oath contrary to their religious persuasion, whenever such a statement was deemed necessary.[33] At an extraordinary Sunday session, on November 3, the convention finally gave its assent to the declaration as amended.

Barrister Charles Carroll, who left the convention on August 27, has been traditionally credited with drafting the declaration. Convincing evidence on the point is lacking, but because the convention sat as a committee of the whole and because numerous alterations were made then, it may be inferred that the final document was not the work of any one man. Among the forty-two articles were scattered provisions that were out of place in a bill of rights, such as that which confirmed the validity of the Annapolis city charter.[34] But to those individual rights which the Pennsylvania and Virginia declarations had proclaimed, Maryland added prohibitions

[30] *Ibid.*, 135-39. No printed copies of this document are extant.
[31] *Ibid.*, 142.
[32] *Ibid.*, 143.
[33] *Ibid.*, 142-43.
[34] Poore, comp., *Constitutions and Charters*, I, 817-20.

against ex post facto laws and bills of attainder. Civilians were exempted from the reach of martial law. Poll taxes were denounced, and paupers were exempted from taxation. A curious section, which declared that "monopolies are odious, contrary to the spirit of a free government, and the principles of commerce, and ought not to be suffered," was probably a reaction to recent commercial experience under the English Navigation Acts.

These men who had spent their lives in the shadow of the Calvert family forbade the future use of titles of nobility or hereditary honors. Unlike the Pennsylvania document, however, the Maryland declaration took the limited view that freedom of speech was guaranteed only to legislators and said nothing about the right of the man in the street to speak his piece. Of course, colonial and English precedents buttressed this provision.

As in the other new states, the matter of religious liberty had provoked considerable discussion, judging from the final article on that tender subject. Akin to the Virginia provision was the Maryland statement that held worship of God to be a duty, but not a natural right as the Pennsylvanians had held. The guarantee of religious liberty was specifically for "persons professing the Christian religion," but no person could be legally molested because of his religious beliefs. The basis for an established church was destroyed but the legislature was allowed to levy taxes "for the support of the Christian religion." Property already in the possession of the Anglican church was guaranteed to that body forever, but to restrict the power of churches as landowners, limits were placed on the amount of property a religious denomination could own.[35] A "declaration of a belief in the Christian religion" was held to be a proper requirement for admission "to any office of trust or profit," and affirmations might be substituted for oaths.

The convention concluded its work by inserting in the

[35] Article LIX.

constitution an article that positively forbade a legislative revision of the declaration of rights "on any pretence whatever."
The language was indeed firm enough.

A full month before the Maryland convention heard the
last rap of President Tilghman's gavel on November 11, the
Delaware convention had formally adopted a bill of rights.
That body had been called to meet at New Castle on August
27, bringing together two factions that varied in political
complexion from extreme radicals eager for independence to
ultra-conservatives who would have been happy to remain
under George III. Caesar Rodney, Whig signer of the Declaration of Independence, had been denied a seat by the voters
of Kent County. Other balloting had resulted in the election
of toryish Charles Ridgely, moderate George Read, and radical Thomas McKean—with the conservative element in the
majority. Independence was already a fact, but the conservatives wanted at least to hold tight reins on the revolution in
their state to see that it did not get out of hand.[36]

The majority of the Delaware convention was willing to
receive certain ideas from other states, however, which did
not radically alter the prewar status of local government. A
declaration of rights was, after all, a mirror of public opinion
that would give the government no new powers and would
positively restrict its control of the individual. Thus the conservatives in Delaware could find nothing worthy of strenuous
objection in a bill of rights. So they accepted the device which
other states had adopted and had more time for other business
by simply borrowing most of their bill of rights from that of
their neighbors.

Before the Delaware delegates had commenced their sessions, copies of the *Pennsylvania Gazette* for August 21 with
a full account of the Pennsylvania Declaration of Rights had
circulated in the three counties that adjoined eastern Mary-

[36] H. Clay Reed, "The Delaware Constitution of 1776," in *Delaware Notes*,
6th ser. (1930), 17-21.

land. The time sequence and the definite similarity of twelve articles led to the presumption that Delaware "drew upon Pennsylvania for certain of the provisions in framing her declaration of rights."[37] This view ignored the debt of Delaware delegates to their friends in Maryland. Professor Max Farrand, writing in 1898, believed that the debt relationship was exactly opposite. Farrand seemed on good ground when he stated that the Maryland declaration followed the Delaware Bill of Rights and this accounted for the similarity of wording in the two documents. He thought it extremely unlikely that a copy of the proposed Maryland declaration, presented by a special committee on August 27, could have traveled from Annapolis to New Castle through private correspondence and concluded that it was "improbable that Delaware could have profited by Maryland's declaration of rights."

New documentary material published in the 1930's revealed that similarities in the two declarations were in fact a result of the use of the Maryland draft by the Delaware delegates, despite the fact that Delaware formally adopted her bill of rights three weeks earlier than Maryland acted. A letter written by George Read, presiding officer of the Delaware convention, to Caesar Rodney after the adoption of the Delaware Declaration of Rights puts the matter beyond reasonable doubt. Read told Rodney:

I had to give you some satisfactory account of the business we have been more particularly engaged in to wit the Declaration of Rights and the plan of Government—as to the first it has been completed some days past but there being nothing particularly in it—I did not think it an object of much curiosity, it is made out of the Pensilvania & Maryland Draughts.[38]

Private correspondence had passed between members of the

[37] Max Farrand, "The Delaware Bill of Rights of 1776," *American Historical Review*, 3 (1897-98), 647.
[38] George Read to Caesar Rodney, September 17, 1776, George H. Ryder, ed., *Letters to and from Caesar Rodney, 1756-1784* (Philadelphia, 1933), 119. See also Reed, "The Delaware Constitution of 1776," *Delaware Notes*, 6th ser. (1930), 23 n.

Maryland and Delaware conventions, many of whom were well known to each other. Sometime between August 27 and the date when the Delaware committee drafted its declaration a copy of the Maryland project had fallen into the hands of Read or one of his colleagues. Read's statement is particularly convincing, for he not only acted as president of the convention but also served as chairman of the committee appointed to draft the declaration of rights. He should have known, if anyone did, the sources of the Delaware Declaration of Rights.

The president's remark that his state had adopted a declaration of rights containing nothing to mark it as out of the ordinary is somewhat misleading. The statement passes over several differences between the Delaware document and other declarations of the same period.[39] Despite liberal borrowing from the Maryland and Pennsylvania declarations (and thus indirectly from the Virginia declaration), the Delaware Declaration of Rights was in a sense more conservative in the use of abstract theories than its predecessors. It is notable that the prefatory statement of the equality of man was missing in this slave state. And unlike the Pennsylvania declaration, which extended civil rights to all men who professed a belief in God, the Delaware Declaration of Rights limited "equal rights and privileges" to Christians.

What the Delaware declaration failed to provide in theory was compensated for in concrete provisions. Though they were generally conservative on most issues, the Delaware delegates adhered to the spirit of their pre-convention oath which bound them to exert their abilities on behalf of the "natural, civil and religious Rights and Privileges" of the citizenry.[40] At the conclusion of their deliberations they borrowed the article from the Pennsylvania and Maryland con-

[39] The Delaware Declaration of Rights was omitted from Poore's *Constitutions and Charters*. The text may be found in Force, comp., *American Archives*, 5th ser., II, 286-87.

[40] *Proceedings of the Convention of the Delaware State* (Wilmington, 1927), 10. Reprint of 1776 edition.

stitutions which declared that a bill of rights should never be violated.[41] Among the provisions of the bill of rights made permanent by this article, two are of special interest—one touching the slave trade, the other religion. If the Delaware convention was unready to declare the equality of all men, at least it was not for the enlargement of the existing slave population. Thus the delegates approved an article which declared that

No person hereafter imported into this State from Africa ought to be held in slavery under any pretence whatever; and no negro, Indian, or mulatto slave ought to be brought into this State, for sale, from any part of the world.

The Delaware constitution makers also considered the separation of church and state vital. Not only was the practice of maintaining an established church forbidden, but ministers were barred from holding "any civil office in this State . . . while they continue in the exercise of the pastoral function."

The ink was scarcely dry on the journals of the Delaware and Maryland conventions when the same sort of drama began to unfold at Halifax, North Carolina. Like their northern neighbors, the inhabitants of North Carolina wanted particular attention paid to what they conceived to be their natural rights. The Orange County constituency warned its delegates that it would not tolerate "depriving any individual of his civil or natural rights unless by way of punishment for some declared offence clearly and plainly adjudged against him by the judging power."[42] The established church was a particularly irksome institution and the citizens therefore asked

that in framing the religious constitution you insist upon a free and unrestrained exercise of religion to every individual agreeable to that mode which each man shall choose for himself and that no one shall

[41] Article XXX of the Constitution of 1776, Poore, comp., Constitutions and Charters, I, 278.
[42] William L. Saunders and Walter Clark, eds., Colonial and State Records of North Carolina (Raleigh, etc., 1886-1914), X, 870h. (Hereinafter cited as N. C. Recs.)

be compelled to pay towards the support of any clergyman except such as he shall choose to be instructed by.[43]

The instructions to the delegates went on to demand that all ministers be permitted to solemnize marriages and that Catholics be barred from office by denying public positions to any person who acknowledged "supremacy ecclesiastical or civil in any foreign power or spiritual infallibility or authority to grant the Divine Pardon to any person who may violate moral duties or commit crimes injurious to the community."[44] This was a far cry from full religious freedom, but it was still further away from the kind of head-cracking intolerance that Nathaniel Ames had commented on a decade earlier.

Other North Carolina communities were equally vocal in their demand for a bill of rights. Waightstill Avery and his four colleagues from Mecklenburg County were specifically enjoined to seek "a bill of rights containing the rights of the people and of individuals which shall never be infringed in any future time by the law-making power or other derived powers in the State."[45] The delegates were to endeavor to produce a bill of rights in strict conformity to the maxim that the people are the source of all power, with guarantees of trial by jury, bans against office-holding by professed atheists, Catholics, or Deists, and freedom of conscience for "all professing christians."[46] Further, the citizens of Mecklenburg County wanted the state congress to submit its product to the voters for their approval or rejection.

A committee of eighteen delegates was chosen at Halifax on November 13 to prepare a bill of rights and a constitution.[47] Enlarged by later appointments, this group included Richard Caswell, president of the congress, the radical Willie Jones, and Thomas Person. This trio shared a large degree of popularity and their selection for this important committee could

[43] *Ibid.*, 870g.   [44] *Ibid.*
[45] *Ibid.*, 870a.   [46] *Ibid.*, 870d.
[47] The journal of the provincial congress is reprinted in Saunders and Clark, eds., *N. C. Recs.*, X, 913-1013.

not have been accidental. Jones and Person were particularly known to be outspoken proponents of popular government, while later events were to prove their zeal for legal safeguards for personal freedom.

For a time pressing affairs of state occupied the congress almost exclusively. The making of a bill of rights and a constitution was relegated to a secondary place. A constitution was reported to the congress on December 6, and discussed paragraph by paragraph during the days that followed without any conclusive action being taken. On December 12 Thomas Jones of Chowan County brought a bill of rights from the committee.[48]   After some discussion this bill of rights was amended and passed the first reading in the congress two days later. Action on the constitution was delayed while the bill of rights passed second and third readings on December 16 and 17 and was "ordered to be engrossed."[49] The hesitation of the congress to approve the constitution before passing a bill of rights has led one historian to state that "the convention looked upon the Bill of Rights as more fundamental than the constitution."[50] In view of the precedents from four sister states, North Carolina congressmen might well have considered the bill of rights a necessary preface to their constitution.

The North Carolina Declaration of Rights added no new safeguards for personal liberty to those which had already been recognized elsewhere. For the first time since the passage of the Virginia Declaration of Rights a state had adopted a bill of rights without adding to or altering the storehouse of ideas concerning liberty. On the other hand considerable material not ordinarily expected in a bill of rights found its way into the document. Although heavy borrowing from earlier bills of rights was obvious, to say that the North Carolina Declaration of Rights "can lay claim to originality neither in

    [48] Ibid., 967.
    [49] Ibid., 973.
    [50] Fletcher M. Green, Constitutional Development in the South Atlantic States, 1776-1860 (Chapel Hill, 1938), 71.

conception nor expression" is perhaps too harsh a judgment.[51] It ignores a unique and significant clause in the twenty-fifth article which recognized the right of citizens to emigrate across the western mountain ranges and erect their own government "by consent of the Legislature."[52] This clause was similar to the Pennsylvania "right to emigrate" provision but it was at odds with the Virginia Declaration of Rights, which took the opposite view of nascent territorial governments in the transmontane region. Hard to justify in a bill of rights was the provision that promised to protect the hunting grounds of certain Indian tribes, and another "rider" which eased the mind of landowners with its guarantee of the validity of old royal and proprietary land titles.

The grassroots movement for disestablishing the church and for banning from office members of certain sects bore fruit in the constitution, rather than in the declaration of rights.[53] Perhaps Willie Jones had a strong hand in this affair, as he was hostile to an organized church and to dogmatic religion generally. The brevity of the article actually left the door open to indefinite extension of religious freedom. The statement, "That all men have a natural and unalienable right to worship Almighty God, according to the dictates of their own consciences," was the most succinct of all the articles on religious freedom passed to that time. The age-old idea that a debtor should remain in prison, already shaken by the Pennsylvania constitution, was virtually ushered out by another constitutional provision. Once again, it was explicitly stated that the Declaration of Rights "ought never to be violated on any pretence whatsoever."

Several claims for the authorship of the North Carolina Declaration of Rights have been advanced, but none comes from the alleged writers themselves. One historian claimed

[51] Enoch W. Sikes, *The Transition of North Carolina from Colony to Commonwealth* (Baltimore, 1898), 69.

[52] Saunders and Clark, eds., *N. C. Recs.*, X, 1005.

[53] *Ibid.*, 1011.

some credit for Richard Caswell, on the ground that the president of the congress exerted much influence in the councils and "was a native of Maryland, and so it is probable a copy of the Maryland Constitution was before them." The further inference is that the Maryland Declaration of Rights contributed considerably more ideas to the North Carolina declaration than that of any other state.[54] In 1834 Joseph Seawell Jones wrote that the declaration of rights and constitution

are said to come from the pen of Thomas Jones, aided and assisted by Willie Jones. I find in one of Governor Johnston's letters, that he alludes to it as Jones' Constitution, and the reader will observe that Thomas Jones was throughout the organ of the committee.[55]

These conflicting claims are based on circumstantial evidence. It is sufficient to note that no direct evidence of authorship has been discovered.

Georgia, the next state to work out a constitution, followed the New Jersey practice to formulate a fundamental code without prefacing it with a bill of rights. The Georgians chose to follow the New Jersey lawmakers by adopting an all-inclusive constitution and thereby preserved the substance of a bill of rights. Many abstract principles, elsewhere included in formal bills of rights, were written into the several articles—including the necessity of frequent elections. Indeed, the Georgia constitution went a step further to provide that eligible voters who "shall neglect to give in his or their ballot at such election, shall be subject to a penalty not exceeding five pounds," unless "a reasonable excuse shall be admitted."[56] Trials were to be held in the vicinity of the alleged crime. Excessive fines and bails were banned, the "principles of the habeas-corpus act"

[54] Sikes, *The Transition of North Carolina*, 69, 69 n.

[55] Joseph Seawell Jones, *A Defence of the Revolutionary History of North Carolina* . . . (Boston, 1834), 287. Quoted in Frank Nash, "The North Carolina Constitution of 1776 and Its Makers," *The James Sprunt Historical Publications*, 11 (1911), no. 2, 21.

[56] Article XII. The entire constitution is reprinted in Poore, comp., *Constitutions and Charters*, I, 377-83.

were guaranteed, and "Freedom of the press and trial by jury [were] to remain inviolate forever."

The Georgia articles pertaining to religion were broad in outlook. "All persons whatever shall have the free exercise of their religion; provided it be not repugnant to the peace and safety of the State; and shall not, unless by consent, support any teacher or teachers except those of their own profession." Another provision barred ministers from serving in the state legislature. Full freedom was nevertheless denied, for only Protestants were to be admitted as members of the lawmaking body.

Although Georgia had been an early haven for "languishing debtors" from England, this constitution adopted on February 5, 1777, made no concession to persons unable to meet their financial obligations. Pennsylvania and North Carolina had already adopted provisions which barred the confinement of penurious debtors. After calling attention to this omission in the Georgia constitution, Professor Saye concluded that the sections protecting the individual citizen were "obviously influenced by the earlier declarations in other States, by the Declaration of Independence," and by the various colonial charter provisions including the Georgia charter of 1732.[57] This much might be said of any state adopting a frame of government in this period, and it can only be concluded that the progeny of debtors were not inclined to be as lenient toward the impecunious as their northern neighbors with presumably a steadier background of frugality.

The claim that Button Gwinnett was responsible for a considerable portion of the Georgia Constitution of 1777 rests mainly on the support of an enthusiastic biographer. It is only known that Gwinnett brought in a committee report on the proposed constitution some eight days before the final draft was approved.[58]

[57] Albert B. Saye, *A Constitutional History of Georgia, 1732-1945* (Athens, Ga., 1948), 101.
[58] Ethel K. Ware, *A Constitutional History of Georgia* (New York, 1947), 32.

The New York constitution which was finally adopted on April 20, 1777, had been on the legislators' docket since the preceding summer. The legislature had drafted a constitution which did not recognize personal rights in a distinct bill of rights, and thus followed the Georgia lawmakers in departing from the precedent of neighboring states. Like the Georgians, too, the New York lawmakers incorporated theories of government and provisions for civil rights in the text of the constitution itself.[59] The sovereignty of the people and the concept of separation of powers were explicitly stated. No citizen was to be "disfranchised, or deprived of any the rights or privileges . . . unless by the law of the land, or the judgment of his peers." An established church was declared "repugnant to this constitution," and laws favoring the Anglican church were repudiated. Quakers were permitted to make affirmation, rather than oath; and they might be excused from militia duty, as non-believers in armed resistance, upon the payment of an exemption fee. Trial by jury was established "inviolate forever." Bills of attainder were outlawed, except those passed during and "before the termination of the present war; and that such acts shall not work a corruption of blood."

New York delegates also believed that they were required "by the benevolent principles of rational liberty . . . to guard against the spiritual oppression and intolerance wherewith the bigotry and ambition of weak and wicked priests and princes have scourged mankind." To do so

the Authority of the Good People of this State Ordain determine and declare that the free Exercise and Enjoyment of Religeous Profession and Worship without Discrimination or preference shall forever hereafter be allowed—within this State to all mankind.[60]

New York, already the sanctuary of Protestants, Catholics, and Jews, thus continued the trend toward greater religious free-

[59] Poore, comp., *Constitutions and Charters*, II, 1328-39.

[60] The 1777 version of this provision is pictured in *Official Document Book, New York State Freedom Train* (Albany, 1950), 24. It reveals the word "toleration" was marked through and replaced with "free Exercise and Enjoyment . . . ," a much broader concept.

dom. Jealous of the possible encroachments of the church, the constitution went on to state that since "the Ministers of the Gospel are by their Profession dedicated to the Service of God & the Cure of Souls," it would henceforth be illegal for any "Minister of the Gospel or Priest of any denomination whatsoever" to hold either a civil or military office in the state.

To the north, an undertaking was afoot in the back country which was eventually to bring a fourteenth state into the Union. While politicians and land speculators in New York and New Hampshire fretted over the growing discontent and disorder in this region, men from the Green Mountains region were charting their own course. Their quarrel with the older governments had grown more acute in the decade preceding the Windsor convention of 1777. Appealing to the right of revolt and the rights of mankind, they effected a revolution which eventually bore fruit with Vermont's admission as a state in 1791. Inasmuch as Vermont began conducting the business of government as a *de facto* body, it seems proper to include here its Declaration of Rights of 1777.

Several months before the Vermont convention met at Windsor, a letter from Dr. Thomas Young of Philadelphia had been circulated among political leaders of the Green Mountain area. Dr. Young, a friend of Ethan Allen's, was one of the radicals who had helped draw up the Pennsylvania Constitution of 1776. Young was prepared to send the seeds of liberty out in broadcast fashion, as his address "To the IN-HABITANTS of VERMONT" indicated. He urged the people to take the Pennsylvania constitution "as a model, which, with a very little alteration, will, in my opinion, come as near perfection as anything yet concocted by mankind."[61] He was aware of the sharp criticism leveled at the Pennsylvania constitution, but labelled its detractors as despots and boasted that the constitution "has bid defiance to their wicked powers."

[61] Rev. Pliny H. White, "Address on the Windsor Convention," Vermont Historical Society, *Collections*, 1 (1870), 63. See also Frederic F. Van de Water, *The Reluctant Republic* (New York, 1941), 182-83.

The Vermont convention accepted Dr. Young's advice with alacrity. The delegates assembled on July 2, 1777. Six days later, they received word from General Arthur St. Clair that the Americans were evacuating Ticonderoga. Before the day ended the Vermont Declaration of Rights and Frame of Government had been approved. Its business finished, the convention adjourned after setting a record for speed in the adoption of a bill of rights and a constitution.

The Vermont Declaration of Rights combined the basic features of the Pennsylvania and Virginia bills of rights. But in two particulars difference was marked. The first article not only made the usual general statement about the freedom and equality of men, but it went further to declare that in view of this truth

Therefore, no male person, born in this country, or brought over sea, ought to be holden by law, to serve any person, as a servant, slave or apprentice, after he arrives to the age of twenty-one years, nor female, in like manner, after she arrives to the age of eighteen years, unless they are bound by their own consent . . . or bound by law. . . .[62]

The Delaware declaration had struck at the slave trade: the Vermont provision apparently was intended to abolish slavery and indentured servitude entirely. The section is more important for its relation to opinion in 1777 than its practical effect, for a slave was a rare sight in Vermont. Freedom of conscience was also allowed, but Protestants were favored over other sects. The final article was tailor-made for men who were considered little more than rebels by several of the states. It declared that "no person shall be liable to be transported out of this State for trial, for any offence committed within this State." Broad as this declaration of rights was in its coverage, it was to be expanded before Vermont was admitted to the Union.

South Carolina adopted a more extensive frame of government early in 1778 after almost two years under a tempo-

[62] Poore, comp., *Constitutions and Charters*, II, 1859.

rary constitution put together before independence had been declared. A bill of rights was not adopted by the General Assembly but, as in New Jersey, Georgia, and New York, the absence of a specific declaration did not mean that safeguards for the people's rights were overlooked. A Presbyterian minister, William Tennent, and Christopher Gadsden are credited with persistent efforts which produced a section stating that "all persons and religious societies who acknowledge that there is one God, and a future state of rewards and punishments, and that God is publicly to be worshipped, shall be freely tolerated."[63] The Protestant religion was declared to be the established religion of the state. The elaborate article even prescribed the manner in which a church might be formed and set down five articles of faith that had to be accepted before the group could "be incorporated and esteemed as a church of the established religion of this State." Despite the marked emphasis on basic doctrinal conformity, a section was inserted in the document which made it illegal to compel a citizen "to pay towards the maintenance and support of a religious worship that he does not freely join in, or has not voluntarily engaged to support." Another article barred ministers from office-holding, and Quakers were excused from taking oaths.

A cluster of articles near the end of the South Carolina constitution provided for a reform of the penal laws that would make punishments "more proportionate to the crime," for observance of the due process of law, for subordination of the military to the civil powers of the state, and for freedom of the press.[64] President Rawlin Lowndes affixed his signature to the Constitution on March 19, 1778.

During the same month in which South Carolina legislators had framed a constitution, the people of Massachusetts had rejected one. By a decisive five-to-one majority the opponents of the proposed constitution voted down an attempt to replace

[63] Green, *Constitutional Development in South Atlantic States*, 108-10.
[64] Poore, comp., *Constitutions and Charters*, II, 162-67.

the old colonial charter.[65] In contrast to Vermont, where the convention lasted six days, Massachusetts and New Hampshire found the constitution-making process long and painful. Conventions in both states initially drew up documents which the people rejected. Not the least of the reasons was the failure to offer the people adequate guarantees of personal safety.

In rejecting the constitution of 1778 the people of Massachusetts made it plain that the omission of a bill of rights had been a mistake. They declared this bill of rights "ought to describe the Natural Rights of Man as he inherits them from the Great Parents of Nature, distinguishing those, the Controul of which he may part with to Society for Social Benefits from those he cannot."[66] The citizens of Plymouth thought a declaration "Clearly Asserting the rights of the people, as men, Christians & Subjects, Ought to have Preceeded the Constitution, and these Rights should be Express'd in the fullest and most unequivocal terms."[67] They felt that the two articles in the constitution of 1778 which promised trial by jury and assured Protestants freedom of religion were an insufficient expression of the full panoply of rights.

Out of the opposition to this constitution came a definite statement, positively delineating an acceptable frame of government. This declaration came from a convention which first met at Ipswich, Essex County, in April of 1778 to consider the proposed constitution and to ascertain whether it conformed to the prevailing pattern on "the natural rights of mankind and the true principles of government."[68] Dominating this gathering of wealth and intellect was 27-year-old Theophilus Parsons, a Harvard-trained lawyer. Parsons forcefully projected

[65] Samuel E. Morison, "The Vote of Massachusetts on Summoning a Constitutional Convention, 1776-1916," Massachusetts Historical Society, Proceedings, 50 (1916-17), 244.

[66] Town of Beverly's instructions of June 1, 1778, quoted in Harry A. Cushing, History of the Transition from Provincial to Commonwealth Government in Massachusetts (New York, 1896), 216.

[67] Town of Plymouth, May 18-June 1, 1778, ibid.

[68] The proposed constitution of 1778 is reprinted in The Journal of the Convention for Framing a Constitution . . . 1779-1780 (Boston, 1832), 255-64.

his ideas on other members of the group, which in time became known as the Essex Junto. Realistic and eager to find a solution that would satisfy both conservatives and radicals, this convention decided that on the matter of personal liberty the rejected constitution fell far short of its mark.

In the work of the Essex convention the shrewd handling of a political strategist is evident. Here was the first instance of a bill of rights used in an effort to "sweeten the taste" of the entire constitution for the voters. Among the eighteen objections of the Ipswich convention was one which declared

That a bill of rights, clearly ascertaining and defining the rights of conscience, and the security of person and property, which every member in a State hath a right to expect from the supreme power thereof, ought to be settled and established, previous to the ratification of any constitution for the State.[69]

The delegates went on record as fearful of personal freedom and property rights unless some satisfactory method of limiting the power of the legislature were devised. The article in the rejected constitution alluding to the rights of conscience was held exceptionable because those rights were not "clearly defined and ascertained." Furthermore, the unsatisfactory article "*allowed* to all the protestants" of Massachusetts freedom of conscience "when in fact, that free exercise and enjoyment is the natural and uncontroulable right of every member of the State."

After placing all of their objections to the old proposal on record, the Essex convention adjourned until May 12. During the interim a committee report was prepared to outline recommendations for an acceptable constitution. This committee report, chiefly Parsons' work, formed the heart of the "Essex Result," a pamphlet which was the principal argument of the county's conservative element.[70] Parsons' report was a powerful statement in support of a constitution based on the

[69] Theophilus Parsons, Jr., *The Memoirs of Theophilus Parsons* (Boston, 1859), 359.
[70] The pamphlet is reprinted, *ibid.*, 359ff.

current ideas of natural rights. He declared that when a person entered society he surrendered certain rights to the government, but others he retained as inalienable. Governments had no leave to interfere with these inalienable rights, which must be set apart in "a BILL OF RIGHTS, previous to the ratification of any constitution." The bill of rights ought to be "the equivalent every man receives, as a consideration for the rights he has surrendered . . . [for] ALLEGIANCE AND PROTECTION ARE RECIPROCAL."

Parsons' report gave some hints as to what a bill of rights ought to contain. Suffrage should be extended to all freemen, and representation

should be so equally and impartially distributed, that the representatives should have the same views, and interests with the people at large. . . . Elections ought to be free. . . . The want of fixed principles of government, and a stated regular recourse to them [is vital]. . . . Standing armies are a tremendous curse to a state.

He suggested that if a future constitutional convention would recognize these principles, political and civil liberty would be assured the good people of Massachusetts Bay.

In response to the numerous town instructions and the manifest desire of the citizens for some statement of personal rights, a second constitutional convention assembled in September, 1779. The delegates undertook the preparation of a declaration of rights after a resolution calling for such a preface to the constitution was approved by a vote of 250 to 1.[71] A committee of thirty-one delegates was appointed to draft both the declaration and the constitution. The membership included John Adams, Parsons, James Sullivan, Robert Treat Paine, James Bowdoin, and Samuel Adams.[72] John Adams, a student of government with long experience in the Continental Congress, apparently was handed the task of drawing up the necessary documents for the committee. The principal evidence of

[71] *Journal of the Convention*, 23.
[72] *Ibid.*, 28-30.

authorship is Adams' own statement made many years later. While the convention was still in progress he wrote merely that he was busy at "my new trade of a Constitution monger."[73] In 1812 he recalled that

This drafting committee, after some weeks of debate, appointed a sub-committee of three members to make a draft. The three were Mr. Bowdoin, Mr. S. Adams, and myself. When we met, Mr. Bowdoin and Mr. S. Adams insisted that I should prepare a plan in writing, which I did. . . . The article relative to religion was not drawn by me, nor by the sub-committee. The Declaration of Rights was drawn by me, who was appointed alone by the Grand Committee to draw it up.[74]

Adams may have been anxious to dissociate himself from the third article because it was the one which caused serious trouble in the convention and later in the town meetings. At any rate his statement that neither he nor the drafting committee had drawn the article was correct. On the eve of his departure for a diplomatic post abroad the convention, after heated debate, adopted a substitute for the committee's recommendation on religious freedom.[75] Otherwise, the language of the original committee report was adopted by the convention with a few minor exceptions.[76]

The troublesome third article grew out of the committee draft, which had as its chief aim the firm entrenchment of a tax-supported Congregational church. Revised in the convention, this article made legislative participation in religious affairs mandatory "in all cases where such provision [for financing the churches] shall not be made voluntarily" by the towns, parishes, and precincts.[77] The third article further permitted the legislature to "enjoin upon all the subjects an attendance" at public worship, although congregations were to remain free

[73] John Adams to Benjamin Rush, November 4, 1779, Adams, ed., *Works of John Adams*, IX, 507.

[74] John Adams to W. D. Williamson, February 25, 1812, Massachusetts Historical Society, *Proceedings*, 13 (1873-75), 300 n-301 n.

[75] *Journal of the Convention*, 46.

[76] The "Grand Committee" report on a declaration of rights is included in the *Journal of the Convention*, 191-97.

[77] *Ibid.*, 223ff.

of state control in their choice of ministers. Taxpayers could still earmark levies for their own sect, "and every denomination of christians, demeaning themselves peaceably, and as good subjects of the Commonwealth, shall be equally under the protection of the law." Finally, the ambiguous article held that "no subordination of any one sect or denomination to another shall ever be established by law."

Satisfied that their labors had produced a worthy product, the Massachusetts delegates sent the constitution to the townships. An attached prefatory letter anticipated the contention over the third article by declaring that the convention had "with as much Precision as we were capable of, provided for the free exercise of the *Rights of Conscience*." Much debate had centered around the third article in the declaration of rights, the letter continued, "and we feel ourselves peculiarly happy in being able to inform you, that though the debates were managed by persons of various denominations, it was finally agreed upon with much more Unanimity than usually takes place in disquisitions of this Nature."[78] While the delegates denied that their powers enabled them to establish one denomination "above another," they formulated an oath of office to exclude "those from Offices who will not disclaim those Principles of Spiritual Jurisdiction which Roman Catholicks *in some Countries* have held, and which are subversive of a free Government established by the People."[79] About the other provisions regarding civil or religious liberty, the letter was silent. The convention had finished its business. It was now up to the people to determine whether the delegates had finished that business properly.

Since the omission of a bill of rights had contributed to the rejection of the constitution of 1778, a careful scrutiny of the proposed declaration of rights was assured. Criticism was general, but, as the delegates had anticipated, more fire was directed at the third article than at any other single provision.

[78] *Ibid.*, 218.   [79] *Ibid.*, 221.

Some critics thought the third article went too far, others not far enough, in establishing a particular mode of worship. Citizens in Ashfield denounced the article as "unconstitutional to human Nature" and without "Precept in the word of God."[80] "True Religion has evidently declined & been corrupted by the interference of Statesmen & Politicians," the Granville town meeting declared. Other citizens believed the article was equivocal. Middleborough townsmen said the article was either "unmeaning or otherwise admits of Different meanings."

From all sides the attack continued. The Reverend Isaac Backus, a leading Baptist minister, used newspaper columns for his attack on the odious article. Bellingham citizens in their town meeting asked for complete freedom of worship, not half measures. "Libertatis Amici" predicted in the *Massachusetts Spy* that numerous taxpayers would never submit to the proposed levies.[81] The town of Westford objected to the article on the grounds that "whenever such Institutions fully executed by the civil authority have taken place among a people, instead of promoting essentially their Happiness and the good order and Preservation of civil government, it has, we believe, invariably produced impiety, irreligion, Hypocrisy and many sore and oppressive evils."[82] The true principles of civil government would be endangered if not "kept Distinct of Religious gospel institutions." The inhabitants of Raynham thought the article ambiguous and expressed fears that if it were not more clearly stated "there will be Danger of Different Societies Quariling and Contending in the law about their Rights which will Tend to the Destruction of Piety, Religion and Morality and Entirely Subvert the Intention of said Third Article."[83] "Philanthropos," a self-styled member

[80] Cushing, *The Transition in Massachusetts*, 266.

[81] *Ibid.*, 267.

[82] Quoted in J. Franklin Jameson, *An Introduction to the Study of the Constitutional and Political History of the States* (Baltimore, 1886), 28.

[83] Samuel E. Morison, "The Struggle over the Adoption of the Constitution of Massachusetts, 1780," Massachusetts Historical Society, *Proceedings*, 50 (1916-17), 371-72.

of the convention, fired broadsides at the article through the pages of the *Independent Chronicle*. The unnamed "delegate" proposed as a substitute an amendment which expressly forbade taxation in support of a religious establishment.

The third article had a few defenders. One of them, "Iraeneus," also claimed service in the recent constitutional convention. "If there is no law to support religion," "Iraeneus" declared, "farewell meeting-houses, farewell ministers, and farewell all religion."[84] He accused opponents of the article of conforming "to a certain junto, composed of disguised Tories, British emissaries, profane and licentious Deists, avaricious Worldlings, disaffected Sectaries, and furious blind bigots."

Some citizens in Brookline apparently thought the article too liberal, and sought a return to the religious practices of the colony in the seventeenth century, "when all dissenters' estates were taxed for orthodox Congregational worship."[85] Abington and five other towns lamented the omission of a section in the constitution which would make the rigors of the old Puritan Sabbath obligatory for all citizens.

Other provisions in the bill of rights were not immune to criticism from the town meetings and pulpits. The town of Dunstable thought the section on freedom of the press (paraphrased from the Virginia declaration) was too liberal, since misguided souls might "Dishonour god by printing herasy."[86] At their town meeting Chelsea citizens asked that the same article be amended to make the printer accountable for defamatory and abusive statements. The Stoughton town meeting wanted freedom of speech explicitly stated. Boston and Milton approved varying degrees of free speech. In the western part of the state some objection was raised to the article which promised judges of the Supreme Judicial Court tenure "as long as they behave themselves well." "We don't see

[84] *Ibid.*, 379-80.
[85] *Ibid.*, 380.
[86] Cushing, *The Transition in Massachusetts*, 268.

that it is any Right or advantage for Officers to be so Independent as There expressed, but a disadvantage," the citizens of Sutton argued.[87] Despite the reassuring address from the convention, some towns still sought guarantees for Protestantism. Lexington wanted due recognition for "the *pious*, noble and *truly heroic Stand*, which *Luther* and the first Reformers" made on behalf of Protestantism. Various towns thought the suffrage restrictions oppressive. Stoughton went so far as to declare "The right of election is not a civil; but it is a natural right, which ought to be considered as a principle corner-stone in the foundation for the frame of Government to stand on."[88]

Amidst the charges and countercharges proponents of the constitution were still hopeful that the necessary two-thirds majority vote would favor the plan. Professor Morison's reconstructed tabulation of ballots indicates that the vote on the third article was 8,885 in favor, with 6,225 against the section. These figures were based on admittedly incomplete sources. Nevertheless, they mirror some of the bitterness engendered by the religious issue in 1780. Furthermore, these results make it appear unlikely that the bill of rights and its partner (the constitution) were approved in the prescribed manner. Many towns proposed amendments and alterations, but these were brushed aside when the delegates reconvened to count the votes and by their findings announced that the required majority vote in the townships permitted the bill of rights and constitution to stand unimpaired. On June 15, 1780, the convention declared that the constitution had been approved "by a very great majority." As Morison has observed, an investigation "of the convention's methods of tabulating the popular vote raises the suspicion that the two-thirds majority was manufactured."[89]

Whether the majority was convention-made or real, the Massachusetts Bill of Rights and Constitution were given to

[87] Morison, "Struggle over the Adoption of the Constitution," 382.
[88] Cushing, *The Transition in Massachusetts*, 269.
[89] Morison, "Struggle over the Adoption of the Constitution," 354.

the people as legally ratified documents with the full force of law. Apart from the exceptionable third article on religion, the declaration represented a collection of provisions from earlier bills of rights rather than an original work. The practice of copying from other bills of rights was convenient. It also indicated that the guaranteed rights of citizens were falling into a stereotyped pattern. Bills of rights were still demanded, but they were no longer a novel piece of business. By 1780 their makers had ceased to break new ground in the enumeration of human rights. Indeed, the third article of the Massachusetts declaration maintained the status quo and operated as a check on the more liberal religious tendencies of the day.

The last of the eight states to formulate a bill of rights during the revolutionary period was New Hampshire. The northernmost state in the Republic had been the first to set up a temporary independent government but it lagged behind the other states in the matter of making a permanent constitution. In the early days of 1776, the New Hampshire Congress at Exeter had adopted a temporary frame of government which was intended to serve the colony only until reconciliation with England could be effected. By late 1777 the instrument was already felt to be inadequate, particularly in view of the action taken in the other states. Accordingly, in June of 1778 a special constitutional convention (separate from the legislature) had been summoned to meet at Concord, "the first such body in the United States or the world."[90] After long deliberation the delegates to this convention produced a constitution prefaced by a brief declaration of rights of the now familiar pattern, including a prohibition on the legislature from passing laws which would "infringe the rights of conscience, or any other natural, unalienable Rights of Men, or contrary to the laws of GOD, or against the Protestant religion."[91]

[90] Allan Nevins, *American States during and after the Revolution* (New York, 1924), 183.
[91] Nathaniel Bouton, ed., *Documents and Records Relating to Towns in New Hampshire* (Concord, 1867-77), IX, 837-38.

New Hampshire voters rejected this constitution. Indeed, rejecting constitutions became almost a habit in New Hampshire before a permanent constitution and bill of rights were finally adopted. The second convention began its first session in the summer of 1781 and did not conclude its business until October of 1783.[92] Among the leaders of this body were Judge John Pickering, "one of the few really learned lawyers in New Hampshire at this period," General John Sullivan, and Dr. Nathaniel Peabody, the physician-patriot.[93]

Somewhat as a trial balloon, the convention sent a proposed constitution to the voters in the fall of 1781.[94] It was prefaced by a bill of rights weighed down with thirty-eight articles. In an address to the people that preceded the documents, the convention declared that this "BILL OF RIGHTS contains the essential principles of the Constitution." "It is the foundation on which the whole political fabric is reared, and is consequently, a most important part thereof." A quotation from the Bible was cited to show that it was necessary to safeguard the rights of conscience.[95] Indeed, the proposed declaration of rights was a wholesale borrowing of the Massachusetts declaration of 1780, with a few additions locally supplied. Most prominent among these additions was the double jeopardy provision, which held that no person could be tried a second time for the same offense if he had once been acquitted. The effect of pleas for an enlightened penal code was evidenced by another article which called for penalties "proportioned to the nature of the offence. . . . The true design of all punishment being to reform, not to exterminate, mankind." Guarantees of habeas corpus were incorporated in the constitution rather than the bill of rights. The legislature was even warned, by a curious provision, "to be exceeding cautious of granting pensions, especially for life."

[92] Jeremy Belknap, *The History of New Hampshire* (Boston, 1791), II, 435.
[93] William A. Robinson in *Dictionary of American Biography*, XIV, 564.
[94] Richard F. Upton, *Revolutionary New Hampshire* (Hanover, 1936), 182-84.
[95] Bouton, ed., *New Hampshire Documents*, IX, 851.

Suspicious voters rejected this convention effort, although there is no evidence that any great stream of criticism was directed at the declaration of rights. Rather, the conservative tone of the constitution proper has been cited as the reason for the unfavorable vote. A third attempt was made in 1782. Possibly the delegates hoped their constituents would note with charity their repeated phrase, in the address which again accompanied their proposals, that "A PERFECT system of Government is not to be expected in the present state of humanity."[96] The declaration of rights which preceded the constitution of 1782 was the proposal of 1781 with a few minor emendations. Despite the constitutional changes, the delegates once more found the people dissatisfied with their product.

Nothing daunted, the convention met to draw up a proposal in June, 1783. Peace with Great Britain was near, and New Hampshire was still making shift with its temporary constitution. Delegates to the convention changed the title, but not the content of the declaration of rights, calling it henceforth the New Hampshire Bill of Rights. Further changes in the constitution proper, particularly regarding the powers of the governor, were wrought. When the votes were counted on October 31, the results must have caused convention delegates to heave a collective sigh of relief. For the work of the convention had, at long last, won the approval of the people.

With the acceptance of the New Hampshire Bill of Rights, the first chapter in the struggle for written guarantees of the rights of citizens on continental America came to an end. Beginning with the Virginia example of 1776 the people of eight states, acting through their representatives, had insisted on explicit statements of the rights which they presumably possessed by virtue of the fundamental laws of nature. Instinctively the people had turned to their states for the guardianship of these rights after severing their connection with the only higher political authority they had ever known.

[96] *Ibid.*, 878.

Until the Confederation went into effect in 1781, the states exercised full sovereignty and recognized no legal authority outside their own borders, although the Continental Congress exercised certain wartime powers. By the end of 1776 a definite pattern of human rights had been established. Essentially, this pattern was furnished by the Virginia Declaration of Rights, modified or enlarged to suit local conditions and demands. Even states which did not prefix their constitutions with a formal bill of rights still had constitutional provisions granting the substance of personal liberty. Both for what they said and what they offered, the bills of rights thus became an important facet of the American political tradition. They brought nearer together than ever before theory and practice, claim and reality.

CHAPTER V

PERSONAL FREEDOM IN THE NEW REPUBLIC

A LTHOUGH most of the new states had set down rights which the people of those commonwealths regarded as immutable in a bill of rights, the instrument designed to maintain the new nation as a perpetual union failed to guarantee personal freedom. The Articles of Confederation, that "Grand Corner Stone" to those who had helped lay it, did not include a single article which assured to citizens freedom of conscience, freedom of the press, or any of the other rights proclaimed in the state bills of rights or constitutions.[1] The omission is explained by the conception of powers of the general government held by Americans in 1777, when the Articles were framed. Since each state was to retain its "sovereignty, freedom, and independence," it followed that all guarantees of freedom for the individual citizen would necessarily come from the state, not the Confederation.

The obligations of a state toward its citizens in the protection of personal liberties had been called to the attention of the Continental Congress in February, 1777—months before Congress had approved the Articles of Confederation. In a debate which arose over the practice of arresting deserters from the Continental army, Thomas Burke of North Carolina sounded a warning which was indicative of prevailing thought. Burke argued that congressional authority could not be exerted on citizens of the states because the precedent might "render Ineffectuall all the Bariers Provided in the states for the Secur-

---

[1] A section of Article V, which held that "Freedom of speech and debate in Congress shall not be impeached or questioned in any court or place out of Congress" could hardly be classed as a guarantee affecting the average citizen.

ity of the Rights of Citizens . . . and the subject of every state was entitled to the Protection of that particular state."[2] This interpretation of the citizen's rights as a state concern prevailed. Thus no demand for a national (or congressional) bill of rights occurred during the years from 1777 to 1786. Only the alarm created by the threatened concentration of power in the second American constitution of 1787 could account for the agitation on behalf of a federal bill of rights.

In the states, however, bills of rights were accepted almost everywhere as a necessary adjunct of the fundamental law. "Every Free Government should consist of three parts, viz. 1st, a Bill of Rights, 2dly, a Constitution. 3dly Laws," a letter in the *Pennsylvania Journal* declared in 1777.[3] The letter was a polemic which drew Thomas Paine into the controversy raging around the Pennsylvania Constitution of 1776. Paine laid down the dictum that a bill of rights "should be a plain positive declaration" of those natural rights which men must retain as either "consistent with, or absolutely necessary toward our happiness in a state of civil government."[4] Although the principles thus enunciated were on the highest plane, Americans deemed unsophisticated language in the wording of laws a distinct virtue. Bills of rights were the "higher law" of the eighteenth century, and they were created to be an instrument of service for every citizen. Christopher Gadsden reflected a common opinion when he wrote on the subject: "For it is essential to a Republic to have its Laws plain and simple, as far as possible, and known to every member of the least attention."[5]

Before recounting various incidents which illustrate a concern for personal freedom during the Revolution, the special role of the loyalists deserves consideration. In general the

[2] Burnett, ed., *Letters of Members of the Continental Congress*, II, 276.
[3] Quoted in Philip S. Foner, ed., *The Complete Writings of Thomas Paine* (New York, 1945), II, 273.
[4] *Ibid.*, 274.
[5] Christopher Gadsden to Francis Marion, November 3, 1782, *South Carolina Historical and Genealogical Magazine*, 41 (1940), 51.

number of Americans who supported the British cause by word or deed was small. The Reverend Ezra Stiles estimated in 1783 that the loyalists "in all the States during this whole eight years of War ... [did not] exceed 15 or *twenty Thousd Souls* out of *three millions*."[6] An accurate count was impossible, of course, for there were plenty of turncoats on the loose whose convictions were charted by the course of the war. When the American army was about, they were patriots. When the British marched in, they hung out George III's banner. Such tories walked the tight-rope, and even when they fell they depended on the confusion of the times to afford them a soft landing place. Looking back on the situation, Jefferson noted that not a single tory had been executed for treason in Virginia—a fact which he attributed to "the lenity of our government, and [the] unanimity of its inhabitants. . . ."[7]

At the early stages of fighting, the patriots were inclined to forgive and forget the loyalists' affiliations. "We shall hail their reformation with increasing pleasure, and receive them to us with open arms," the North Carolina provincial congress declared in May, 1776.[8] Time turned this feeling of leniency to rancor. Social ostracism was the least they suffered from their neighbors. To the army they always represented a possible "fifth column." Washington called them the "abominable pests of Society," and their presence (even in small numbers) caused him to approve a system of test oaths and the use of somewhat arbitrary methods by troops sent to render the loyalists ineffectual.[9]

Local circumstance involving loyalists differed. Tory property was ordinarily confiscated by the states, while obstreperous loyalists were often jailed, tarred and feathered, and generally

[6] Dexter, ed., *Stiles Diary*, III, 61.
[7] Jefferson, *Notes on the State of Virginia*, William Peden, ed. (Chapel Hill, 1955), 226.
[8] Quoted in Hugh T. Lefler and Albert R. Newsome, *North Carolina* (Chapel Hill, 1954), 217.
[9] Washington to the Committee of Suffolk, L. I., May 16, 1776, Fitzpatrick, ed., *Writings of Washington*, V, 48-49.

denied liberties enjoyed by the patriots. Loyalist clergymen were not exempted from the fury of mobs. Stubborn church-men who insisted on offering prayers for the king and royal family were usually forced to close their doors, but as late as January 1, 1777, the Reverend Edward Winslow of Braintree, Massachusetts, was able to pray for George III and his family "without any interruption or prohibition" from local authori-ties or mobs.[10]   In 1776 the Reverend Thomas Barton, an Ang-lican missionary at Lancaster, Pennsylvania, reported to au-thorities of the Society for the Propagation of the Gospel in Foreign Parts some of the indignities suffered by tory church-men—"Some of them have been dragged from their horses, assaulted with stones & dirt, ducked in water; obliged to flie for their lives, driven from their habitations & families, laid under arrests & imprisonments!"[11]   Popular opinion became so overwhelming against any toleration of loyalists that many were in time driven to desert either their convictions or their homes. To say that loyalists were denied personal freedom is true, but no modern state has ever permitted wartime dis-affection or treason to go unchecked. The magnanimous ac-tions of the Americans, and particularly Washington, toward the loyalists on numerous occasions only supports the view that, all things considered, the loyalists probably fared rather well.[12]

As for the patriots, the precise effect of the state bills of rights upon the preservation of their personal freedom in the new Republic during the Revolutionary era is difficult to meas-ure. At the close of the Confederation period, Madison ex-pressed the frank view that "experience proves the inefficacy of a bill of rights on those occasions when its controul is most needed." "Repeated violations of these parchment barriers

[10] Edward Winslow to the Secretary, January 1, 1777, William S. Perry, ed., *Historical Collections Relating to the American Colonial Church* (Hartford, 1870-73), III, 589.

[11] Thomas Barton to the Secretary, November 25, 1776, *ibid.*, II, 490.

[12] See the statement made by Washington's aide, Tench Tilghman, quoted in Nathaniel W. Stephenson and Waldo H. Dunn, *George Washington* (New York, 1940), I, 394-95.

have been committed by overbearing majorities in every State," he declared. "In Virginia I have seen the bill of rights violated in every instance where it has been exposed to a popular current."[13] Jefferson agreed that "the Declaration of rights is like all other human blessings alloyed with some inconveniences . . . but the good . . . vastly overweighs the evil."[14] Jefferson shared the growing belief that it was far better to have safeguards for personal freedom on the statute books than to trust the discretion of state authorities or the whims of a legislative majority. Tangible evidence of continued vigilance for civil liberty during the Revolutionary era may be found in the numerous petitions, memorials, and court cases which were based on some guarantee of personal rights. As the state bills of rights were taking form they also acquired meaning in judicial precedents which were being established. By 1789 significant developments in the establishment of personal liberty had been achieved through the state courts.

No single issue among the various points covered by the bills of rights caused so much discussion or legislative action as freedom of religion. All citizens could expect equal treatment under the bills of rights except those whose religious convictions placed them in the minority. Thus a Congregationalist, Baptist, Catholic, and Anglican might have joined to support guarantees of a free press or trial by jury; but when it came to the matter of complete freedom of religion, a stirring argument and perhaps a bloody nose or two were likely. Legal incrustations upheld the established church in many of the new states. The drive to gain religious freedom, therefore, was in fact an effort to separate church and state completely. This meant that in New England the various splinter groups of Protestantism were arrayed against the established Congregational church, while in the South the dissenters toiled to sever state support from the older Anglican churches.

[13] James Madison to Thomas Jefferson, October 17, 1788, *Documentary History of the Constitution of the United States* (Washington, 1894-1905), V, 87.
[14] Thomas Jefferson to James Madison, March 15, 1789, *ibid.*, 161.

Foremost among the groups demanding unequivocal religious freedom were the Baptists. Their historic aversion to official ties between church and state was based on the conviction that civil authorities who touched religious affairs were transgressors in a field reserved "for Christ [who] only is the king and lawgiver of the church and conscience."[15] Half measures would not satisfy them. Prosecution only whetted their zeal. That spirit which had motivated Roger Williams a century earlier now sparked their persistent attempts to strike down the last vestiges of the legally established churches.

In Virginia certain events focused attention on the established Anglican church, which remained as the official state church despite the promise in the Declaration of Rights that citizens might enjoy the free exercise of religious practice. Both the dissenters and the Anglicans had able champions. Jefferson was constantly pressing the attack, applauded by the dissenters. Among the conservative opposition was that skilled and popular political figure, Edmund Pendleton, who was unwilling to break old ties with the traditional church. A showdown battle between the two forces had long been brewing. The Anglicans generally were on the defensive after the "New-Light Stir" of George Whitefield's tremendous revivals during the Great Awakening of the 1740's.[16] The Reverend Elijah Craig of the Blue Run Baptist Church was imprisoned in Culpeper County before the Revolution for preaching dissenting doctrine, whereupon his lawyer warned the court that Baptists "were like a bed of camomile; the more they were trod, the more they would spread."[17] Craig was jailed but continued preaching from a jail cell and was later incarcerated

[15] From the remarks of John Smyth, leader of a group of exiled Baptist refugees in Holland. Quoted in Lyman H. Butterfield, "Elder John Leland, Jeffersonian Itinerant," in American Antiquarian Society, *Proceedings*, 62, part 2 (1952), 164.

[16] Wesley M. Gewehr, *The Great Awakening in Virginia, 1740-1790* (Durham, 1930), 91.

[17] David Benedict, *A General History of the Baptist Denomination in America* (Boston, 1813), II, 291-92. Similar indignities are reported in Mays, *Edmund Pendleton*, I, 262-65.

in Orange County for the same offense, but he continued his activities. The biographies of the dissenting ministers abound with reports of fist fights and jail sentences in vain efforts to halt their preaching to the people.

To many dissenters the article on religion in the Virginia Declaration of Rights was "as the rising sun of Religious liberty, [meant] to relieve them from a long night of Ecclesiastical bondage," but its wholesome effect had not been completely satisfactory.[18] During the same month that the Virginia declaration was proclaimed, the Baptists of Prince William County dispatched to the convention their petition calling for permission "to maintain their own ministers and none others" and asked "that they be married, buried, and the like," without paying the clergy of other denominations.[19]

Buttressing the Baptists at this early stage of the drive were the Presbyterians, who noted through the Presbytery of Hanover an awareness of the recent state papers. They dispatched to the Virginia legislature a memorial alluding to the stirring language of the declaration, which they conceived as a pledge "to secure the free exercise of religion according to the dictates of our consciences; and we shall fall short in our duty to ourselves . . . were we . . . to neglect laying before you a statement of the religious grievances under which we have hitherto labored, that they may no longer be continued in our present form of government."[20] The petition movement grew throughout the summer and fall of 1776 in Virginia. A typical document from dissenters in Albemarle and Amherst counties requested "that every religious denomination may be put upon an equal footing, independent of another."[21]

[18] Petition of Prince Edward County, quoted in Mays, *Edmund Pendleton*, II, 133.

[19] William Taylor Thom, *The Struggle for Religious Freedom in Virginia: The Baptists* (Baltimore, 1900), 55.

[20] W. H. Foote, *Sketches of Virginia, Historical and Biographical* (Philadelphia, 1850), 323-24, quoted in William Warren Sweet, *Religion in the Development of American Culture, 1765-1840* (Chicago, 1952), 13.

[21] Thom, *Struggle for Religious Freedom in Virginia*, 58.

The Anglican clergy did not take these attacks with meek submission. They offered a petition of their own, claiming that "it would be inconsistent with justice either to deprive the present incumbents of parishes of any rights or profits they hold or enjoy, or to cut off from such as are now in orders and unbeneficed, those expectations which originated from the laws of the land. . . ." Furthermore, these churchmen declared that Christian doctrines with their resultant "tendency to produce virtue among men . . . can be best taught and preserved in their purity in an established church. . . ."[22] To the radical element in Virginia, this must have seemed to be a most reactionary document, and the more it was read the worse it sounded. A feeble voice was raised for the Anglicans by another sect, however. The Methodists maintained a nominal connection with the Church of England throughout the war years and their guiding light, John Wesley, reversed an earlier stand to denounce American revolutionaries. Their position probably retarded the growth of the group, but they did support the Anglicans in this important church-state controversy.[23]

The pressure of the dissenters' entreaties was recognized in November, when the House of Delegates went on record in favor of legislation which would abolish any existing law "which renders criminal the maintaining any opinions in matters of religion" other than the orthodox Anglican view. As the year came to a close, the Virginia lawmakers passed a bill which removed from the statute books all laws requiring church attendance or restricting religious opinion, and exempted dissenters from making a contribution to support the established church. "This act, in effect, destroyed the establishment," Professor Eckenrode observed.[24] At the time this result was not so apparent. Jefferson indicated that the accomplishments were insufficient, and explained that more

---

[22] Quoted in Mays, *Edmund Pendleton*, II, 134-35.
[23] *Ibid.*
[24] H. J. Eckenrode, *Separation of Church and State in Virginia* (Richmond, 1910), 53.

was not achieved because "although the majority of our citizens were dissenters . . . a majority of the legislature were churchmen."[25]

Jefferson correctly surmised that the struggle for absolute freedom of religion in Virginia was far from ended by December of 1776. In the years that followed, dissenting churchmen sent petition after petition to the General Assembly calling for complete religious freedom.[26] A Baptist petition was accompanied by a poem written by the Reverend David Thomas, who was disturbed by the legal encumbrances which denied his sect full liberty of conscience:

> Tax all things; water, air, and light,
> If need there be; yea, tax the *night*:
> But let our brave heroick minds
> Move freely as celestial winds.
> Make vice and folly feel your rod,
> But leave our consciences to God.[27]

The Baptists remained in the front ranks of the dissenters in Virginia as hostility to the established church spread. In October of 1779 their General Convention, which met at Nottaway Meeting House in Amelia County, approved the recommendation of Reverend Jeremiah Walker in support of the "Bill for Establishing Religious Freedom" which Thomas Jefferson and his friends were seeking to pass into law. The convention resolution declared that Jefferson's proposal "puts religious freedom upon its proper basis; prescribes the just limits of the power of the state . . . and properly guards against partiality towards any religious denomination."[28] Although taxes for the established church were no longer imposed, there were other grievances equally irritating. Since the law did not

---

[25] Paul Leicester Ford, ed., *Writings of Thomas Jefferson* (New York, 1892-99), I, 54.

[26] See Lewis P. Little, *Imprisoned Preachers and Religious Liberty in Virginia* (Lynchburg, 1938), 481-83.

[27] Benedict, *History of the Baptists*, II, 479.

[28] Robert B. Semple, *A History of the Rise and Progress of the Baptists in Virginia* (Richmond, 1810), 65.

recognize marriages performed by dissenting ministers, the legality of these ceremonies was a nice question which plagued the families involved. Sly remarks about the children born of these marriages sometimes led to physical violence. The dissenters of Amelia County were joined by other church groups early in 1780 when petitions were forwarded to the state legislature demanding that their marriage ceremonies be made lawful.[29] These petitions went to the Committee for Religion, headed by George Carrington, which found them worthy of consideration. On recommendation of the committee a bill which granted dissenters the right to be legally married by their own ministers was enacted into law in December, 1780.[30]

When supporters of the established church threatened the Methodists, Presbyterians, Baptists, and other sects in Virginia with a bill calling for state subsidies for "teachers of the Christian religion," the old antagonisms were renewed. On August 13, 1785, the Baptist General Committee approved a petition which denounced the proposal as "repugnant to the spirit of the Gospel," and certain to be "destructive of religious liberty."[31] The teaching bill was the last determined effort in Virginia to subsidize a favored sect. Its defeat a few months before the passage of Jefferson's "Bill for Establishing Religious Freedom" signaled virtually complete separation of church and state.[32] With the assistance of James Madison, who marshalled much of his support from dissenting Virginians beyond the tidewater region, Jefferson's bill was adopted in 1786.

Even this extensive act did not wholly satisfy the Baptists. They were still unhappy about the Incorporation Act of 1784, passed by the House of Delegates "in a quick strategic move

[29] Thom, Religious Freedom in Virginia, 68.
[30] Hening, ed., Statutes at Large . . . of Virginia, X, 61-62.
[31] Thom, Religious Freedom in Virginia, 76.
[32] Eckenrode took the view that the 1787 "repeal of the incorporation act [for the Protestant Episcopal Church] definitely marks the separation of church and state in Virginia." See his Separation of Church and State, 129.

by friends of the [Anglican] Church to preserve for it the extensive property it held under the old establishment."[33] Elder John Leland, who had something of the back-country lawyer in him, probably was responsible for the Baptist petition to the legislature some months after Jefferson's bill had passed. This petition declared the Incorporation Act inconsistent with Article XIV on religion in the Declaration of Rights, and contrary to

the express words of the IV Art. of the Bill of Rights, which prohibits rewards or emoluments to any Man, or set of men, except for services rendered the State; and what services that Church has rendered the State, either by her Clergy or Laity, more than other Churches have done we no [know] not.[34]

Parts of the Act were repealed the following year, but more than a decade passed before this last vestige of the established church was eradicated in Virginia.

Less dramatic, but equally important to thousands of Georgians, was a similar quarrel which reached a high pitch after the Revolution ended. Religious assessment bills had been defeated in the Georgia legislature in 1782 and 1784, but a measure for the public support of religion was approved 43 to 5 early in 1785.[35] There was no stipulation as to the kind of minister to be employed, that choice being left to the petitioners from the heads of thirty families in each county. The bill provided a tax rebate to counties for the maintenance of a minister, and Baptists would have gained more by its use than any other denomination, since they were the fastest growing sect in the state. Still, the principle involved was deemed dangerous by the Baptist leaders, so they opposed the whole plan. Accordingly, in 1786, the Baptist Association presented a remonstrance to the Georgia legislature, where it was tabled. The bill seems to have been allowed to die a quiet death, how-

[33] Butterfield, "Elder John Leland," 177.
[34] Eckenrode, *Separation of Church and State*, 119; also quoted in Butterfield, "Elder John Leland," 178.
[35] Reba C. Strickland, *Religion and the State in Georgia in the Eighteenth Century* (New York, 1939), 166-67, 176-77.

ever; and before the century ended Georgians had placed a religious freedom provision in their new constitution which nullified this law.

New England was the scene of still another battle over the issue of religious freedom. In Massachusetts the militant and zealous Baptists were again in the forefront of opposition to the established Congregational Church. Their ministers were the most outspoken critics of the state-supported church. Particularly notable was the Reverend Isaac Backus, who had been preaching sermons on the subject since 1770. Before the Revolution began Backus had expounded on "A Plea for Liberty of Conscience," and he had lobbied for religious liberty at the First Continental Congress in 1774. Backus was foremost among those opposed to Article III of the Massachusetts Declaration of Rights, chiefly because it had entrenched the established church. Under Backus' guidance the Baptists petitioned the Massachusetts General Assembly for disestablishment of the state church, using strong language "against the injustice of being taxed where we are not represented." After the Declaration of Rights was adopted in 1780 they demanded that the provisions on freedom of conscience be observed. They noted that many promises were made

which never were fulfilled; and when the State Constitution was formed, the Bill of Rights was made to look one way, but priest and constables have gone another. . . . notwithstanding all these declarations, many have been molested and restrained in their *persons, liberties,* and *estates,* on religious accounts.[36]

The appeal of the Baptists eloquently pointed out the disparity between theory and practice. Its effect was negligible, however. Not until the 1830's did Massachusetts end the practice of supporting an established church.

But in Connecticut a limited concession to separatists from the established church was granted by a law passed in 1777. The law exempted those persons from supporting the estab-

[36] Benedict, *History of the Baptists,* II, 271.

lished church who could furnish proof that they were contributing to a separatist church. The dissenters' protest, which had begun three decades previously, continued however, and in 1784 the Connecticut legislature further relaxed the old code by permitting dissenting groups to organize churches on the same conditions which bound the state-supported Congregational Church. The close tie between the established church and the state remained. Those citizens, dissenters as well as members of the state church, still ran the risk of paying fines if they failed to take their religious obligations seriously.[37]

Even in Pennsylvania, where the harmony of religious groups had often excited wonder, a few citizens labored under restrictions imposed on them because of their religious preference. An indication of their resentment reached the Federal Constitutional Convention at Philadelphia in 1787 when Jonas Phillips, a Jewish citizen of Philadelphia, sent a petition requesting a change in the Pennsylvania constitution. Apparently unfamiliar with the nature of the Convention, Phillips asked the repeal of a clause in the state constitution which demanded of officeholders recognition of the New Testament as a divinely inspired work. Phillips declared that

to swear and believe that the new testement was given by devine inspiration is absolutely against the Religious principle of a Jew. and is against his Conscience to take any such oath—By the above law a Jew is deprived of holding any publick office or place of Government which is a Contridectory to the bill of Right Sect. 2.[38]

Despite the validity of complaints in Massachusetts, Pennsylvania, and elsewhere, the wide gap between the language of religious provisions in the state bills of rights and the actual workings of religious groups had been considerably narrowed by 1787. Prodded by the dissenters, Virginia legislators had enacted a definitive statute of religious freedom. In New Eng-

[37] Paul W. Coons, *The Achievement of Religious Liberty in Connecticut* (New Haven, 1936), 22.
[38] Max Farrand, ed., *The Records of the Federal Convention of 1787* (New Haven, 1911-37), III, 78.

land the religious issue was in ferment, but the dissenters still waited for action on their proposals for complete freedom. Twelve years after the Revolution had begun, full religious freedom had been attained only in Rhode Island and Virginia. Test oaths, established churches, and other stumbling-blocks checked the complete realization of liberty of conscience in the other states.[39]

Guarantees of freedom of the press in the state bills of rights had been welcomed by printers who could see in their enactment a ban against any form of an American licensing act. Some thoughtful persons felt that freedom of the press led to abuses, however, and the most famous of American printers, Benjamin Franklin, speaking as a citizen, voiced their complaint. Franklin declared that "few of us, I believe, have distinct Ideas of its [freedom of the press] Nature and Extent. . . . if it means the Liberty of affronting, calumniating, and defaming one another, I, for my part, own myself willing to part with my Share of it when our Legislators shall please so to alter the Law, and shall cheerfully consent to exchange my *Liberty* of Abusing others for the Privilege of not being abus'd myself."[40]

Libel laws were enacted, but any attempt by the states to touch the press directly was bound for defeat as the Massachusetts stamp tax placed on newspapers and almanacs in 1785 demonstrated. The odious connotations attached to a stamp act did not escape editors, who claimed that their right to maintain a free press had been violated. The *Massachusetts Centinel* called the act "the first *Stone* in the *fabrick of Tyranny*," and, unperturbed by this mixing of metaphors, declared that the tax would end freedom of the press.[41] When the act was repealed in 1788 the *Massachusetts Spy* applauded.

[39] Sanford H. Cobb, *The Rise of Religious Liberty in America* (New York, 1902), 501.
[40] Albert H. Smyth, ed., *The Writings of Benjamin Franklin* (New York, 1907), X, 37-38.
[41] Clyde A. Duniway, *The Development of Freedom of the Press in Massachusetts* (Cambridge, 1906), 136 n.

Heaven grant that the FREEDOM of the PRESS, on which depends the FREEDOM of the PEOPLE, may in the United States, be ever guarded with a watchful eye, and defended from *Shackles* . . . until the trump of the celestial Messenger shall announce the final dissolution of all things.[42]

Another incident in Massachusetts involving freedom of the press occured in 1787, when George Brock and Gideon Pond were accused of seditious libel. They were indicted for publishing articles which lauded the motives behind Shays's Rebellion. By pardoning the two men before their case could reach a trial court, however, the state authorities avoided a test of the issue of freedom of the press.[43]

A free press had long been the goal of Americans who believed that an atmosphere of free expression was most conducive to the general welfare. Franklin's complaint indicates that some publishers lacked discretion and good judgment, but the problem thus posed involved the responsibilities of a free press. In Massachusetts the cry "freedom of the press" was successfully used to avoid the tax-gatherer's visit, and had helped exonerate editors whose writings had lauded armed resistance. The exact limits of a free press had not been defined, and while the definition was being shaped in libel and sedition statutes the printers were left to rely on their own common sense in the conduct of their affairs.

During the period following Yorktown the state courts found that freedom of the press, along with other guarantees made by the state bills of rights, often posed difficult problems. For cases involving property, wills, and contracts precedents were abundant. For cases involving civil rights there were neither precedents nor easy answers. Such a case arose in Pennsylvania when Eleazer Oswald, a Philadelphia printer, claimed that both freedom of the press and the right of trial by jury had been denied him. As the publisher of the *Independent Gazetteer*, Oswald was sued for libel in 1788 on the

[42] *Ibid.*, 137.   [43] *Ibid.*, 142.

charge of having "inserted in his newspaper several anony-
mous pieces against the character of Andrew Browne, the
master of a female academy, in the city of Philadelphia." This
information apparently was a threat to the enrollment in
Browne's school.[44] Oswald took his case to the people in a
printed "address to the public," which declared his enemies
were attacking him under the guise of an attempt to get
justice. What their actions demonstrated, Oswald charged,
was "that my situation as *a printer, and the rights of the press
and of freemen,* are fundamentally struck at." He further
intimated that he could expect no fairness from Browne's
friends on the court bench.

This outburst was too much for the judges, who promptly
hailed Oswald into court on a contempt charge. Oswald's
counsel claimed the contempt proceedings violated the Pennsylvania Declaration of Rights, which guaranteed to accused
persons a trial by jury. The lawyer also said that if Oswald
testified before the court his answers would constitute evidence
that might be used against him, in violation of another of the
provisions in the declaration of rights designed to protect
citizens.[45]

Chief Justice Thomas McKean overruled the defendant's
objections on the ground that the Pennsylvania Declaration
of Rights did not authorize libel under the guise of a free
press; and that the right of a court to decide upon contempt
charges was a basic power of the bench which the state declaration did not modify. McKean agreed with the prosecuting
attorney, William Lewis, when he charged that Oswald's
"silence corroborates the evidence" and really deprived the
accused man of an opportunity to defend himself. Oswald was
fined £10 and sentenced to a month in jail.

But Oswald refused to let the matter die. After his release he sent a memorial to the General Assembly asking for

[44] Respublica *v.* Oswald, *Pennsylvania Reports,* 1 Dallas 319.
[45] *Ibid.,* 328.

impeachment of the Supreme Court.. The court was not without friends in the legislature. William Lewis, who had prose-
cuted Oswald, was a member of the Assembly and he stoutly
defended the trial. The state declaration of rights had not
been violated, Lewis said, since it was a restraint upon the
General Assembly and not a cloak to "tolerate and indulge
the passions and animosities of individuals." Lewis declared
that it was equally false to charge that the printer's right to
trial by jury or to avoid self-incriminating testimony had been
subverted. He denied that all cases were destined for a trial
by jury under the Pennsylvania Declaration of Rights. Nor,
said Lewis,

can anything more explicitly demonstrate that the framers of the
constitution were aware of some cases, which required another mode
of proceeding, than their declaring that 'trials shall be by jury as heretofore?'—Who will assert that contempts were ever so tried? Who
will hazard an opinion, that it is possible so to try them?[46]

Oswald also had supporters in the legislature. They
claimed that a study of the bill of rights and constitution of
the state would reveal the injustice of the court decision.
Thomas Findley said "it would be fatal, indeed, to the cause
of liberty, if it was once established, that the technical learning
of a lawyer is necessary to comprehend the principles laid
down in this great political compact between the people and
their rulers." Findley and the other adherents of Oswald were
unable to carry the impeachment. The majority in the General Assembly sustained the action of Chief Justice McKean
and his colleagues on the bench.

Oswald's inability to find in the state bill of rights the
protection he sought was not a universal experience in the
Confederation period. On the contrary, there were other indications that the state tribunals were rather more inclined
to give accused persons the full benefit of provisions in the bills
of rights. Following the Revolution the courts heard numerous

[46] *Ibid.*, 329d.

cases which involved the rights of persons who had been deprived of property during the war because of their adherence to the British cause. In North Carolina a 1787 decision was based on the state constitution, which promised every citizen that his property would not be taken away arbitrarily, without a trial by jury. If the legislature could usurp that right, said the court, "it might with as much authority require his life to be taken away without a trial by jury." The act of 1785 which denied that right to citizens, was therefore declared "abrogated and without any effect" in an early pronouncement of the doctrine of judicial review. This decision reinforced similar opinions rendered by courts in New Jersey, Rhode Island, and New Hampshire between 1780 and 1786.[47]

In another case involving the right of trial by jury the courts of South Carolina proved to be equally attentive to personal rights. The decision involved the arrest and fine of a Charleston tavern keeper who had been jailed for selling liquor without a license. The city court of wardens levied a fine of £50, the non-payment of which sent tavern-keeper McMullen to a prison cell. McMullen was released and brought before the state Superior Court on a writ of habeas corpus, where he was freed of all charges. The judges held that his treatment in the lower court had deprived him of the right to a trial by jury and therefore was "irregular and void."[48] Justice John Grimke of South Carolina also prepared the way for a ban on ex post facto laws when he declared in 1787 that one act of that character, already approved by the state legislature, was a violation of the law of nations.[49]

Further evidence that the courts were guarding the personal liberties of the people came from the state of Connecticut, which, like South Carolina, did not have a separate bill of

[47] Bayard v. Singleton, *North Carolina Reports*, 1 Martin 48. See also Charles G. Haines, *The Role of the Supreme Court in American Government and Politics, 1789-1835* (Berkeley and Los Angeles, 1944), 17-18.

[48] McMullen v. City Council of Charleston, *South Carolina Reports*, 1 Bay 46, 49.

[49] Porter v. Dunn, *ibid.*, 53-58.

rights. There the charge of committing an illegal search and seizure, which had been a Revolutionary grievance against the crown, was placed squarely on the doorstep of a state official. The matter arose when Benjamin Frisbie's premises were searched in 1787 for a cache of stolen pork. The Connecticut Superior Court ruled that the warrant which preceded the search of Frisbie's home and his arrest had been a general warrant, and was therefore "clearly illegal."[50] Connecticut courts also blocked state prosecutors from using the testimony of accused persons in seeking their conviction. On at least two occasions during the Confederation period the Superior Court made it plain to prosecutors that citizens could not be asked or expected to give evidence against themselves.[51] The Connecticut high court established an important state precedent in 1788 when it handed down a decision declaring that criminal cases should be tried in the vicinity of the crime. A decision in 1783, which forbade the second trial of a citizen for the same offense once he had been acquitted, was reinforced by a similar verdict on "double jeopardy" in 1787.[52]

Occasionally the courts pondered the question of personal liberty in circumstances which made the administration of justice difficult. This situation confronted the Pennsylvania Supreme Court in People v. Doan. Aaron Doan of Bucks County had been "attainted of outlawry for a felony" while a fugitive in British-occupied New York during the war. Doan apparently returned to Pennsylvania and was seized in 1784 under authority of the attainder. His execution was ordered, but the question of his right to a trial by jury was raised. John Dickinson, president of the Supreme Executive Council, sent a message to the judges concerning the propriety of the pending execution in the light of the state declaration of rights, which guaranteed trial by jury. Was there any precedent for

---

[50] Frisbie v. Butler, *Connecticut Reports*, 1 Kirby 213-15.

[51] State v. Pheps, *ibid.*, 282; State v. David Thomson, *ibid.*, 345.

[52] Gilbert v. Marcy, *ibid.*, 401-02; Hannaball v. Spalding, *Connecticut Reports*, 1 Root 86; Coit v. Geer, *ibid.*, 1 Kirby 269.

ordering an execution by judicial proceedings on an attainder, Dickinson asked, and did an attainder violate the Declaration of Rights "which establishes, with such strong sanctions, the right of trial by jury"? The justices answered that there was a precedent for the action, created by the rulings of the Council itself after the Declaration of Independence had been promulgated. They also held that Doan had in effect refused a regular trial when he became a fugitive.[53] The decision helped speed Doan toward a hangman's noose without the benefit of a jury trial.

Experience during the Confederation period also demonstrated the effect of that popular phrase, found in most of the state bills of rights, which declared "all men free and equal." The wording caused echoes in states other than Virginia, where the language of Mason's draft had been challenged on the floor of the convention of 1776. The conservative faction pointed an accusing finger at the clause as a distinct disavowal of slavery but the "constituent member" argument, that slaves were not constituent members of society and therefore not covered by the assertion, was used to dispel fears that the statement applied to Negroes.[54] Such was not the case in Massachusetts, where the first article of the state Declaration of Rights enunciated in 1780 the freedom of all mankind. The historian Jeremy Belknap insisted that this article

was inserted not merely as a moral or political truth, but with a particular view to establish the liberation of the negroes on a general principle, and so it was understood by the people at large. . . . Many blacks, taking advantage of the publick opinion and of this general assertion in the bill of rights, asked their freedom, and obtained it.[55]

The status of the slave in Massachusetts was clarified when Nathaniel Jennison, the owner of Quock (or Quack) Walker,

[53] Respublica v. Doan, Pennsylvania Reports, 1 Dallas 85-93.
[54] See ante, Chapter II.
[55] "Queries Respecting the Slavery and Emancipation of Negroes in Massachusetts, Proposed by the Hon. Judge Tucker of Virginia, and Answered by the Rev. Dr. Belknap," Massachusetts Historical Society, Collections, 1st ser., 4 (1795), 203.

was charged in May, 1781, with beating and imprisoning the Negro. Jennison was tried in the Supreme Judicial Court in 1783, found guilty of assault, and fined £2. The court held that "the idea of slavery is inconsistent with our own conduct and Constitution."[56] "This decision was a mortal wound to slavery in Massachusetts," Belknap said. He reported that the New Hampshire Declaration of Rights of 1784 was interpreted as referring to the freeing of Negroes born after the declaration, clearly following Massachusetts in adopting and enforcing the "free and equal" clause.[57] The list of 158 slaves on the New Hampshire census rolls for 1790, however, indicates that there was no clear-cut case as effective as the Massachusetts decision had been in ending slavery.[58]

The writ of habeas corpus also was successfully used in Connecticut in 1784 to free Jack Arabas, a former slave who had served three years in the Continental army. Connecticut had no declaration of rights but the Superior Court granted a habeas corpus on the ground that Arabas "was a freeman, absolutely manumitted from his master by enlisting and serving in the army as aforesaid."[59] In Maryland, attorney Jeremiah T. Chase, counsel for a mulatto who sought her freedom in the early 1780's, quoted Blackstone to the court and carried his point that "All persons are free by nature . . . and he that holds another in slavery must show . . . by what means the vassal was deprived of the inestimable blessing of liberty."[60]

Assuredly, no perfect system for protecting the rights of citizens had been devised by 1789, but a clear pattern of the development of personal liberty in the new nation had emerged. This pattern had been worked out in the state bills of rights and state court decisions. State courts had proved to be particularly instrumental in the process of enforcing guaran-

[56] Massachusetts Historical Society, *Proceedings*, 1st. ser., 13 (1873-75), 294.
[57] Massachusetts Historical Society, *Collections*, 1st ser., 4 (1795), 204.
[58] Bouton, ed., *New Hampshire Documents*, IX, 896 n-98 n.
[59] Arabas *v.* Ivers, *Connecticut Reports*, 1 Root 92-93.
[60] Toogood *v.* Scott, *Maryland Reports*, 2 Harris and McHenry 28.

tees in the bills of rights. The watchdog value of the courts was recognized by Gouverneur Morris in 1785, when he noted the power of judicial review was "dangerous; but unless it somewhere exists, the time employed in framing a bill of rights and form of government was merely thrown away."[61] In states where no bill of rights existed common law precedents were utilized, although courts probably preferred written documents as a basis for decisions.

Continued vigilance for personal liberty was demonstrated by legislators as late as 1786, when Vermont enacted a second declaration of rights. This post-Revolution declaration was a slightly altered version of that proclaimed by the disputed territory in 1777, with certain changes apparently dictated by experience under the borrowed Pennsylvania Declaration of Rights. The changes included a section promising citizens justice "without being obliged to purchase it," and guaranteeing elections "without corruption." Free speech for legislators was promised, thus establishing legislative immunity. The power of suspending laws was limited to the legislature. Only the last alteration seemed to protect directly the individual Vermonter, and this nineteenth article stated that a citizen of Vermont could not be subject to martial law "in any case" unless he was serving in the army or militia.

Meanwhile, New York took steps to correct the omission of a bill of rights from her state constitution. Early in 1787 the New York legislature passed a thirteen-point bill which was, in effect, a declaration of rights. The law contained most of the elements considered essential in such a document—safeguards against arbitrary arrest, provisions for free elections, and prohibitions on the billeting of soldiers. The Virginia article on excessive fines and cruel punishments was borrowed verbatim.[62] Less than a month later, an additional act was passed which guaranteed to citizens the writ of habeas corpus

[61] Jared Sparks, The Life of Gouverneur Morris (Boston, 1832), III, 438.
[62] Laws of the State of New York (Albany, 1886-1887), II, 344-45.

along with a "trial in the vicinage" clause of the type found in other state bills of rights. By late February of 1787 citizens of New York, in common with most of their neighbors, could regard their personal liberty as protected by written law from the caprice of unreasonable government or irrational men.

Widespread dissatisfaction with the Articles of Confederation in the postwar years did not grow out of the absence of provisions safeguarding personal liberty, which was a state concern. Even staunch supporters of the Confederation admitted its weaknesses, and a movement to amend the Articles was in progress when more ambitious plans for an entirely new constitution were launched. The Continental Congress had appointed a "Grand Committee . . . to report such amendments to the confederation" in August, 1786. This committee was not expected, however, to concern itself with a broadening of the protections for personal liberty, or of making such protection a function of federal or national government.[63] The committee did note the need for a federal court system, and its recommendations for a federal judiciary included a provision "that the trial of the fact by Jury shall ever be held sacred, and also the benefits of the writ of *Habeas Corpus.*"[64] These recommendations were not acted upon, probably because the existing state bills of rights and numerous precedents made such legislation unnecessary under the Articles of Confederation.

Although Congress had neither authority nor excuse for enacting a declaration of rights for the inhabitants of the states, it was obliged to take action on behalf of the citizens living in the territories under its jurisdiction. Settlers in the country north and west of the Ohio had petitioned Congress for a frame of government which would afford them a legal code, a court system, and administration similar to those of the eastern states.[65] For three and a half years Congress had debated the

[63] Ford, ed., *Journals of the Continental Congress,* XXXI, 494.
[64] *Ibid.,* 497-98.
[65] See the memorial of the "Inhabitants of Cahokia, November 10, 1784," in Clarence W. Alvord, ed., *Illinois Historical Collections,* 2 (1907), 567-73.

question without reaching a firm decision. Then in a sudden burst of activity during July of 1787 the delegates settled the whole matter. In the space of five days committee reports were discussed and amended, then the bill was hustled through the customary three readings to a final vote.[66] This legislation, which bore the caption "Ordinance of the government of the territory of the United States North West of the river Ohio," is known to history as the Northwest Ordinance of 1787.

Outwardly the Northwest Ordinance appeared to have been conceived in haste. Actually, it was the product of a steady evolution of ideas in which the committee work of the best minds of Congress had figured: Jefferson, Madison, Monroe, and Rufus King being among the contributors. Conflicting claims and the doubtful status of the region beyond the western border of Pennsylvania had been virtually cleared by the Virginia cession of the Northwest country in 1784, one of the "solid accomplishments of the Confederation."[67] Jefferson prepared a plan of government for this region shortly after Congress formally accepted the cession which became the nucleus of subsequent proposals. Some of Jefferson's imaginative ideas in the plan have been given undue emphasis—such as his scheme to name the created territories "Polypotamia" and "Assenisipia" and other fanciful titles—while the solid foundations of a territorial system are often overlooked. The plan explicitly set down a method which provided for the orderly transition of a settlement from the frontier to membership in the Union "on an equal footing with the said original states."[68] It also contained a resolution

That after the year 1800 of the Christian æra, there shall be neither slavery nor involuntary servitude in any of the said states, otherwise than in punishment of crimes, whereof the party shall have been duly convicted to have been personally guilty.

[66] Peter Force, "The Ordinance of 1787, and Its History," in William P. and Julia P. Cutler, Life, Journals and Correspondence of Rev. Manasseh Cutler, LL.D. (Cincinnati, 1888), II, 418.
[67] Boyd, ed., Jefferson Papers, VI, 571-74.
[68] Ibid., 604.

Congress struck out this provision on April 19, 1784, by a strictly sectional north-south vote. The Ordinance of 1784 was accepted by Congress a few days later, but was subsequently repealed after Jefferson had moved to his new post as Minister to France. Another Ordinance, enacted in 1785, contributed notably to Jefferson's earlier scheme by providing a surveying system which embodied the Republic's basic policy of land distribution. Still this program was not made effective until 1787, as Congressmen and land speculators haggled over the entire western lands problem.

Significantly, personal rights had been of little concern to the committees charged with reporting a plan for governing the western territory until September of 1786, when a recommendation to Congress took cognizance of the omission. Then a brief section was added which read:

And to secure the rights of personal liberty and property to the inhabitants and others, purchasers in the said districts it is hereby

Resolved, That the inhabitants of such districts shall always be entitled to the benefits of the Act of Habeas Corpus, and of the trial by Jury.[69]

No mention was made of other specific guarantees included in the state bills of rights. But the resolution was noteworthy as the first step toward congressional action on personal rights. The substance of this resolution appeared in slightly altered wording in a bill introduced into Congress on May 10, 1787. The proposed bill did not reach a vote, however, and died before the third reading.

Once the idea of preserving individual rights had been injected into the discussion, the committee permitted an overhauling of the legislation that made up for earlier oversights. On July 11, when the committee reported a revised bill, the two safeguards of personal liberty suggested initially had grown into a full bill of rights for the inhabitants of the Northwest Territory. This document—the Ordinance of 1787—

[69] Ford, ed., *Journals of the Continental Congress*, XXXI, 670.

in the handwriting of Nathan Dane guaranteed full civil rights "as articles of compact between the original States and the people and [future] States in the said Territory" and was forever to "remain unalterable unless by Common Consent." Like the state bills of rights of the Revolution the civil rights provisions of the Northwest Ordinance were fundamental law beyond change by ordinary legislation. Little that was new or unfamiliar was added. By the same token the traditional provisions were included to an item: freedom of religion, trial by jury, habeas corpus, reasonable bail and moderate fines. Cruel and unusual punishments were prohibited. Inviolability of contract and the sanctity of private property were both assured. As in previous bills of rights liberty and property went hand in hand. "No man shall be deprived of his liberty or property but by the Judgment of his peers or the law of the land."

The exact details of the story of this first "federal" bill of rights are difficult to reconstruct. It is clear, however, that Nathan Dane was not solely responsible for its contents. Three days after Congress had enacted the Ordinance Dane wrote his fellow delegate from Massachusetts, Rufus King, that the committee had been "rather pressed" and had wanted to "adopt the best system we could get." Concerning the well-known prohibition on slavery Dane wrote:

When I drew the ordinance (which passed, a few words excepted, as I originally formed it) I had no idea that States would agree to the sixth article, prohibiting slavery, as only Massachusetts of the Eastern States, was present, and therefore omitted it in the draft: but finding the House favorably disposed on this subject . . . I moved the article, which was agreed to without opposition.[70]

In his recommendation Dane followed the course laid out by Jefferson, who had attempted to ban slavery from the West three years earlier. Manasseh Cutler, skillful lobbyist for the

[70] Nathan Dane to Rufus King, July 16, 1787, Burnett, ed., *Letters of the Continental Congress*, VIII, 631-32.

Ohio Company, had concerned himself with the bill which Dane was drafting. "The amendments I proposed have all been made except one," Cutler noted in his diary.[71] Cutler was reasonably certain of support from some congressional delegates he was dealing with, but he thought "Dane must be carefully watched, notwithstanding his professions."

Dane himself furnished the best evidence on the sources of the bill of rights provisions in the Ordinance of 1787. Forty-three years later, when he was the sole survivor of all the framers of that historic piece of legislation, he denied that he had ever claimed originality for his draft. "The Ordinance of '87 was framed, mainly, from the laws of Massachusetts," he admitted. In further explanation he said, "If any lawyer will critically examine the laws and constitutions of the several States, as they were in 1787, he will find the titles, six articles, &c., were not to be found anywhere else so well as in Massachusetts."[72] The road from Virginia to the Northwest had passed through Boston.

The importance of the Northwest Ordinance in American history has been frequently assessed from various points of view. Together with the Land Ordinance of 1785 it was part of the solid achievement of the much belabored Confederation government. It established a frontier policy for the United States along liberal lines which allowed for a measure of self-government in the dependent territories and for their admission as states on terms of equality with the original thirteen. One of the most celebrated provisions abolished slavery in this vast area of the nation. The bill of rights is frequently passed over in these appraisals of the significance of the Northwest Ordinance. Nevertheless the fact that specific guarantees of personal freedom were included in the act which established the form of government for the territories is important for two reasons. For the first time, civil rights became a factor in

[71] Cutler, Life of Cutler, I, 293.
[72] Nathan Dane to Daniel Webster, March 26, 1830, Massachusetts Historical Society, Proceedings, 1st ser., 10 (1867-69), 479.

national legislation. Secondly, the example of the bill of rights introduced in revolutionary Virginia had run a full course through the Union and was in effect passed on to those states yet to come. In short, the Northwest Ordinance marked the end of one phase of the history of American bills of rights and the beginning of another in which the problem of individual liberty was placed in a new perspective.

CHAPTER VI

THE FEDERAL CONVENTION

THERE WAS no general agreement as to the merits of the call for a convention which would revise the Articles of Confederation. All shades of opinion were represented in the contemporary correspondence of political figures and the newspapers of the day. Public criticism of affairs under the Confederation caused a Philadelphia newspaper to declare that "our situation is neither so bad as artful designing men have represented, nor is it likely to continue long so bad as it now is."[1] On the other hand, the political situation so alarmed John Adams that he admitted the lack of attendance in Congress was "Proof of something so bad that I dare not name it."[2] And Washington himself rebuked the suggestion that his influence might be used to good advantage in the areas, such as western Massachusetts, where matters were getting out of hand. "Influence is no Government," the General answered. "Let us have one by which our lives and liberties and properties will be secured; or let us know the worst at once."[3]

Significantly, in the newspaper articles and private correspondence calling for a change in government, there was no complaint about infringement on the rights of individual citizens. Criticism was directed at the existing form of government because of its inability to preserve order and protect prop-

[1] *Pennsylvania Gazette*, September 6, 1786. See also Merrill Jensen, *The New Nation* (New York, 1950), 194-257. Jensen states that "There is nothing in the knowable facts to support the ancient myth of idle ships, stagnant commerce, and bankrupt merchants in the new nation."
[2] John Adams to Rufus King, June 14, 1786, Charles R. King, *The Life and Correspondence of Rufus King* (New York, 1894-1900), I, 182.
[3] George Washington to Henry Lee, October 31, 1786, Fitzpatrick, ed., *Writings of Washington*, XXIX, 34.

erty, and because of its weakness in the fields of both foreign and domestic affairs. The states alone protected civil rights; the rights of property formed another category, a category with many zealous guardians.

The delegates who met in Philadelphia came to draft the blueprint for a strong central government. Missing from the assemblage of notables that included the first men of each state was Jefferson. After his discouraging experience as governor of Virginia he had taken the ministerial post to France, and from his diplomatic headquarters Jefferson sent forth volumes of letters that were to influence the course of ratification. The fact that the debates were secret and the element of time involved in ocean communication prevented Jefferson from being abreast of the situation. Jefferson's absence conceivably left a responsibility on George Mason's shoulders, for both were devoted, experienced champions of personal freedom. Madison would have been an able and probably a willing lieutenant, but the two Virginians went their separate ways during the convention. Other delegates with experience in drafting either bills of rights or legislation protecting personal liberties were William Samuel Johnson of Connecticut, and George Read and John Dickinson of Delaware. To none of these could Mason look for support of his proposals for a bill of rights in the last moments of the debate, however, for the overriding topic of the convention was the powers of the federal government—not individual liberty.

Of course, there was nothing unusual in the fact that the personal rights of citizens were not a topic of discussion in the preliminary debates. Under the Confederation, these rights had been under state protection. There was no reason to assume that this protection had been lifted as long as the nature of the new government was unknown.

Many Americans probably shared the thoughts expressed by Madison's kinsman who noted the Convention was at work and commented:

The Truth is, I believe, the Outlines of the American governments are as well drawn, in order to promote public and private Happiness, and to secure that greatest possible Portion of Liberty, which we have so successfully contended for, as human sagacity could possibly devise. These Outlines only require to be skilfully filled up, perhaps in some Cases to be somewhat extended. . . . The least that ought to be done surely, is to make a fair Experiment.[4]

One point seems clear. Satisfaction among the general public regarding personal rights was established. Thus neither Mason nor his colleagues at Philadelphia found it necessary to come into the convention hall ready to serve as watchdogs for civil liberty.

The main business of the convention, as Washington had explained to Madison, was to draft "a liberal, and energetic Constitution, well guarded and closely watched, to prevent incroachments, which might restore us to that degree of respectability and consequence, to which we had a fair claim, and the brightest prospect of attaining."[5] Mason was impressed with the magnitude of their task and ventured to say that the revolt against Great Britain was "nothing compared to the great Business now before us," since the happiness or misery of unborn millions was involved.[6] Mason and most of the Virginia delegates at Philadelphia were convinced that a stronger national government was necessary, but the method of erecting it was far from settled.

Indeed, virtually all the delegations represented varying viewpoints which in some cases clashed with their own state and sectional interests. General Henry Knox's ideas coincided with the thinking of more than one delegate. Washington's wartime chief of artillery thought "the vile State governments are sources of pollution, which will contaminate the American

[4] Rev. James Madison to James Madison, June 11, 1787, in Massachusetts Historical Society, *Proceedings*, 2nd ser., 17 (1903), 465-66.
[5] George Washington to James Madison, November 5, 1786, Fitzpatrick, ed., *Writings of Washington*, XXIX, 52.
[6] George Mason to George Mason, Jr., June 1, 1787, Mason Papers, Library of Congress.

name for ages . . . smite them in the name of God and the people."[7] But the various plans presented to the Convention made no attempt to obliterate the states. Advocates of both the Virginia and New Jersey plans were committed to the preservation of states as political units. Although these "blue-prints" provided the basis for a compromise on the balance of power between the large and small states, neither plan mentioned the rights of individual citizens. Nor did Charles Pinckney concern himself with civil rights in the original draft of his plan.[8] Rather, all the proposals conceded that the states must be preserved with diminished powers, while a federal government was to be erected possessing paramount power over the states.

During the early debates Mason attempted to stake out a federal position regarding the rights of citizens. This had not been possible under the Articles of Confederation.[9] Foreseeing the strengthened role of the national government, Mason cautioned the Convention to move slowly in this vital realm. "He admitted that we had been too democratic but was afraid we s[houl]d. incautiously run into the opposite extreme," Madison noted. Mason went on to ask the Convention "to attend to the rights of every class of the people," and added that he favored a policy which "would provide no less carefully for the rights—and happiness of the lower than the highest orders of Citizens."[10] James Wilson and Madison agreed with Mason on the point, but Elbridge Gerry of Massachusetts was equally positive that the people were "the dupes of pretended patriots" and not to be trusted without checks on their freedom. "The

[7] Henry Knox to Rufus King, July 15, 1787, King, ed., *Life of King*, I, 228.
[8] See Farrand, ed., *Records of the Federal Convention*, III, 595-609; J. Franklin Jameson, "Studies in the History of the Federal Convention of 1787," American Historical Association, *Annual Report for 1902*, I, 117-20; Andrew C. McLaughlin, "Sketch of Pinckney's Plan for a Constitution, 1787," *American Historical Review*, IX (1903-04), 735-47. By a scholarly use of the materials, and aided by the discovery of an important manuscript, Jameson and McLaughlin were able to reconstruct the contents of the original Pinckney plan.
[9] Farrand, ed., *Records of the Federal Convention*, I, 34.
[10] *Ibid.*, 49.

evils we experience flow from the excess of democracy," he said, knowing that his colleagues were sworn to secrecy.[11]

Throughout the early proceedings of the Convention the delegates were obviously not disturbed about the future course of personal freedom in the Union. Broader questions fundamental to erecting a national government occupied their attention, although the delegates who wanted no infringement of state sovereignty were at work. James Wilson, a thorough republican though an advocate of strong national government, wanted the people to possess the franchise as "the legitimate source of all authority." This attitude was thoroughly compatible with the provision in the Virginia Declaration of Rights, often repeated elsewhere, which held that "all power is vested in, and consequently derived from, the people. . . ." With free elections secured, it seemed unlikely that any other right would be in jeopardy. Roger Sherman made it plain that there must be a limitation on the powers of the national government to handle foreign affairs, defense, commerce, and tariffs. Almost as an afterthought he added, "All other matters civil & criminal would be much better in the hands of States."[12] Mason agreed, but saw danger signs that the arrangement might not suit all delegates because the federal government probably would have direct powers that might be exercised on the individual citizen.

The author of the Virginia Declaration of Rights foresaw a new relationship between citizens and the national government which was in the making. The old reliance upon the states as guarantors of personal liberty appeared to be on uneasy ground. Thus delegates who favored strong state governments perceived what was happening, and they grew alarmed. On June 20 Mason flatly declared that he "never would agree to abolish the State Gov[ernmen]ts. or render them absolutely insignificant." Luther Martin of Maryland supported Mason, assuring his fellow delegates that the people looked to the states for security of their lives, liberties, and properties, and

[11] *Ibid.*, 48.   [12] *Ibid.*, 133.

would continue to do so.[13] When fears that the individuality of states would be swallowed up by the national government were voiced, Wilson took the floor to combat the notion. The proposed federal government would be as anxious "to preserve the rights of the States as the latter are to preserve the rights of individuals," Wilson insisted.[14] Despite the assurances, however, the seed of doubt had been planted regarding the rights of individual citizens.

Nor would crusty Luther Martin let the issue die quietly. With considerable warmth he defended the states, called for a narrow limitation of the powers of the national government, and wanted to deny it the right to operate directly on individual citizens. The people, Martin contended, "as such have little to do but with their own States," and the states "will take care of their internal police and local concerns."[15] His three-hour speech was an argument on behalf of the states, and his contention that citizens looked to the local governments for protection was confirmed by experience in every state.

In contrast with Martin's tirade, the extreme views of Alexander Hamilton represented a position entirely consistent with his idea that the state governments constituted so much unnecessary furniture for a strong national government. He attacked Martin's whole line of reasoning, then for extra measure added that the national government should have power over the individual citizens as well as over the states.[16]

Charles Pinckney of South Carolina saw no need to bog the debate down on the question of federal-state relationships. He reminded his colleagues that "strong government" was not necessarily "oppressive government." Good Federalist that he already was, Pinckney concluded that the best way to assure civil and religious liberty was to create a national government that would guarantee a stable society.[17] Certainly, at this stage of debate, the delegates generally agreed with Oliver Ells-

[13] *Ibid.*, 341.
[15] *Ibid.*, 437-39.
[17] *Ibid.*, 402.

[14] *Ibid.*, 356.
[16] *Ibid.*, 479.

worth when he said his eyes were turned to the state governments for the preservation of his rights. "From these alone he could derive the greatest happiness he expects in this life," the Connecticut delegate said. In his defense of the small-state position, Ellsworth made the most of the close contact between the citizens and their state governments. Rufus King, who wanted no obstacles to bar the path of a strengthened national government, was reassuring. He promised Ellsworth and other small-state delegates that the rights of all states would be maintained under a national government "as the fundamental rights of individuals are secured by express provisions in the State Constitutions."[18] With such unanimity of opinion revealed in open debate, it seems natural that the drafting committee presumed there was no place on their agenda for a separate bill of rights.

For almost a month, as the delegates steered their way through the strenuous debate without touching on the matter of personal liberty, there apparently was a general agreement that the new national government would not infringe the state bills of rights. However, when a method of electing the chief executive came before the Convention, Mason once more asserted his concern for civil liberty. "The pole star of his political conduct" was "the preservation of the rights of the people," and he held that public officials "should at fixed periods return to that mass from which they were at first taken, in order that they may feel & respect those rights & interests, Which are again to be personally valuable to them."[19] The language was familiar to those who knew the wording of the Virginia Declaration of Rights, which provided that elected officials "should at fixed periods, be reduced to a private station." Mason thought this point so essential that he called it "the very palladium of Civil liberty." Moments later the Convention adjourned, leaving Mason's words of caution to the discretion of the Committee of Detail which was charged

[18] *Ibid.*, 493.   [19] *Ibid.*, II, 119-20.

with preparing a draft constitution for submission to the whole body.

The fragmentary notes of the Committee of Detail preserved by Mason and James Wilson reveal slight concern for personal rights. One explanation for the omission, already made apparent by the debate in the Committee of the Whole, was contained in the suggestions for a preamble written by Edmund Randolph. A preamble setting forth the ends of government had been proper in the first state constitutions, Randolph declared, but would be improper here "since we are not working on the natural rights of men not yet gathered into society, but upon those rights, modified by society and . . . interwoven with what we call . . . the rights of states."[20] However, this same report of the Committee of Detail bears an emendation in the handwriting of John Rutledge which called for a jury trial in criminal cases in the state where the offense was committed.[21] A similar provision was contained in another report written by Wilson and edited by Rutledge.[22] The jury trial clause, which the Committee of Detail chose to adopt without specific advice from the floor, marked the first recognition of individual rights by the Convention.

The Convention reassembled on August 6, after the great compromises on representation had been reached in committee during the adjournment. Throughout the grueling days ahead, when the temperature soared upward on Doctor Franklin's thermometer, the spirit of compromise continued to hold discussion within bounds. The report of the Committee of Detail kept the delegates busy for more than a month, until the final days of the Convention.

As the general frame of the constitution became more clearly discernible, the enormous powers of the national government caused a small band of delegates to call for guarantees of personal liberty. Charles Pinckney submitted to the Committee of Detail on August 20 a list of propositions which

[20] *Ibid.*, 137. [21] *Ibid.*, 144.
[22] *Ibid.*, 173.

amounted to a bill of rights. Among Pinckney's recommendations was a ban against religious tests for any federal officeholder.[23] Mason, recalling ideas in the Virginia Declaration of Rights, had asked for a prohibition on standing armies a few days earlier. Before the week ended, Gerry and James McHenry of Maryland also moved for the insertion of a clause declaring that "The Legislature shall pass no bill of attainder nor ex post facto law."[24] These scattered proposals (not all accepted) indicated a reviving interest in guarantees of personal liberty.

Once the move to gain a complete enumeration of rights failed, the delegates who favored these guarantees were forced to propose the provisions in a piecemeal fashion. The prohibition on bills of attainder met no opposition, but several delegates doubted the necessity of mentioning ex post facto laws. Daniel Carroll, who favored the proposition, said experience showed that state legislatures "had passed them, and they had taken effect." Wilson observed that prohibitions in state constitutions had been meaningless, and "it will be useless to insert them in this Constitution." When put to a test, however, the Convention approved the part on bills of attainder unanimously, and voted for the ex post facto ban by a large majority.[25] Pinckney's suggestions for a guarantee of habeas corpus and for trial by jury in criminal cases received similar approval when they reached the Convention on August 28. Before the day ended the prohibition on passing bills of attainder or ex post facto laws was extended to the states when Rutledge's motion to that effect was adopted. Pinckney finally introduced his prohibition on religious tests for officeholders on the Convention floor, where it was adopted unanimously. Roger Sherman charged that it was unnecessary on the grounds that the prevailing liberal spirit of the times was a sufficient guarantee

[23] Ibid., 341-42.
[24] Ibid., 375.
[25] James Madison to George Washington, March 18, 1787, Documentary History of the Constitution, IV, 95.

that such tests would not be required. But his colleagues preferred to trust a written law rather than an unwritten sentiment.

The debate on the method of ratifying the proposed constitution gave dissatisfied delegates an opportunity to air their grievances. Madison, who sided with the majority and apparently believed at this time that private rights were adequately protected by the states, wanted the proposed plan of government placed before special conventions elected by the people. Madison paraphrased the Virginia Declaration of Rights when he said:

> The people were in fact, the fountain of all power, and by resorting to them, all difficulties were got over. They could alter constitutions as they pleased. It was a principle in the Bills of rights, that first principles might be resorted to.[26]

Gerry and Mason were worried about the Constitution itself, and they sought postponement of the ratification article. Dissatisfied with the plan, Mason even went so far as to say "he would sooner chop off his right hand than put it to the Constitution as it now stands." Various concessions to state sovereignty might make the document acceptable, he hinted, but unless certain points were properly settled "his wish would then be to bring the whole subject before another general Convention." The impatient majority refused to heed Mason's words, and the plan of ratification by conventions was therefore adopted by an overwhelming margin. It was now apparent that Gerry, Mason, and probably Randolph would oppose the final draft of the Constitution unless the majority did an about-face and made greater concessions to their views.

Not until the Convention reached its final week did the opposition, labelled as Antifederalists, come out with propositions calculated either to win support or to make a second convention necessary. Their program unfolded when the question of jury trials for civil cases arose on September 12,

[26] Farrand, ed., *Records of the Federal Convention*, II, 476.

and Gerry argued that juries were needed "to guard ag[ain]st. corrupt Judges." "A general principle laid down on this and some other points would be sufficient," Mason added. Then, for the first time since the Convention had been in session, Mason expressed a wish that "the plan had been prefaced with a Bill of Rights, & would second a Motion if made for the purpose—It would give great quiet to the people; and with the aid of the State declarations, a bill might be prepared in a few hours."[27] Gerry fell in with Mason and made the desired motion that a committee be formed to prepare a bill of rights. Mason promptly seconded.

Roger Sherman of Connecticut was the only delegate whose opposition to the proposed bill of rights is recorded. Sherman prefaced his remarks by saying that he was for securing the rights of the people whenever it was necessary. In the present case, however, a federal bill of rights was not requisite. "The State Declarations of Rights are not repealed by this Constitution; and being in force are sufficient," Sherman explained. He argued that where the rights of the people were involved, Congress could be trusted to preserve them.

Mason countered with the charge that henceforth the federal government and federal laws would "be paramount to State Bills of Rights." His brief plea was unavailing, as the delegates (voting as state units) unanimously opposed the motion to form a bill of rights committee.

Neither Mason nor Gerry accepted this vote as a final verdict. Again the strategy of the piecemeal adoption was employed. On September 14 Mason unsuccessfully sought to preface the militia clause in Article I with the words, "And that the liberties of the people may be better secured against the danger of standing armies in time of peace," although his Virginia colleagues supported him. It was a busy day for Mason, who then moved to strike out the clause prohibiting bills of attainder or ex post facto laws—on the ground that

[27] *Ibid.*, II, 587-88.

their limitation to criminal cases was not sufficiently clear. Gerry supported Mason, but most of the delegates were not willing to share this apprehension. Then Pinckney joined Gerry in demanding a declaration "That the liberty of the Press should be inviolably observed," but once more Sherman claimed such a provision was completely unnecessary. The "power of Congress does not extend to the Press," Sherman said, and he was backed up by the majority.[28]

Mason's attempt to get a bill of rights adopted bit-by-bit was a failure, even though he had several delegates who were anxious to aid in the work. Pinckney and Gerry joined forces to call for a provision in Article III guaranteeing that "trial by jury shall be preserved as usual in civil cases." Nathaniel Gorham opposed the suggestion, contending that the use of juries differed from state to state. This was true, of course, and rather than risk future wrangling over what the term "usual" connoted in various parts of the country the delegates preferred to let the matter slide.

When the Convention drew to a close on the final day of debate before the engrossed copy of the Constitution was to be signed, Mason voiced his fear that the powerful federal government being created would become oppressive. Mason's position as a leader seeking a bill of rights was shaken during these concluding moments when he saved a futile, eleventh-hour effort not for personal liberty, but for a notion which would have prevented the passage of navigation acts before 1808 unless approved by a two-thirds majority in Congress. As a Virginia planter this was a natural suggestion, but it was this move which echoed in the delegates' minds as they turned homeward—not the pleas for a bill of rights.

Desperate measures were the last resource of the Anti-federalists. In this salvaging operation they fell back on the call for another Federal Convention as a last maneuver. Randolph had been urging it for some days. Now Mason followed

[28] *Ibid.*, 617-18.

Randolph to predict dire consequences for the Republic if the Constitution were adopted, but expressed his willingness to sign if provisions were made for a second convention to receive amendments from the states. Charles Pinckney said that he found faults, but that he feared general confusion and civil war more, and would sign. Gerry listed his objections, most of them aimed at the powers of Congress. "He could however he said get over all these, if the rights of the Citizens were not rendered insecure," and the gravest error here was "to establish a tribunal without juries, which will be a Star-chamber as to Civil cases." Like Randolph and Mason, Gerry held out for a second convention.

After more than three months of debate, some of it intemperate and nearly all of it in sweltering temperatures, the delegates made short work of Randolph's motion for another Federal Convention, defeating it unanimously. Moments later the Convention voted on the Constitution as it now stood. Madison reported "All the States ay." Two days later the engrossed copy was signed, only Randolph, Gerry, and Mason abstaining.

The proposed Constitution went forward to the states buttressed by the tremendous prestige of a recommendatory letter from Washington. Few, if any, of the delegates expected the necessary nine states to ratify the proposed Constitution quickly. Grave doubts were expressed by men who had led the movement from the Annapolis convention days forward, and for a variety of reasons. Madison wrote Jefferson at his diplomatic post in Paris that while the public was still unaware of the contents of the Constitution, the Convention was "equally in the dark as to the reception which may be given to it on its publication."[29] Most of the delegates, although they did not favor the entire plan, considered it at least a partial remedy for the new nation's ills and far better than nothing at all. These two groups combined later to form the hard core

[29] James Madison to Thomas Jefferson, September 6, 1787, *ibid.*, III, 78.

of the Federalist or pro-Constitution party. Marshaled in opposition were local politicians like Robert Yates, John Lansing, and Luther Martin, who completely rejected the Constitution, viewed the whole procedure with alarm, and left the Convention before the final draft was approved. This small element furnished valuable allies for men of the stamp of Gerry and Mason, who did not completely reject the Constitution but who desired numerous amendments, or, better still, a second convention after the states had examined the document. The two groups pooled their resources to fight against ratification, thereby forming the nucleus of the anti-Constitution or Antifederalist party.

Before the Convention adjourned the lines of opposition were forming, not only in Philadelphia, but in New York, Richmond, and other communities where leaks of information had gained friends or created enemies for the Constitution. Only when lifelong friends suddenly came to a parting of ways was it clear that certain issues—such as a bill of rights— had deserved much more attention than the Convention chose to give them. "Col. Mason left Philada. in an exceeding ill humour indeed," Madison again reported to Jefferson. "A number of little circumstances arising in part from the impatience which prevailed towards the close of the business, conspired to whet his acrimony. He returned to Virginia with a fixed disposition to prevent the adoption of the plan if possible. He considers the want of a Bill of Rights as a fatal objection."[30]

There is no way to gauge the combined effects on George Mason of the Philadelphia summer heat, a chronic case of gout, and the frayed nerves produced by the long sessions of debate. But the record of those debates, which was not made public at the time, clearly shows that Mason did not mention the bill of rights until the Convention business was in the eleventh hour. He had given a bill of rights outspoken support and concrete form in Virginia eleven years earlier and

[30] Madison to Jefferson, October 24, 1787, *ibid.*, 135-36.

had seen his ideas spread. There is no ready answer to explain why Mason delayed mention of a bill of rights until the last days of the Convention. The "Objections to this Constitution of Government" which Mason wrote on the blank pages of his copy of the "Committee on stile and arrangement" report were written at a somber hour. This report had been placed in the hands of the delegates on September 13, and Mason apparently wrote down his objections either on the same day or in the few days remaining before he departed for Gunston Hall. His attitude was plainly hostile to the Constitution, for on numerous points which he considered vital his wishes had been disregarded by the Convention. It is not then surprising that in his opening sentence Mason shaped a powerful weapon for opponents of the Constitution. "There is no Declaration of Rights, and the laws of the general government being paramount to the laws and constitution of the several States, the Declaration of Rights in the separate States are no security." Mason then went into a detailed criticism, which included disapproval of the fact that there was "no declaration of any kind, preserving the liberty of the press, or the trial by jury in civil causes; nor against the danger of standing armies in time of peace."[31] Then his argument shifted to other matters touching on the powers of the federal government.

Manuscript copies of the "Objections" were circulated among Mason's friends, and in time printed copies were distributed throughout the Republic. Mason's protest against the omission of a bill of rights was supported by Richard Henry Lee, a fellow Virginian with long experience in public affairs who was now a member of the Continental Congress. While the Convention was still in progress Lee visited Philadelphia where he found the delegates "very busy & very secret," but not so tight-lipped that he was deprived of valuable hints about their work. Lee approved of what he heard. He thought that a "departure from Simple Democrocy [sic] seems indis-

[31] Ibid., II, 637-40.

pensably necessary," and judged that the public was ready for almost any government promising stability. He did, however, hope that the tendency toward strong government would be "so controuled as to secure fully and completely the democratic influence acting within just bounds."[32] But when the Constitution in its final form reached New York Lee was alarmed and immediately set to work "forming propositions for essential alterations in the Constitution, which will, in effect, be to oppose it."[33] Lee joined Melancton Smith of New York in an attempt to have the Continental Congress wash its hands of the affair, intimating that the Convention had exceeded its powers.[34] When this effort failed, Lee took the ground that amendments to the proposed Constitution by Congress were necessary. Again he was rebuffed by his colleagues.

Lee then drew up a set of proposals which he sought to tack on the document before it was transmitted to the state conventions by Congress. These began, as had Mason's objections, with a clear call for a bill of rights. Lee claimed that the declarations of rights adopted by most of the states were proof of the people's demand for a bill of rights. Therefore a federal declaration of rights must make explicit guarantees for freedom of religion, freedom of the press, and trial by jury in both criminal and civil cases. He demanded a ban on standing armies in peacetime, on excessive bail or fines, and on unreasonable searches and seizures of persons and property. He wanted assurances of the right of assembly and petition by the people, of free and frequent elections, and of the independent status of judges.[35] Lee's other objections indicated general concurrence with Mason on the errors and omissions in the Constitution, a fact which did not escape Madison's ob-

[32] Richard Henry Lee to [Francis Lightfoot Lee?], July 14, 1787, Ballagh, ed., *Letters of Lee*, 424.
[33] Edward Carrington to James Madison, September 23, 1787, Burnett, ed., *Letters of Members of the Continental Congress*, VIII, 647.
[34] Ford, ed., *Journals of the Continental Congress*, XXXIII, 540-41.
[35] Burnett, ed., *Letters of Members of the Continental Congress*, VIII, 648-49.

servation.[36] Congress rejected these amendments and adopted the ratification plan recommended by the Convention. Although Lee's measures failed, his voice was joined with Mason's in the opposition.

While Mason's "Objections" were rushed into print, an attempt to discredit him was made by circulating a report that an Alexandria mob had insulted him while he was en route to Gunston Hall because of his refusal to sign the Constitution. No evidence was offered to support the rumor.[37] Mason's pamphlet supplied ammunition for the "Address of the Sixteen Seceding Members of the Legislature of Pennsylvania" on September 29 when the anti-Constitution group walked out of the General Assembly, alleging steamroller tactics by their opponents. Their criticism of the Constitution included lack of a declaration of rights. Thus they lamented the failure to guarantee freedom of the press, jury trial in civil cases, and annual elections. Equally important to the sixteen members was a prohibition on standing armies.[38] From Gunston Hall Mason dispatched a copy of the "Objections" to neighboring Mount Vernon, and assured Washington that his complaints were not numerous but in some cases were of capital importance.[39] Washington had barely received the letter before he wrote Madison concerning the two dissenting Virginians. "The political tenets of Colo. M. and Colo. R. H. L. are always in unison," he declared. The General thought Lee was at the bottom of their recalcitrance and blamed him for the difficulties caused in the Pennsylvania legislature. Washington also forwarded Mason's "Objections" to Madison. "To alarm the

[36] James Madison to George Washington, September 30, 1787, ibid., 651-52.

[37] Rowland, Life of Mason, II, 181; James Madison to Thomas Jefferson, October 24, 1787, Farrand, ed., Records of the Federal Convention, III, 136. The Pennsylvania Gazette, October 17, 1787, reported, "We hear from Virginia, that GEORGE MASON has been treated with every possible mark of contempt and neglect, for neglecting to sign the Federal Constitution, and that PATRICK HENRY, Esq; is using his influence in the state, in promoting its adoption."

[38] Rowland, Life of Mason, II, 183. See also E. Bruce Thomas, Political Tendencies in Pennsylvania, 1783-1794 (Philadelphia, 1938), 137.

[39] George Mason to George Washington, October 7, 1787, Rowland, Life of Mason, II, 182.

people seems to be the groundwork of his plan," Washington said.[40]

Meanwhile, Lee had sent a copy of his proposed amendments to Mason, with a note expressing his fear of the power of their opponents. "In this state of things the patriot voice is raised in vain from such changes and securities as reason and experience prove to be necessary against the encroachments of power upon the indispensable rights of human nature," he wrote. Lee mentioned the names of public men in Virginia, Maryland, and South Carolina who were "sensible and independent" and who would probably agree that the Constitution "should be sent back with amendments reasonable, and assent to it withheld until such amendments are admitted."[41] He also sent a copy of the proposed alterations to Samuel Adams, a fellow-toiler in "the Vineyard of liberty," who was not without influence in Massachusetts.[42] To Washington he sent another letter expressing his fear that the Constitution, unamended, would endanger "the just rights of human nature."[43]

Gerry was meanwhile at work in Massachusetts. Like Mason he believed it necessary to defend his recent refusal to sign the Constitution. Gerry wrote to the presiding officers of the state legislature that "the liberties of America were not secured by the system, [and] it was my duty to oppose it." He thought it a most grievous fault "that the system is without the security of a bill of rights." Given the proper amendments, Gerry concluded, the Constitution might offer the people good government and preserve their liberty.[44]

Thus the opposition to the Constitution mustered strength against what it recognized to be formidable opponents. Con-

[40] George Washington to James Madison, October 10, 1787, Fitzpatrick, ed., Writings of Washington, XXIX, 285-86.
[41] Richard Henry Lee to George Mason, October 1, 1787, Ballagh, ed., Letters of Lee, II, 438-40.
[42] Richard Henry Lee to [Samuel Adams], October 5, 1787, ibid., 445.
[43] Richard Henry Lee to [George Washington], October 11, 1787, ibid., 449.
[44] Elbridge Gerry to President of Senate and Speaker of House of Representatives of Massachusetts, October 18, 1787, Farrand, ed., Records of the Federal Convention, III, 128-29.

sidering the difficulties of communication, the organizational work went on rapidly, aided by the obvious agreement among the leaders as to what constituted the most vulnerable point in the Constitution. They saw other and perhaps more objectionable flaws in the document, such as the failure to ban navigation acts and the nebulous provisions for elections, but none proved so potent a weapon for the Antifederalists as the failure to include a bill of rights. In the early stages of their leadership of the opposition, Mason and Lee determined to couple the demand for a bill of rights with other concessions desired from the Federalists.[45] Lee spoke to Mason of "our plan"—a scheme to coordinate with public men in other states their opposition measures. The general reception of at least a part of their objections indicated that they had struck a responsive chord with a considerable part of the people. Other Antifederalists did use the same argument, but Lee and Mason used it first. Thereafter "no Bill of Rights!" was the main chant of the opponents of ratification.

The Federal Convention had been called to revise the Articles of Confederation with the object of strengthening the national government. Until the final sessions there was no discussion of a full bill of rights, although attempts had been made to gain guarantees for personal rights in a piecemeal fashion. In dismay over the creation of a national government that would completely dominate the state governments, Mason and several other delegates ultimately seized upon the omission of a bill of rights in directing criticism at the Constitution. In twentieth-century political terms, was the bill of rights only a "phoney issue" used in an attempt to thwart ratification? This harsh judgment would not appear to be justified, for

[45] *Ibid.*, 367. It is noteworthy that only a few weeks before Mason's death in 1792, a document was set down in Thomas Jefferson's handwriting marked "ex relatione G. Mason" which stated that Mason decided to oppose the Constitution only in the last stages of the 1787 Convention. "The Constn as agreed to till a fortnight before the Convention rose was such a one as he wd have set his hand & heart to." Yet at that time no mention of the Bill of Rights had been made on the Convention floor.

although the Antifederalists had other and perhaps more cherished designs, the omission of a bill of rights was to many opponents of the Constitution the chief stumbling block to ratification.

Thus the Antifederalists girded themselves for the political warfare ahead, having already discerned a vulnerable chink in the Federalist armor which was to become the chief target of the opposition attacks. The Federalists, failing to realize the importance of a bill of rights, miscalculated public opinion and found themselves on the defensive almost from the outset of the ratification struggle.

CHAPTER VII

THE RATIFICATION STRUGGLE

ALTHOUGH Richard Henry Lee and George Mason gave the opponents of the Constitution their best argument against ratification from the popular standpoint, they did not attempt to form committees of correspondence in every state to carry on the fight. Their plans were not so skilfully laid as those of the Federalists. Mason was primarily concerned with Virginia's reaction, possibly because he thought his home state would set an example for the rest of the Republic to follow. Lee, possessed of more energy and strategically located in New York, was a leader of the Antifederalist movement in its early stages and aided the cause with his "Letters by a Federal Farmer," one of the most respected offerings of the opposition press throughout the entire ratification period. Governor George Clinton, a powerful figure in New York politics, determined to oppose the Constitution and proved himself more capable of leading the dissenting elements than either Lee or Mason as the struggle progressed. But during the earliest stages of the fight, Antifederalists from Massachusetts and New Hampshire southward based their opposition on hints thrown their way by pamphlets from the desks of Lee and Mason.

One indication of the Antifederalist strategy came only a few days after the Federal Convention had finished its business. Edmund Randolph wrote both Lee and Mason suggesting the propriety of an act by the Virginia legislature calling for another federal convention to consider the amendments put forward by the states.[1] Randolph's suggestion fitted the plans of Lee and Mason. In a reply to Randolph, Lee agreed that "the plan for us to pursue will be to propose the necessary amendments, and express our willingness to adopt it with the amendments; and to suggest the calling a new convention for the purpose of considering them."[2] Mason and Patrick Henry took the proposal into the Virginia House of Delegates and saw it enacted into law as a part of the legislation calling for a state convention to meet the following June to consider the proposed Constitution.[3] Governor Randolph dispatched the invitation to the other states late in December, but a postal delay (blamed on uncooperative mail-handlers) prevented any effective action on the scheme. Even in New York, where an Antifederalist majority dominated the legislature, action on the plan to call for a second convention was delayed until February. The New York legislators were inclined to favor another convention, but in the meantime a state convention was scheduled for June.

Indirectly allied to the Antifederalist cause through no political maneuver were the various Protestant elements which feared any hint of a church-state connection. As the ratification campaign developed these religious bodies proved to be among the most dependable of the Antifederalist allies. Professor Sweet concluded that the Presbyterians opposed the adoption of the Constitution with an almost complete unanimity largely because they feared the possibility of established churches in the several states. Baptists were also generally anti-Federalist, for fear that the Constitution did not afford sufficient safeguards for religious freedom.[4] The Antifederalist

[1] Edmund Randolph to James Madison, September 30, 1787, Moncure D. Conway, *Forgotten Chapters in the Life of Edmund Randolph* (New York, 1888), 95. Randolph alludes to his letter to Mason.
[2] Richard Henry Lee to Edmund Randolph, October 16, 1787, Ballagh, ed., *Letters of Lee*, II, 450-55.
[3] Edward P. Smith, "The Movement Towards a Second Constitutional Convention in 1788," in J. Franklin Jameson, ed., *Essays on the Constitutional History of the United States, 1775-1789* (Boston, 1889), 60-61.
[4] Sweet, *Religion in the Development of American Culture*, 89.

strategy capitalized—in a bungling sort of way—on the worst fears of these groups by innuendo and expressions of doubt, without attempting to organize this sizable opposition through influential leaders or the denominations generally.

While both Federalists and Antifederalists thus worked overtime on behalf of their causes, events in America were being closely watched from abroad by several experienced observers. John Adams, American minister to England, received his first news of the Constitution from Gerry. His immediate reaction was favorable to the Constitution, but he was uneasy about one particular point. "What think you of a Declaration of Rights?" Adams asked Jefferson. "Should not such a Thing have preceeded the Model?"[5] His letter was sent across the English channel to Paris, where Jefferson was serving as the American minister to France. Jefferson was inclined to approach the proposed frame of government with prudence. His first impression was that a few amendments to the old Articles of Confederation might have accomplished the same result and saved "the good, old & venerable fabrick, which should have been preserved even as a religious relique."[6] Then Madison relayed to Jefferson information about the plan and scores of newspapers, which by the end of 1787 were devoting most of their news columns to the ratification contest and the attendant polemics. Jefferson saw merit in the suggestion for a second federal convention, but he saw more harm in another assembly called for the same purpose as the late meeting at Philadelphia. After carefully studying the Constitution, he wrote Madison a candid letter explaining his approval of certain sections, while taking exception to others and to the omissions. Jefferson was pleased with the separation of powers, the promised vigor of the government, and the grant of power to levy and collect taxes. The compromise on representation "captivated" him, and several other important features, such as the

[5] John Adams to Thomas Jefferson, November 10, 1787, *Documentary History of the Constitution*, IV, 369.
[6] Thomas Jefferson to John Adams, November 13, 1787, *ibid.*, 377.

veto power of the executive, received his approval. The bulk of his letter was reserved for what he found distasteful.[7]

"I will now add what I do not like," Jefferson wrote, "first the omission of a bill of rights providing clearly & without the aid of sophisms" for the whole catalog of civil rights commonly accepted as fundamental in America. To these guarantees for personal freedom, Jefferson added a restriction against government-granted monopolies. The argument that James Wilson was employing in Pennsylvania, that these rights were beyond the scope of a general government and clearly unnecessary, was to Jefferson "a gratis dictum" that might please a Philadelphia audience but which left him uneasy. Whereas the second section of the Articles of Confederation had assured to each state the retention of its sovereignty and jurisdiction in all cases where specific powers had not been delegated to the central government, no such assurance was found in the proposed Constitution. The lack of uniformity in the states on the matter of jury trials in civil cases should have stimulated the Convention to conclude that errant states must have their mistakes pointed out, "to have established a general right instead of a general wrong." Then as an afterthought, Jefferson scribbled between the lines of his letter a closing remark. "Let me add that a bill of rights is what the people are entitled to against every government on earth, general or particular, & what no just government should refuse, or rest on inference."

Further reflection on the need for a bill of rights soon caused Jefferson to take a firm position. To Colonel William S. Smith, in the American legation at London, Jefferson revealed his own ideas on how a bill of rights might be added to the Constitution. If I were in America now, Jefferson wrote,

I would advocate it [Constitution] warmly till nine [states] should have adopted, & then as warmly take the other side to convince the remaining four that they ought not to come into it till the declaration

[7] Thomas Jefferson to James Madison, December 20, 1787, *ibid.*, 411-15.

of rights is annexed to it. by this means we should secure all the good of it, & procure so respectable an opposition as would induce the accepting states to offer a bill of rights. this would be the happiest turn the thing could take.

After Jefferson shaped this idea of ratification he made no secret of it. He alluded to the scheme in letters dispatched to his closest friends in America during the early winter months of 1788, so that any circulation of his letters at home meant that the idea would be known from New York south to the Carolinas.[8]

When Jefferson later learned that his early thoughts on a bill of rights were in harmony with the Antifederalist viewpoint, he denied any partisan bias. Even before his views were known, however, many Federalists claimed that the Antifederalist strategy was unmistakable. The demands for a bill of rights were too widespread to be coincidental. Richard Henry Lee had praised the Constitution faintly, but he was more insistent upon another that would be "properly amended." Lee further asked if another federal convention could not better produce a governmental fabric "fit for freemen to wear?"[9]

Staunch Federalists denounced such tactics. Christopher Gadsden complained to Jefferson that

These subtil, dextrous long-train'd, systematical Opponents well knowing the Constitution recommended must be approv'd of in toto, or not [at] all, therefore wou'd seem to approve of it as highly as any the most zealous for it, only with an *All But*, which *But* alter'd wou'd gain they wou'd pretend universal Satisfaction, that it may be defer'd for that mighty reasonable *But* to another Convention hoping that will never happen & so the Bubble burst of Course.[10]

More than denunciation was required to achieve ratification.

[8] Thomas Jefferson to Colonel William S. Smith, February 2, 1788, *ibid.*, 470. See other Jefferson letters dated February 2, 6, 7, and 12, *ibid.*, 469, 479-80, 481-82, 501-02.

[9] Richard Henry Lee to Samuel Adams, October 5, 1787, Ballagh, ed., *Letters of Lee*, II, 447.

[10] Christopher Gadsden to Thomas Jefferson, October 29, 1787, *Documentary History of the Constitution*, IV, 356.

If a bill of rights or a second convention was the Antifederalist goal, as Gadsden and his friends believed it was, then Federalist efforts would have to be exerted on behalf of the Constitution as it stood when the Convention adjourned. Well-organized Federalist party machinery was soon working in the important states to counteract Antifederalist moves and promote their own cause.

To the Federalist leaders the great issue involved in the ratification tug-of-war was "to make the revolution a blessing instead of a curse."[11] Thus they wasted no time in gaining the initiative in the campaign. Their opponents constantly complained that they were trying to hurry the people into approval of the Constitution before it could be studied properly and opinions formed by reason rather than passionate, partisan appeals. Federalists retorted that reason dictated the necessity of adopting the Constitution without delay. But they realized that their position was not invulnerable because the desires of every group were not completely satisfied. Henry Knox foresaw the necessity for compromise at the outset when he suggested to Washington that concessions to the opposition might be expedient. "Every well founded objection which shall be stated in the course of the discussions on the subject should be fairly considered," he wrote, "and such fundamental Laws enacted as would tend to obviate them."[12]

Knox's conciliatory attitude was not shared by Alexander Hamilton. When the Antifederalists in New York began their attack on the Constitution with a claim that the proposal would drastically curb the liberties of the people, Hamilton diagnosed the argument as sheer demagoguery. "It is the plan of men of this stamp to frighten the people with ideal bugbears, in order to mould them to their own purposes," he charged. "The

[11] David Humphreys to Alexander Hamilton, September 16, 1787, Frank L. Humphreys, *Life and Times of David Humphreys* (New York, 1917), I, 423.
[12] Henry Knox to George Washington, October 3, 1787, *Documentary History of the Constitution*, IV, 312.

unceasing cry of these designing croakers is, My friends, your liberty is invaded!"[13]

Other Federalists thought Hamilton's inclination to dismiss the Antifederalist attack on the issue of personal liberty without serious concern was somewhat rash and dangerous. "I confess I cannot help doubting the negative quality which it conveys," William Pierce confided to a close friend, "as some of the greatest men I ever knew have objected to the government for no other reason but because it was not *buttoned with a Bill of Rights;* men whose experience and wisdom are sufficient to give authority and support to almost any opinion they may choose to advance."[14]

One of the first Federalists to perceive the potency of the Antifederalist demand for a bill of rights was James Wilson. Wilson's early answer to the opposition constitutes one of the most notable of all the Federalist replies to the question which had alarmed so many Americans. So forceful was Wilson's rebuttal that it was maintained as the principal Federalist answer to the demand for a bill of rights until the final pro-Constitution argument on the subject was written by Hamilton in the *Federalist* LXXXIV. Less than a month after the Federal Convention had adjourned, Wilson spoke on behalf of the Constitution before a group of citizens in Philadelphia. In his defense of the document, Wilson quickly turned to the attacks centered on the omission of a bill of rights. The powers of Congress would come from positive grants explicitly stated in the Constitution, Wilson said, and every power not granted to Congress was reserved by the people.[15]

This distinction being recognized, will furnish an answer to those who think the omission of a bill of rights, a defect in the proposed constitution; for it would have been superfluous and absurd, to have stipulated

[13] Paul L. Ford, ed., *Essays on the Constitution* (Brooklyn, 1892), 289.
[14] William Pierce to St. George Tucker, September 28, 1787, from *Georgia Gazette*, March 20, 1788, in *American Historical Review*, 3 (1897), 315.
[15] Paul L. Ford, ed., *Pamphlets on the Constitution* (Brooklyn, 1888), 155-57.

with a federal body of our own creation, that we should enjoy those privileges, of which we are not divested either by the intention or the act that has brought that body into existence.

Since the proposed plan of government held no power over such liberties as freedom of the press, Wilson argued, a formal declaration would have been "merely nugatory." In fact, Wilson added, a formal declaration on the subject would have been harmful because it "might have been construed to imply that some degree of power was given," if the Convention had attempted to define the extent of that power. Wilson disposed of the claim that trial by jury in civil cases was to be abolished by asserting that lack of uniformity on this point was demonstrated in the varying practices among the states.

The failure to prohibit a standing army was another opposition criticism that Wilson wanted to shatter completely. He alluded to the army garrisons then maintained on the banks of the Ohio River. That army had been raised under the Articles of Confederation, yet everybody saw that it was necessary if the frontier was to remain peaceful. Any abuse of the power could be checked by Congress, which would be directly responsible to the people. But the burden of Wilson's argument was that Congress could not misuse powers that it did not possess. And if there were mistakes in this Constitution, Wilson concluded, "the seeds of reformation are sown in the work itself, and the concurrence of two thirds of the congress may at any time introduce alterations and amendments."[16]

News of the ratification contest reached Washington at Mount Vernon, where the revolutionary hero had retired in order to view the struggle without becoming directly involved. Washington was not impressed with the objections raised to alleged danger for personal liberty. Although he professed himself to be no blind admirer of every part of the Constitution, he considered the demand for a bill of rights as a smoke screen raised to conceal the other reasons which would not

[16] *Ibid.*, 161.

stand exposure "in open day."[17] After the Pennsylvania convention began, Washington declared that most of the Antifederalist literature he had seen appeared to be calculated to frighten the people. To speak of a bill of rights or other amendments was folly. "Every attempt to amend the Constitution at this time is, in my opinion, idly vain," he concluded.[18] Throughout the contest for ratification Washington was inclined to regard opponents of the Constitution as selfish men fighting for personal motives rather than principles. Washington's personal feelings toward the opposition leaders may account for his failure to consider the bill of rights movement a matter of great concern.

As the seat of the Federal Convention, the city of Philadelphia had quickly divided into two camps over the Constitution. The address of the seceding sixteen who attempted to block the call for a state ratifying convention was but the first round in the bitter quarrel. Writing as "Centinel" in the *Independent Gazetteer,* Judge Samuel Bryan immediately challenged Wilson's speech of October 6, which had maintained that the Constitution would erect a government of declared powers with others reserved for the people. Judge Bryan claimed that under the sweeping powers granted to the federal government, whose acts would be the supreme law of the land, Congress could restrain and regulate printers until freedom of the press was destroyed. "After such a declaration, what security does the *Constitutions* of the several States afford for the *liberty of the press and other invaluable personal rights,* not provided for by the new plan?" Bryan asked. Trial by jury in civil cases was to be abandoned, thus permitting English merchants to sue for alleged debts with a much greater chance of collection. A standing army would become a "grand machine of power and oppression" raised to tempt an ambitious man who had dictatorial designs. Personal rights would be

[17] George Washington to Bushrod Washington, November 10, 1787, Fitzpatrick, ed., *Writings of Washington,* XXIX, 312.
[18] George Washington to David Stuart, November 30, 1787, *ibid.,* 323.

lost because the state declarations of rights would be super-seded. This transfer of power to a strong central government made a bill of rights absolutely necessary. "For universal experience," wrote Bryan, "demonstrates the necessity of the most express declarations and restrictions, to protect the rights and liberties of mankind, from the silent, powerful and ever active conspiracy of those who govern."[19] Finally, "Centinel" declared, there was little real hope that Congress would grant a bill of rights to the people once the Constitution was ratified. The fifth article which contained the details of amending procedure was "mere sound." He sadly concluded that it would take a revolution to erect a bill of rights once Congress was in power.

Delaware had already ratified the Constitution with considerable haste and by a unanimous vote, but the Federalists were looking to Pennsylvania, where the first genuine test of their strength was expected. There factions bred out of the controversies under the Pennsylvania Constitution of 1776 had carried their quarrels over into the ratifying convention. Many of the men satisfied with the state constitution took sides with the Antifederalists, while their old enemies often supported the plan offered by the Federal Convention. Robert Whitehill, William Findley, and John Smilie, all from the western part of the state, had supported the state constitution and were now outspoken champions of the Antifederalist cause. A Federalist writer claimed that Whitehill had conspired with "a disaffected member of the federal convention, from Virginia, in a closet conversation," and had taken the cue for his opposition from that man—probably George Mason.[20] Whitehill and his friends, in their "Address from the Seceding Members," had provoked Wilson's reasoned answers to their charge that a bill of rights constituted a grievous omission from the handiwork of the Federal Convention. Now the Federalist

[19] *Centinel No. II,* broadside, Rare Book Room, Library of Congress.
[20] *Pennsylvania Gazette,* October 3, 1787.

press took up the cudgels. The *Pennsylvania Gazette* published the letter of "Avenging Justice," who charged that the Antifederalist claims that freedom of the press would be abolished were spread by a group armed with abominable falsehoods.[21] "How despicable must the cause of that opposition be, which has recourse to such means to effect its purpose!" But the charge that freedom of the press was endangered was to persist even after the state convention had ended with a Federalist victory.

The Pennsylvania convention had been summoned to meet on November 20. The Antifederalists considered the early call a bit of strategy designed to stifle full discussion. They viewed it as a Federalist plot which had to be met with vigorous opposition, and the press was their chief method of resistance. In this campaign the Antifederalist strategy was directed along the lines suggested earlier by Mason and Lee. Was the Constitution "to be so hastily adopted or rejected, that it cannot admit of a revision?" asked an "Old Whig."[22] If the state conventions did not approve it, their objections could be forwarded to the Continental Congress, he suggested, and another convention called. A second convention could form a federal government by carefully avoiding the mistakes made by the first meeting. Then the "Old Whig" added: "It will not be done without a *careful attention to the framing of a bill of rights*." "Centinel" observed that the first attempt to draft a constitution did not mean that other efforts were unnecessary. "A future general Convention being in possession of the objections, will be the better enabled to plan a suitable government," "Centinel" added.[23] To the Federalist argument that nobody in the enlightened year of 1787 would be foolish enough to suggest that freedom of religion should be denied to Americans "An Old Whig" replied that he was convinced that human nature had not changed, and

[21] *Ibid.*, October 17, 1787.
[22] *Philadelphia Independent Gazetteer*, October 29, 1787.
[23] *Ibid.*, October 5, 1787.

They are idiots who trust their future security to the whim of the present hour. . . . What is there in the new proposed constitution to prevent his [a conscientious objector] being dragged like a Prussian soldier to the camp and there compelled to bear arms?

This argument was aimed at the pacific Quakers. Without a bill of rights, the "Old Whig" said, liberty of conscience and all the other personal rights would depend "on the will and the pleasure" of their rulers.[24]

The Federalist press in Pennsylvania had ready answers for their opponents. Early in October, they claimed "there was a fixed resolution of the antifederal junto to oppose the federal government, *long before* it made its appearance."[25] They charged that the Antifederalists opposed the Constitution because it would diminish their own powers in state politics. When their opponents continued to insist on amendments prior to ratification the Federalists gave them a new name—"amend-mentites"—then compared them "to the Israelitish spies, who brought up an evil report of the land of Canaan."[26] Tench Coxe, writing as "An American Citizen," pointed out that the Articles of Confederation lacked a bill of rights, a fact which had not excited any opposition to that earlier constitution. Neither the old constitution nor the new one mentioned liberty of the press or personal rights, he declared, "because they are already provided for *by the state constitutions.*" Anything related to personal rights was actually out of place, as Wilson had demonstrated, "*in a contract among sovereign states.*"[27] Nothing was said about the privilege of eating and drinking in the Constitution, Coxe noted with sarcasm, but he doubted that any man was seriously afraid that his right to dine was endangered by the silence of the Constitution on this point.

Sarcasm became a favorite weapon of the Federalists. A week before the state convention met the *Pennsylvania Gazette*

[24] *Ibid.,* November 1, 1787.
[25] *Addresses to the Citizens of Pennsylvania* (Philadelphia, 1787), 1.
[26] *Pennsylvania Gazette,* November 19, 1787.
[27] *Addresses to the Citizens of Pennsylvania,* 4.

carried "A Receipt for an Antifederal Essay," which contained as its ingredients

WELL-BORN, nine times—*Aristocracy*, eighteen times—*Liberty of the Press*, thirteen times repeated.—*Liberty of Conscience*, once.—*Negroe slavery*, once mentioned—Trial by jury, seven times—*Great Men*, six times repeated—*MR. WILSON*, forty times—and lastly, GEORGE MASON'S *Right Hand in a Cuttingbox*, nineteen times—put them altogether, and dish them up at pleasure. These *words* will bear boiling, roasting, or frying—and, what is remarkable of them, they will bear being served, after once used, a dozen times to the same table and palate.[28]

In western Pennsylvania Hugh Brackenridge joined the Federalists to poke jibes at the "Anties." Writing in the Pittsburgh *Gazette*, Brackenridge called the demand for a bill of rights a sham. The Antifederalists were yelling

> That the convention in great fury,
> Have taken away the trial by jury;
> That liberty of press is gone,
> We shall be hang'd each mothers son;
> Say Lord knows what, as comes in head,
> Pretences for a scare crow made.[29]

But most of the writing was in a heavier vein, particularly around Philadelphia, as the opening session of the convention drew nearer. Pamphlets from other states reached the city and were circulated as "the latest advice" from New York, Boston, and Baltimore. Before the convention set about its business, Federalists could quote "Publicus," the "Federalist," and "Landholder," and other pamphleteers enrolled in their cause, while Antifederalists were equally assured of the truth in George Clinton's "Cato," Richard Henry Lee's "Federal Farmer," and Mason's "Objections." Even the most violently partisan newspapers followed the curious custom of occasionally printing without comment a fiercely biased article clipped from an opposing journal.

[28] *Pennsylvania Gazette*, November 14, 1787.
[29] Quoted in Russell J. Ferguson, *Early Western Pennsylvania Politics* (Pittsburgh, 1938), 83.

While the call for a bill of rights grew louder in Pennsylvania, Lee had published the first of his letters over the signature of a "Federal Farmer." These pamphlets had been broadcast throughout the areas where strong Antifederalist sentiment existed. Lee hammered away at the Federalist argument that a bill of rights was impractical. There were certain fundamental rights which should form the groundwork of every constitution, Lee declared, and he believed "a complete federal bill of rights to be very practicable."[30] Lee went on to point out the danger of a standing army, and the limitation on jury trials. The few allusions to personal rights in the Constitution as it stood were a half-hearted attempt to form a bill of rights, Lee explained, but a full catalog of personal liberties was required. Freedom of religion, jury trials, a prohibition on unreasonable warrants of search and seizure, freedom of the press—all were necessary in a national compact that would serve "for ages and millions yet unborn."[31] Lee urged the people to appraise the Constitution with caution, and recommended the calling of "state conventions some months hence, which shall examine coolly every article, clause, and word in the system proposed, and to adopt it with such amendments as they shall think fit."[32]

Lee plainly feared the power of the federal government, and by amendments he meant not a bill of rights alone, but curbs on the national government in the sphere of federal-state relations. There was a sectional aspect to ratification, illustrated in one case by the southern fear that navigation laws passed by the national government would benefit northern shipping (hence an uncomplimentary paragraph in Mason's "Objections" was omitted from the northern editions).[33] But in the case of Lee's arguments, as with dozens of others advanced by

[30] Ford, ed., *Pamphlets on the Constitution*, 290-91.
[31] *Ibid.*, 314-17.
[32] *Ibid.*, 324.
[33] James Madison to George Washington, December 20, 1787, *Documentary History of the Constitution*, IV, 417.

the Antifederalists, the demand for a bill of rights constituted a common ground on which citizens from every section of the Republic could take a stand. The opponents of the Constitution were playing politics on a grand scale. The bill of rights was their greatest political asset in every part of the nation because it represented an issue that transcended sectional interests.

In the midst of mounting tension on the ratification question the Pennsylvania convention met to deliberate and vote. Delegates elected in the larger cities were generally favorable to the Constitution, while many of the western delegates were in the Antifederalist camp. James Wilson addressed the delegates in an effort to dispose of the objections raised because of the omission of a bill of rights. Five states had no declaration of rights, yet could gentlemen honestly say that the inhabitants of South Carolina, New Jersey, New York, Connecticut, or Rhode Island (and he might have added Georgia) were oppressed? Wilson went on to say that by their example these states had proved that a bill of rights was not an essential of a republican government. Wilson recurred to his earlier argument, that the Constitution was an instrument of enumerated powers only, thus making a bill of rights unnecessary.[34] To enumerate all the rights of mankind would be impolitic and dangerous, he insisted, for errors of omission might pave the way for greater wrongs. But, Wilson said, the Federalists were asked

What harm could the addition of a bill of rights do? If it can do no good, I think that a sufficient reason to refuse having any thing to do with it. But to whom are we to report this bill of rights, if we should adopt it? Have we authority from those who sent us here to make one?[35]

Apparently the western delegates thought the convention did possess that authority, for on December 12 Robert Whitehill presented to the body a petition from 750 inhabitants of Cum-

[34] Jonathan Elliot, ed., *The Debates in the Several State Conventions on the Adoption of the Federal Constitution* (Philadelphia, 1888), II, 435-37.
[35] *Ibid.*, 454.

berland County. The petitioners asked that the Constitution be adopted only with the addition of amendments, including a bill of rights. Whitehill then offered the convention fifteen proposed amendments, which were turned down by a vote of 46 to 23. The Antifederalists were not a match for their opponents, and before the day ended the Constitution itself was ratified by an identical vote.[36]

Friends of the Constitution promptly applauded the Pennsylvania ratification as a signal victory, which indeed it was, since a setback for the Constitution at this stage might well have been disastrous. The Antifederalists called a "rump convention" of their own, at which twenty-one of the twenty-three delegates who had voted against ratification issued their own manifesto, "The Address and Reasons of Dissent of the Minority of the Convention." Published on December 18, the address indicated that many delegates were still sour about the entire affair. Their objections were presented under three headings, one of which was that "a bill of rights was indispensable to ascertain and establish 'those unalienable and personal' rights of man." Among these rights was a guarantee of trial by jury in all cases. The address also denounced standing armies in time of peace, and federal control over state militia.[37] At Carlisle, where news of ratification was greeted with a riot, an Antifederalist pamphlet appeared denouncing the ratifying convention. The pamphlet accused Benjamin Rush of expressing his delight over the lack of guarantees for personal liberty. Rush was quoted as saying, "I am happy sir, to find that the convention hath not disgraced this constitution with a bill of rights." The question raised by the "Anties" was "Whether ought Pennsylvania to reward such declarations with a suit of tar and feathers, or a hempen necklace."[38] Cumberland County Antifederalists also framed a note of thanks to the minority

[36] Thomas, *Political Tendencies in Early Pennsylvania*, 147.
[37] *Ibid.*, 149.
[38] *The Government of Nature Delineated* . . . (Carlisle, 1788), 176, quoted in Butterfield, ed., *Letters of Benjamin Rush*, I, 455.

which had labored in vain on behalf of "the drooping cause of liberty."[39] The Federalists had won, but it appeared that their victory was not being accepted with good grace by all of their opponents.

New Jersey followed the lead of Pennsylvania before the week was over by ratifying the Constitution. In New Jersey there was less discussion and the vote for ratification was unanimous. On January 2, 1788, Georgia also ratified unanimously.

In Connecticut, where an early convention had been called by the Federalist leaders in state politics, Oliver Ellsworth and Roger Sherman entered the lists with essays favoring the Constitution in strong terms. Ellsworth, writing as "The Landholder," devoted a whole article to an answer to Mason's "Objections." Mason had refused to sign the Constitution, Ellsworth declared, because his motion asking that no navigation act could be passed without the consent of two-thirds of Congress had failed. But he thought that all of Mason's other objections were mere window dressing.[40] Wilson's argument against a bill of rights was used by Ellsworth in answering the demand for guaranteed liberties. Declarations of rights were "insignificant," Ellsworth explained, since the people constitute the source of all political power anyway. He ridiculed the claim that the Constitution was silent about freedom of the press. Freedom of the press was not mentioned, "Nor is liberty of conscience, or of matrimony, or of burial of the dead," Ellsworth declared, but "it is enough that congress have no power to prohibit either, and can have no temptation."[41]

Using the pseudonym of "A Countryman," Roger Sherman went further than Ellsworth in denouncing the demand for a bill of rights. Those who urged this objection had reached

[39] John B. McMaster and Frederick D. Stone, eds., *Pennsylvania and the Federal Constitution, 1787-1788* (Lancaster, 1888), 497.
[40] Ford, ed., *Essays on the Constitution*, 161-62.
[41] *Ibid.*, 164.

the "sublimity of *nonsense* and *alarm*," he wrote, by thundering against the Constitution "in every shape of *metaphoric terror*, on the subject of a *bill of rights*."[42] The rights of men demanded more than paper protection, Sherman asserted. "The only real security that you can have for all your important rights must be in the nature of your government." Sherman frankly admitted that the proposed Congress might invade the liberties of the people if it abused its powers. But there was a check on the Congress in the self-interests of the legislators. "If the members of Congress can take no improper step which will not affect them as much as it does us, we need not apprehend that they will usurp authorities not given them to injure that society of which they are a part," Sherman explained. This was a new argument that buttressed Wilson's earlier statement. The meager records of the Connecticut convention reveal no objections over the omission of a bill of rights in a state which had more than a hundred years of experience with written guarantees for personal liberty. The convention ratified the Constitution on January 9 by an overwhelming vote of 128 to 40.

At about the same time that Jefferson's thoughts had crystallized into a definite plan in favor of amendments containing a bill of rights, the Massachusetts convention reached a climax. After debate which had consumed almost a month this important New England state seemed ready to reject the Constitution by a narrow margin. The floor fight had been enlivened by the introduction of amendment proposals by desperate Federalists. These proposals were made necessary by the continued criticism directed against the Constitution over the omission of a bill of rights and other issues ever since copies of the document had first been distributed during the preceding fall months. The *American Herald* columns carried over the signature of "John De Witt" a prediction late in October that, once the Constitution was adopted, amendments could be made

[42] *Ibid.*, 218.

only by open rebellion.[43] Antifederalist printers suspected a
conspiracy among Federalists in the post offices when they
found their source of news from the south cut off by uncooperative post riders. The address of the Pennsylvania minority,
printed in the Philadelphia newspapers on December 18, failed
to reach Boston until after the ratifying convention adjourned
on February 9.[44]

Despite the lack of news from other states, the Antifederalists in Massachusetts found sufficient material for their
use. "A Watchman" complained in the *Worcester Magazine*
that while liberty of conscience was slighted in the Constitution,
the prohibition on religious tests might permit a Mohammedan
to become president. This writer also lamented the lack of
guarantees for a free press and freedom of speech.[45] A handbill distributed on the streets of Boston in mid-November had
cited thirteen "DISADVANTAGES of FEDERALISM," including the lack of a bill of rights, restraint of a free press, a
standing army, "*Habeas Corpus* done away . . . And, 13th,
Religion Abolished." The handbill concluded that these reasons, "and many more, require the plan to be *amended*, and
made *conformable* to the Circumstances of the People."[46] Citizens in the western part of the state were no less attentive to
the question of a bill of rights. In Berkshire County, the
Great Barrington Antifederalists lost by a narrow vote their
proposals to send a delegate to the state convention instructed
to complain over the failure of the Constitution to preserve
personal freedom. Harvard, in Worcester County, sent objections to the omission of a bill of rights and instructed its
delegate to vote against the Constitution on the ground that it
would "soon bring the good people of the United States under
Despotism." Northward in the Maine country, similar fears

---

[43] Quoted in Samuel B. Harding, *The Contest Over the Ratification of the
Federal Constitution in the State of Massachusetts* (New York, 1896), 24.

[44] George Bryan to John Ralston, March 7, 1788, in *Pennsylvania Gazette*,
March 26, 1788.

[45] Harding, *Ratification in Massachusetts*, 36.

[46] *Ibid.*, 53-54.

were expressed. Thomas B. Wait, a Falmouth printer, declared that there was "a certain darkness, duplicity and studied ambiguity of expresion [sic] running thro' the whole Constitution which renders a Bill of Rights peculiarly necessary."[47]

James Winthrop is believed to have written the "Letters of Agrippa," which were Antifederalist propaganda pamphlets that found a ready circulation. "Agrippa" answered the argument advanced by James Sullivan in his "Letters of Cassius," that a bill of rights would not protect the people if their representatives did not stand in awe of the electorate. If the Congress wanted "to use their efforts to effect the establishment of an aristocratical or despotick government, would a bill of rights be any obstacle to their proceedings?" Sullivan asked.[48] Any plan of government, "Agrippa" answered, which appointed a legislature without any checks preserving the rights of individual citizens constituted a forfeiture of power by the people. States had recognized this fact by enacting bills of rights, he observed, and it was a shrewd deception to say that rights not given to Congress are reserved for the people.[49]

Samuel Adams, the venerated patriot of the Revolution, had written critically of the Constitution and was apparently convinced that it must be defeated in the ratifying conventions. He warned Richard Henry Lee that the proposed government consolidated powers dangerously, then lamented "that the Seeds of Aristocracy began to spring even before the Conclusion of our Struggle for the natural Rights of Men, Seeds which like a Canker Worm lie at the Root of free Governments."[50] Adams, assumed to be an Antifederalist, was elected to the convention as a delegate from Boston. Gerry, though not a delegate, was induced by that group to sit in on its sessions because of his knowledge of the Federal Convention. Rufus

[47] Thomas B. Wait to George Thatcher, January 8, 1788, quoted in ibid., 39.
[48] Ford, ed., Essays on the Constitution, 28.
[49] Ibid., 95-96.
[50] Samuel Adams to Richard Henry Lee, December 3, 1787, Cushing, ed., Writings of Adams, IV, 325.

King, Nathaniel Gorham, and Theophilus Parsons were among the Federalist leaders. The Antifederalists had let their opponents carry the debate. They came to the convention convinced of the dangers in the Constitution and were somewhat impatient. John Hancock, elected president of the convention, was believed to lean toward the Antifederalist view. In addition to a jealous regard for personal and state rights, the Antifederalists were convinced that there were inherent errors in the Constitution. One of these errors was the ban on religious tests, which many delegates considered as an affront to religious men. Parsons tried to explain the meaning of this provision to the convention, but on this and other points the Antifederalists and their friends remained convinced that alterations were necessary, and that without amendments they could not vote in favor of the Constitution.[51]

The Federalists then held a caucus and a compromise was proposed. Parsons was charged with drafting a set of recommendatory amendments. These conciliatory articles were to be forwarded with the ratified Constitution, the Federalists told Hancock. The amendments were turned over to Hancock, who presented them to the convention as his own handiwork.[52] Samuel Adams, who had been pressed by some Boston mechanics and artisans to side with the Federalists, arose to praise the amendments Hancock had offered, thus indicating to the Antifederalists that one in their ranks was wavering. Charles Jarvis offered the clinching argument. "The Constitution is a great political experiment," he said, hence the acceptance of the proposed amendments would remove many of the objections voiced in the debate. Now that recommendatory amendments were proposed, the way was cleared for approval of the new frame of government.[53]

On the following day, the Antifederalists renewed their plea for a prefatory bill of rights rather than amendments. "Any

[51] Parsons, *Memoir of Theophilus Parsons,* 97-98.
[52] *Ibid.,* 78.
[53] Elliot, ed., *Debates,* II, 154.

gentleman in that Convention could form one in a few hours, as he might take the bill of rights of Massachusetts for a guide," one delegate asserted. Parsons again brought forward the familiar answer that Congress had no power to touch personal rights.[54] Other delegates expressed doubt that amendments could be "interwoven in the Constitution." Despite the Federalist concession, ratification was still uncertain. At the last moment Samuel Adams introduced an amendment to the proposed group offered by the Federalists. It was in effect a bill of rights and it caught the Federalists off guard.[55] Upon hearing phrases about "liberty of the press" and the "rights of conscience" again some Antifederalists who had been wavering began to stiffen. Considerable confusion was noted in the Federalist ranks. Jeremy Belknap declared that Adams attempted to withdraw the proposition when he "perceived the mischief he had made . . . but some of the Anti leaders revived it, and he was obliged finally to *vote against it*."[56] Belknap thought that Adams' motive was not an attachment to the cause of civil liberty, but rather an effort to gain public favor. Adams' past record and his earlier professions on personal liberty, were in contradiction of his final vote against his own motion. Defeat of the Adams resolution signaled victory for the Federalists. Still the Antifederalists were only narrowly outvoted when the ballot came later in the day, 187 yeas to 168 nays. Isaac Backus, present as a delegate from Middleborough, broke with the Baptist clique which opposed ratification. In justifying his vote for the Constitution, Backus noted that the

[54] *Ibid.*, 162.

[55] Adams' proposal was: "And that the said Constitution be never construed to authorize Congress to infringe the just liberty of the press, or the rights of conscience; or to prevent the people of the United States, who are peaceable citizens, from keeping their own arms; or to raise standing armies, unless when necessary for the defence of the United States, or of some one or more of them; or to prevent the people from petitioning, in a peaceable and orderly manner, the federal legislature, for a redress of grievances; or to subject the people to unreasonable searches and seizures of their persons, papers or possessions." *Debates of the Massachusetts Convention of 1788* (Boston, 1856), 86-87.

[56] Jeremy Belknap to Ebenezer Hazard, February 10, 1788, Massachusetts Historical Society, *Collections*, 5th ser., 3 (1877), 17-18.

"exclusion of any hereditary, lordly power, and of any religious test, I view as our greatest securities in this constitution."[57]

As the first state to send along recommendatory amendments with ratification, Massachusetts established a precedent
which remaining states could follow unless they approved the
Constitution as it stood. These nine articles included proposals
that all powers not delegated by the Constitution be reserved
for the states, enjoined Congress not to use its powers in regulating elections unless the circumstances were unusual, and
asked that Congress be prohibited from levying direct taxes
and creating monopolies. The necessity for grand jury indictment was upheld, along with the need for jury trials in
civil actions between citizens of different states. Freedom of
conscience, freedom of speech, and liberty of the press—so
frequently mentioned by the Antifederalist minority—were
overlooked. The door was opened, however, for other states
to add suggestions as they ratified the Constitution.

The proposed amendments found the various party leaders
viewing the maneuver with mixed feelings. Madison thought
that the introduction of amendments was a blemish on the ratification but that they were "in the least offensive form."[58]
Washington believed that the presence of amendments and the
small majority lightened the impact of ratification on the Antifederalists. "As it is, it operates as a damper to their hopes,
and is a matter of disappointment and chagreen to them all."[59]
When Jefferson heard of the recommendatory amendments
he completely revised his opinion on ratification. Instead of
his previous thought that nine states should ratify while four
held out for amendments, he now confessed that the "plan of
Massachusetts is far preferable, and will I hope be followed

[57] Isaac Backus, *A History of New England* . . . , David Weston, ed. (Newton, Mass., 1871), II, 335.
[58] James Madison to George Washington, February 15, 1788, *Documentary
History of the Constitution*, IV, 505.
[59] George Washington to Henry Knox, March 3, 1788, Fitzpatrick, ed.,
Writings of Washington, XXIX, 434.

by those who are yet to decide."[60] Jefferson still considered a bill of rights necessary, and the Massachusetts proposal which limited the powers of Congress was only a half-way solution to this problem. "It will do too much in some instances & too little in others," Jefferson predicted; "it will cripple the federal government in some cases where it ought to be free, and not restrain it in some others where restraint would be right." Further consideration of the Massachusetts method of ratifying confirmed Jefferson's views. By June he could declare

if the states which were to decide after her should all do the same, it is impossible but they must obtain the essential amendments. It will be more difficult if we lose this instrument, to recover what is good in it, than to correct what is bad after we shall have adopted it.[61]

Not all America was in accord with Jefferson's conciliatory mood, however, even after his revised views became known in his homeland. Edmund Randolph called the Bay State amendments "a paltry snare." A few were admissible, he conceded; but others seemed pointed at the South, and the rest were milk-and-water.[62]

Meanwhile, express riders carried the news from Massachusetts to other states, where it was cited by the Federalists as proof that the Constitution would soon become the law of the land. But in New Hampshire, where a ratifying convention had met on the heels of the Massachusetts adjournment, optimistic Federalist reports of an earlier day proved false. From the outset it was apparent that a majority of the delegates were positively pledged by their towns to vote against the Constitution. Somewhat dismayed, the Federalists decided that only a temporary adjournment could save their cause. They hoped that with additional time they could persuade dissenting townsmen to take a different view of the Constitution. This

[60] Thomas Jefferson to Edward Carrington, May 27, 1788, *Documentary History of the Constitution*, IV, 631-32.

[61] Thomas Jefferson to William Carmichael, June 3, 1788, *ibid.*, IV, 680-81.

[62] Edmund Randolph to James Madison, February 29, 1788, Conway, *Life of Randolph*, 101.

strategy was employed, and the Convention delegates approved the adjournment which saved New Hampshire for the Federalists.[63]

The ratification by Massachusetts had disappointed Gerry, but he was determined to carry the Antifederalist cause forward with even more vigor. He wrote a pamphlet, "Observation on the New Constitution, and on the Federal and State Conventions," under the pseudonym of "a Columbian patriot." Gerry advised the remaining states either to reject the Constitution or to delay their proceedings until a second federal convention could be called.[64] There was no security for the individual citizen's rights in the whole plan, Gerry stated. Thinking men could detect the falsity of Federalist claims "that the whole constitution is a declaration of right."[65] Over sixteen hundred copies of the pamphlet were printed in New York by the Antifederalists for distribution through their state, though the Albany committee complained that its style was "too sublime and florid for the common people in this part of the country."[66]

There was nothing florid or sublime in Francis Hopkinson's lampoon of the plea for a bill of rights in his essay, "The New Roof," which assumed there would be an early ratification of the Constitution. Widely reprinted, Hopkinson's parody asserted that a "bill of scantling" for the new roof was useless and improper, since the "timber was to be cut from our own lands . . . [and] the wood always was and always would be the property of the family."[67] More ridicule was heaped on those who demanded a bill of rights by "One of the People," who said that Americans were becoming as attached to forms of government with bills of rights in the same way "that has obtained among the Hollanders upon the

---

[63] C. Gibbs to George Washington, February 24, 1788, *Documentary History of the Constitution*, IV, 520.

[64] Ford, ed., *Pamphlets on the Constitution*, 21.

[65] *Ibid.*, 12-13.

[66] *Ibid.*, 1.

[67] *Pennsylvania Gazette*, January 9, 1788.

subjects of foot-stoves and houses."[68] A bill of rights, he declared, was a British idea which degraded the thoughtful American! "Let these truths sink deep into our hearts: that the people are the masters of their rulers . . . and that a master reserves to himself the exclusive care of all property, and *every thing else* which he has not committed to the care of those servants." The revamped Wilson rebuttal thus was old wine poured into a new bottle.

The Federalists expressed genuine concern over the position taken by some of the religious groups which were constantly gaining more adherents. "A Baptist," writing in the Philadelphia *Freeman's Journal,* expressed alarm over possible curbs on freedom of conscience in the Constitution. "A real Baptist" answered the charge that a dominion of bishops would be established, then cast doubt on the true affiliation of the other writer. "The artifice and *low* cunning of such violent partisans will not add to *their* [Antifederalist] *strength* a single convert," he predicted.[69] While the official status of the *Journal* writer might have been doubtful, there was no question about the definite opposition various religious sects were throwing in the path of ratification. When the Virginia General Baptist Committee met in Goochland County on March 7, 1788, the Constitution was warmly debated by the delegates. Their discussion centered on whether the document "made sufficient provision for the secure enjoyment of religious liberty; on which, it was agreed unanimously, that, in the opinion of the general committee, it did not."[70] Opposition of this nature jolted the Federalists into recognizing that legalistic arguments were ineffectual with a portion of the citizenry. James Madison, however, was a known friend of religious liberty and he still dismissed all arguments for a bill of rights as so much misguided factionalism. In the *Federalist* XXX-VIII he explained that proponents of a bill of rights were

[68] *Ibid.*
[69] *Ibid.,* January 30, 1788.
[70] Semple, *History of the Baptists in Virginia,* 76-77.

unable to agree among themselves on what they desired. Madison strengthened his case by noting that the public demand for a national bill of rights had not been heard prior to 1787.[71]

Even after a state had ratified the Constitution, the opposition was not content to accept defeat docilely. In certain parts of Pennsylvania tempers continued to flare when the Constitution was mentioned. Open riots took place in the western counties; blood was shed, and civil disorder only stressed the bitter antagonism between the opposing factions. Hugh Brackenridge ridiculed the repeated charges that personal liberty would be destroyed by the new Constitution. He sarcastically admitted that the failure to include a bill of rights had been an error, but

There was no occasion for a bill of *wrongs;* for there will be *wrongs* enough . . . the *rights of conscience* are swept away. The Confession of Faith, the Shorter Catechism, and the Pilgrim's Progress are to go. . . . The *liberty of the press;* that is gone. . . . Not so much as the advertisement for a stray horse, or a runaway negro, can be put in any of the Gazettes. . . . The *trial by jury,* that is knocked in the head, and all that worthy class of men, the lawyers, who live by haranguing and bending the juries, are demolished . . . I would submit to any candid man, if in this constitution there be the least provision for the privilege of shaving the beard? or is there any mode laid down to take the measure of a pair of breeches?[72]

More serious and important than the taunts of a frontier editor were the preparations made in Maryland for the convention called for April. Strong opposition was expected by the Federalists in Luther Martin's home state, where William Paca, Samuel Chase, and Jeremiah Chase had been organizing the Antifederalists. When the Constitution was first circulated Samuel Chase had told a large crowd in Annapolis that the document was certain to abolish their state bill of rights and

[71] E. H. Scott, ed., *The Federalist and Other Constitutional Papers* (Chicago, 1894), I, 204-07.
[72] *Pittsburgh Gazette,* March 1, 1788, quoted in Ferguson, *Early Western Pennsylvania Politics,* 94-95.

constitution.[73] A short time later he had written a denunciation of a petition calling for ratification without amendments
or alterations. For almost two months Martin's "Genuine Information," a purported speech to the state legislature on the
Constitution, greeted readers of the *Maryland Gazette*. This
lengthy blast at the Constitution contained few allusions to
personal liberty, and the section on trial by jury erroneously
declared that this barrier against arbitrary power would be
removed in all cases arising under federal laws.[74] Later, Martin claimed that he had prepared a bill of rights to offer at the
Federal Convention but friends had convinced him that it
would have been a useless gesture.[75] Now Martin demanded
either amendments prior to ratification or a second federal
convention. He heatedly denounced the "political quacks" who
are using the pretense of curing governmental ills to "urge you
rashly to gulp down a constitution, which in its present form,
unaltered and unamended, would be as certain death to your
liberty, as arsenic could be to your bodies."[76]

Professor Philip A. Crowl asserts that the Constitutional
question was viewed with marked apathy by Maryland voters.
While it is probably true "that the initiative in the fight against
the Constitution was taken not by debt-burdened farmers but
rather by a small faction of lawyers and merchants within the
ruling oligarchy," it is also important to note that this minority
party organized some resentment among the ordinary citizens
by their campaign.[77] Daniel Carroll stated that an incendiary
handbill from the Antifederalist press was distributed by John
Mercer and Jeremiah Chase. The broadside carried a list of
personal guarantees under the heading "BILL of RIGHTS"
and included "NO EXCISE," "NO POLL TAX," and
"No whipping militia, nor marching them out of the state,

[73] Ford, ed., *Essays on the Constitution*, 325.
[74] Farrand, ed., *Records of the Federal Convention*, III, 221-22.
[75] Ford, ed., *Essays on the Constitution*, 364-66.
[76] *Ibid.*, 377.
[77] See Philip A. Crowl, "Anti-Federalism in Maryland, 1787-1788," *William and Mary Quarterly*, 3rd ser., 4 (1947), 449.

without consent of the general assembly." These demands greatly alarmed the people, Carroll declared. "I am assured when they attended the polls, a wildness appeard in many which show'd they were realy frightend by what they had just heard."[78] Antifederalist labors resulted in victories in Anne Arundel, Baltimore, and Harford counties. Despite scattered local victories, however, the election returns favored a large Federalist majority.

The Maryland convention might have ratified the Constitution with a minimum of ceremony had not a dozen duly elected Antifederalists determined to offer amendments to accompany the document. William Paca attempted to offer a series of alterations on April 24, but he was howled down before he could read the proposals. The Federalists listened to other objections, but finally lost patience with Paca and his friends. A roll call vote on the ratification question showed 63 ayes and 11 nays. Paca at once declared that he had voted for the measure "under the firm persuasion, and in full confidence that such amendments would be peacably obtained so as to enable the people to live happy under the government."[79] If these amendments were not adopted, Paca declared his unalterable opposition to the Constitution. In a conciliatory mood the Federalists yielded to a request for a drafting committee that might shape amendments for the convention. Thirteen proposed amendments were fashioned by this committee in a report, while fifteen others were rejected. The acceptable amendments offered a curb to the power of Congress, guarantees for trial by jury, a "double jeopardy" clause, a prohibition against general warrants, freedom of the press, and other provisions found in the state bills of rights. These proposals clearly went far beyond the innocuous suggestions made by the Massachusetts convention. Other proposals which touched on the power of Congress in regulating elections, poll taxes, navi-

[78] Daniel Carroll to James Madison, May 28, 1788, *Documentary History of the Constitution*, IV, 636-41.
[79] Elliot, ed., *Debates*, II, 549.

gation acts, the right of petition, a disavowal of an established religion, and military exemption for conscientious objectors were turned down.[80]

Under the deluge of suggestions the Federalists on the committee apparently lost patience with Paca and his supporters. They refused to permit a report of the committee to go before the convention. Their action was sustained by the convention, although a request to record the vote was refused. The convention then adjourned. The Antifederalists refused to accept defeat gracefully, however, and they issued the entire twenty-eight proposed amendments in pamphlet form as a kind of minority report.[81] It was plainly a propaganda technique that could not influence the final action of the convention. But men of Luther Martin's stamp were accustomed to having the last word.

News that Maryland had ratified brought a shift of attention to South Carolina. Reports on the progress of ratification continued to overshadow other items in most newspapers. Rumors received the garb of truth in the press, some of them as far from the truth as the persistent report that Rhode Island had called a convention that would undoubtedly ratify the Constitution. The fact was that the Rhode Island legislature had sent the Constitution to the towns instead of calling a convention. In the town meetings the Constitution had been defeated, 237 yeas to 2,708 nays, but Federalists consoled themselves with a report that many friends of the Constitution had refused to vote as a protest against the legislative action.[82] South Carolina had called a convention for May after hearing Charles Pinckney assure the House of Representatives that his earlier fears over personal rights had been ill-founded. Arthur Simkins, Patrick Calhoun, and James Lincoln, all elected from the district of Ninety-Six, did not share Pinckney's optimism,

[80] *Ibid.*, 550-53.
[81] *Ibid.*, 555-56.
[82] John Collins to the President of Congress, April 5, 1788, *Documentary History of the Constitution*, IV, 555.

particularly on the matters of freedom of the press and religious freedom. Lincoln wanted to know why there was no bill of rights.[83] Pinckney borrowed the Wilson argument to answer Lincoln, declaring that Congress had no expressed power to touch civil rights. Then, Pinckney added, there was another reason which the South Carolina delegates had considered when a bill of rights was discussed at Philadelphia. Bills of rights usually began with a statement to the effect that all men are born free and equal. "Now," said Pinckney, the delegates realized that it would "make that declaration with a very bad grace, when a large part of our property consists in men who are actually born slaves."[84]

Pinckney's answer that slavery had kept the Federal Convention from seriously considering a bill of rights was both novel and astute. The powerful Rawlins Lowndes had already signified his intention to use state control of slavery and paper money as a basis for his opposition to the Constitution. Pinckney said that if the South insisted on slavery, it must be consistent and not talk about the natural freedom of all mankind. The Federalists realized too that Lowndes was a dangerous opponent, for he had taken up the cry of the northern Antifederalists and was talking about a second convention. Lowndes, General Thomas Sumter, and their associates received powerful support in their attempt to prevent the calling of a convention and were barely defeated by a 76 to 75 vote.

Alarmed by the close ballot in the legislature, the Federalists braced themselves for further blasts from their opponents. Their task was made infinitely easier when Lowndes was denied a seat in the convention by his pro-Constitution constituents in Charleston.[85] Without his leadership the Antifederalists were on the defensive from the outset, and when General Sumter moved for a delay of the convention until October,

[83] Elliot, ed., *Debates*, IV, 300, 312-15.
[84] *Ibid.*, 316.
[85] Rawlins Lowndes to John Lamb, June 21, 1788, Isaac Q. Leake, *Memoir of the Life and Times of General John Lamb* (Albany, 1850), 308.

they were completely overwhelmed. Despite Patrick Dollard's warning that his constituents in Prince Frederick District would resist the Constitution until "your standing army, like Turkish janizaries enforcing despotic laws, must ram it down their throats with the points of bayonets," the convention ratified the Constitution on May 23, 1788.

As a gesture of appeasement to the Antifederalists the South Carolina convention adopted several recommendatory amendments. "We had a tedious but trifling opposition to contend," Edward Rutledge acknowledged. "We had prejudices to contend with and sacrifices to make. Yet they were worth making for the good old cause."[86]

News favorable to "the good old cause" from South Carolina was joyfully received by friends of the Constitution elsewhere. The eighth state was now under the "new roof." Approval by one more state convention assured a trial for the Constitution, and there were reassuring reports that both New Hampshire and Virginia were eager to become the ninth member of the new federal circle.

Antifederalist sources were equally confident that Mason, Henry, and Lee had not been idly contemplating affairs in Virginia. As practical politicians, they were most inclined to look for success in those states where the Antifederal leaders were most powerful—that is—in office. Virginians had mapped the major strategy in the campaign, and their success would prove a stumbling block to the entire ratification process. The New York Antifederalists, leaving nothing to chance, had set up the "Federal Republican Committee" as a clearing house for information. In May, General John Lamb communicated with leaders of the opposition in New Hampshire and Virginia. His message bore an admonition that preservation of the rights of mankind depended upon a willingness "to use our best endeavors to procure amendments to the System previous to

[86] Edward Rutledge to John Jay, June 20, 1788, Henry P. Johnston, ed., *The Correspondence and Public Papers of John Jay* (New York, 1890-93), III, 252-53.

its adoption."[87] More important was Governor Clinton's letter to the Virginia chief executive, Edmund Randolph. Written May 8, it hinted at the possibility of an agreement between the two states and joint action on the proposed amendments prior to ratification. But for reasons which Randolph adjudged sufficient the Clinton letter was not sent to the convention in Virginia at all and was not forwarded to the Virginia legislature until the eve of ratification, when a quorum was lacking.[88]

All these machinations occurred behind the scenes, however. The public knew only that since the previous fall the two factions had been waging an earnest political battle over the Constitution. Many Antifederalist objections had been raised, but the demand for a bill of rights was among the earliest party maneuvers. This demand persisted, and no other single objection to the Constitution struck a more responsive chord of popular appeal. The Federalists saw in this demand an attempt to overthrow the whole Constitution, and they viewed even recommendatory amendments as useless if not harmful.

Still, the demand for a bill of rights was so widespread the more realistic Federalists saw that if much could be gained and little lost by conceding it, a compromise on the point might be necessary. No promises had been made, however, and to the average citizen it must have seemed that the days of the Confederation were numbered. Since 1776 most Americans had lived under a state constitution and bill of rights. Jefferson had predicted that after the Revolution ended the American democratic process would "be going down hill." Did the evidence presented by the Antifederalists confirm this dire prediction of tobogganing liberty? And if so, what did the Federalists propose to do about it?

[87] John Lamb to Nathaniel Peabody, May 18, 1788, *Historical Magazine*, 3rd ser., 2 (November, 1873), 280-81.

[88] E. Wilder Spaulding, *New York in the Critical Period, 1783-1787* (New York, 1932), 261.

CHAPTER VIII

THE GREAT COMPROMISE

WHATEVER HOPES the Federalists might have harbored regarding a hurried ratification gradually gave
way to a genuine fear that the whole scheme might fail. To
save their plan a bold strategy was required, and like many
strokes of political wisdom before and since it was applied to
give the desired object all the aspects of a sugar-coated pill.
Over four decades later, John Marshall was able to review
the events leading up to this compromise on a bill of rights
without the partisan bias he held in 1788. Then Marshall
conceded that during the political battles of 1787-88

Serious fears were extensively entertained that those powers which
the patriot statesmen . . . deemed essential to union, and to the attain-
ment of those invaluable objects for which union was sought, might
be exercised in a manner dangerous to liberty. . . . In almost every
convention by which the constitution was adopted, amendments to
guard the abuse of power were recommended. . . . In compliance with
a sentiment thus generally expressed, to quiet fears thus extensively entertained, amendments were proposed by the required majority in
congress, and adopted by the states.[1]

Thus did the Chief Justice of 1833 recall the offering made
by Federalists in 1788 to win over those who lumped most of
their objections under the phrase: "There is no bill of rights."

From where they stood in 1788, however, many of the
Federalists saw little evidence that they were on the threshold
of triumph. Hamilton believed himself surrounded by Antifederalists in New York and judged the whole cause in the light
of local circumstances. Washington's former aide, Tobias Lear,
declared that the Antifederalists were tireless in spreading their

[1] In Barron v. Baltimore, 7 Peters 250.

doctrines in New Hampshire. Their design was to frighten the people into believing that adoption of the Constitution meant that "the rights & liberties of all American Citizens would be destroyed."[2] The *Pennsylvania Gazette* circulated the report that £2,000 had been raised and spent by the Antifederalists through committees of correspondence.[3] So great was the opposition to ratification that Benjamin Franklin took up his pen to declare that "popular Opposition to a public Measure is no Proof of its Impropriety, even tho' the Opposition be excited & headed by Men of Distinction."[4] Indeed, it appeared to many observers that the Federalists had won only in the states most disposed toward ratification from the beginning. The rest of the fight would consist of assaults on the main citadels of Antifederalism.

The earlier adjournment of the New Hampshire convention in the face of known hostility to the Constitution made the outlook for the June convention appear bleak to the Federalists. Joshua Atherton, a leader of the opposition, was in communication with the Federal Republican message center in New York, and had assured General John Lamb of his belief that to ratify and then propose amendments was "to surrender our all."[5] Lamb in turn warned Nathaniel Peabody, another powerful figure in New Hampshire politics, of the importance of organized opposition which could unite in proposing amendments. Lamb was sure that accord among the Antifederalists in New Hampshire, Virginia, and New York would produce the desired alterations in the Constitution.[6] The effectiveness of this cooperation was acknowledged by Nicholas Gilman, a New Hampshire delegate to Congress and Federalist to the

[2] Tobias Lear to George Washington, June 2, 1788, *Documentary History of the Constitution*, IV, 676.

[3] *Pennsylvania Gazette*, March 12, 1788.

[4] *Federal Gazette*, April 8, 1788, *Documentary History of the Constitution*, IV, 571.

[5] Joshua Atherton to Gen. John Lamb [n. d.], Smith, "Movement Towards a Second Convention," in Jameson, ed., *Essays on Constitutional History*, 66.

[6] John Lamb to Nathaniel Peabody, May 18, 1788, *Historical Magazine*, 3rd ser., 2 (November, 1873), 280-81.

core. Gilman blamed many of the difficulties that his party faced on Henry and Mason, and declared that

Had it been pleasing to the preserver of Man, in the Super abundance of his tender mercies to, to [sic] have removed P———y with M———n to the regions of darkness, I am induced to think the new System of Government would have been adopted—but the delay in our back-sliding State has rendered it much more doubtful in my mind that it has been at any period since the Completion of the plan.

Like Lear, Gilman reported that the Antifederalists were well organized and "indefatigable in their exertions."[7]

In spite of their strenuous efforts the Antifederalists found themselves on the defensive at the New Hampshire convention. A committee was appointed to frame amendments, but the Antifederalists could not muster sufficient support to make ratification conditional until the amendments were in force.[8] Atherton's opposition was in part based on his aversion to the slave trade. He reputedly told the convention that by voting for the Constitution "we become *consenters to,* and *partakers in*, the sin and guilt of this abominable traffic, at least for a certain period, without any positive stipulation that it should even then [1808] be brought to an end."[9]

The committee on amendments borrowed the nine articles drafted by Theophilus Parsons for Massachusetts, but it did go a few steps further than the Essex County conservative in their recommendations. The committee asked for a three-fourths majority in Congress for the support of a standing army, a ban on the public quartering of soldiers, an assurance that Congress would make "no Laws touching Religion, or to infringe the rights of Conscience," and for the right of citizens to bear arms.[10] These amendments, adopted to allay the sus-

[7] Nicholas Gilman to John Sullivan, March 23, 1788, Burnett, ed., *Letters of Members of the Continental Congress*, VIII, 709.

[8] James W. Patterson, "Ratification of the Constitution of the United States by New Hampshire," New Hampshire Historical Society, *Proceedings*, 2 (1888-95), 34.

[9] Elliot, ed., *Debates*, II, 203.

[10] *Documentary History of the Constitution*, II, 142-43.

picions expressed in town meetings, materially assisted the cause of the Constitution. It was ratified by the New Hampshire convention by a ten-vote majority on June 21.

The New Hampshire ratification gave the Constitution the assent of nine states, thus assuring it a trial. Without the concurrence of Virginia and New York, however, no permanent union or government could be maintained. The current belief was that Virginia would continue as the most populous and wealthy state in the Republic. A union without Virginia was inconceivable, and factions formed over the ratification issue which posed a grave threat to political unity in the state. Mason, Lee, and Henry were all men of parts, respected in their home state for their abilities, past services, and present opinions. All three were outspoken in their criticism of both the spirit and the letter of the Constitution. Madison was capable of defending the document, but he was still a young man without the experience and influence of his seasoned opponents. Jefferson was abroad. Washington, whose presence might have awed the opposition, chose to remain at Mount Vernon rather than to serve in the state convention. When the delegates gathered at Richmond early in June of 1788 there must have been considerable apprehension among men on both sides of the assembly hall—Federalist and Antifederalist alike.

Beginning with the party contest in Pennsylvania the demand for amendments had grown to such proportions that it could no longer be ignored. Since the Massachusetts convention had adopted the Federalist compromise, every subsequent ratification found the majority willing to concede on the issue of amendments. In Virginia there had been rumors as early as February that Washington himself was in favor of amendments. The General was urged to deny publicly the truth of the report, particularly since the argument for amendments had "the most weight with the common class."[11] Washington did not follow his correspondent's advice, but the demand for

[11] David Stuart to George Washington, February 17, 1788, *ibid.*, IV, 508.

a declaration of rights disturbed him. He wrote Lafayette "there was not a member of the convention, I believe, who had the least objection to what is contended for by the Advocates for a *Bill of Rights* and *Tryal by Jury*." The convention had by-passed the bill of rights simply because it was unnecessary. The question of trial by jury was left "as a matter of future adjustment."[12] Madison was giving in by degrees. "Recommendatory alterations are the only ground that occurs to me," he conceded in April.[13]

With the stakes so high it was natural that the tempo of the pamphlet warfare would increase. David Stuart complained that Mason's "Objections" were placed in every house in his county. Whether Lee and Mason gained converts or not their works continued to circulate among the reading public. "R. H. Lees Publication has been read with Attention, and he has been detected in mistaking Facts," a Federalist letter-writer declared. "The Necessity of *Mason's*, and his Bill of Rights, has been done away by *Aristides*."[14] "Aristides" was Alexander Contee Hanson, the Maryland Federalist whose articles in the *Maryland Journal* had been issued as a pamphlet. His answers to the opposition were considered definitive only by Federalist partisans, for his judgment was that political bugbears rather than genuine wrongs had been attributed to the Constitution. The bill of rights argument, Hanson wrote, was the stronghold of Antifederalism. He assailed the demand for a bill of rights in terms borrowed from James Wilson, then added,

The restraints laid on the state legislatures will tend to secure domestic tranquility, more than all the bills, or declarations, of rights, which human policy could devise. It is very justly asserted, that the plan contains an avowal of many rights. It provides that no man, shall suffer by expost[*sic*]facto laws or bills of attainder. It declares that

[12] George Washington to Marquis de Lafayette, April 28, 1788, Fitzpatrick, ed., *Writings of Washington*, XXIX, 478-79.

[13] James Madison to Edmund Randolph, April 10, 1788, *Documentary History of the Constitution*, IV, 573.

[14] *Pennsylvania Gazette*, April 16, 1788.

gold and silver only shall be a tender for specie debts; and that no law shall impair the obligation of a contract.[15]

Hanson hinted that the prohibition on paper money probably drew more foes of the Constitution together than any move for a bill of rights. He also imputed the motives for demanding a new convention to men interested only in gains for their state or themselves.[16]

Other Virginians besides Lee and Mason took to the public prints with Antifederalist messages. Writing as "A Plain Dealer," Spencer Roane attacked the inconsistencies in Governor Randolph's ambiguous letter, stating his reasons for not approving the Constitution at the Federal Convention. He declared that Randolph's whole argument sounded too much like a defense of the Constitution. Roane sniped at Randolph, and also struck a blow for a bill of rights. "A Constitution ought to be like Cæsar's wife, not only good, but unsuspected," Roane declared, "since it is the highest compact which men are capable of forming, and involves the dearest rights of life, liberty and property."[17] It was a where-there-is-smoke-there-is-fire approach that could influence thinking in a parable-quoting society.

The work of the Virginia Antifederalists was proceeding but as yet their plans were not disclosed to the public. Lee suggested to Mason a private meeting of the leading "friends to amendments . . . to see how far it may be safe to press either for modes of amendment or the extent of amendments, and to govern our actions accordingly."[18] Lee had heard "candid friends to this system admit that amendments may be made to improve the plan," which convinced him that the Virginia convention could recommend amendments and allow the new Congress two years to secure the changes. The acceptance of

[15] Ford, ed., *Pamphlets on the Constitution*, 241-43.
[16] *Ibid.*, 246.
[17] Ford, ed., *Essays on the Constitution*, 392.
[18] Richard Henry Lee to George Mason, May 7, 1788, Ballagh, ed., *Letters of Lee*, II, 466-67.

amendments represented a compromise whereby the sincerity
of the Federalists could be tested while the good features of
the Constitution would be retained. Of course, Lee declared,
there must be "a just security given to civil liberty." This
plan would bring harmony to the states, quiet the opposition,
and avoid the necessity of "risking the convulsion of conventions." Lee was already retreating from his earlier strong
Antifederalist stand. In the proposed amendments he suggested that "*localities* ought to be avoided as much as possible."
He thought the Massachusetts recommendations generally
good, but pointed out that they omitted guarantees of a free
press. This and several other additions, including a trial by
jury and a check on the possible coalition between the president
and senate, Lee thought necessary in framing a set of amendments which would insure success to their plan.[19] Lee also
wrote Edmund Pendleton a long letter suggesting the same
method of obtaining amendments but emphasizing the civil
liberties which needed the sanction of amendments.[20]

Patrick Henry did not share Lee's conciliatory attitude.
He served warning that he would carry his opposition to the
Constitution beyond what the Federalists considered the limits
of decency. Jealous of the rights of the southern states, Henry
was doubly suspicious of a consolidated government. He had
turned down a proffered place on the Virginia delegation to the
Federal Convention, frankly declaring that he declined the
appointment because he "smelt a rat." Henry was second only
to Washington in prestige with the people of Virginia, and
his well-known opposition to the Constitution was sufficient
reason for pessimism in the Federalist ranks. Madison believed Henry capable of an attempt to disrupt the Union if the
Constitution were ratified. This estimate of Henry's opposition seemed justified after he arose in the Convention and
shouted, "I declare, that if *twelve states and an half* had

[19] *Ibid.*, 468-69.
[20] Richard Henry Lee to Edmund Pendleton, May 22, 1788, *ibid.*, 469-74.

adopted it, I would with manly firmness, and in spite of an erring world, reject it."[21] Without amendments, Henry said, the Constitution was unpalatable. Neither Lee, who was unable to attend the convention but still exerted considerable influence, nor Mason was believed to be so intransigent in their opposition.

Other forces which the Federalists found arrayed against them were the ministers and congregations of some of the dissenting religions. The unanimous disapproval of ratification by the Virginia General Baptist Committee in March, 1788, reflected the attitude of thousands of communicants spread over the entire state. A friend warned Madison that the Antifederalists numbered as allies,

in a General way the Baptus's, the Prechers of that society are much alarm'd fearing Religious liberty is not suffisiently secur'd thay pretend to other objections but that I think is the principle objection, could that be Removed by sum one Caperble of the Task, I think thay would become friends to it, that body of people has become very formible in pint of Elections.[22]

The writer, Joseph Spencer, also enclosed the objections of Reverend John Leland, a powerful Baptist leader, which were headed by a complaint over the lack of a bill of rights. Leland mentioned liberty of the press but most grievous of all, he thought, was the insufficient security of religious freedom. No religious oath was required of officeholders, and a national church might be established at any time. Leland concluded that

if Oppression does not ensue, it will be owing to the Mildness of administration & not to any Constitutional defence, & if the Manners of People are so far Corrupted, that they cannot live by republican principles, it is very Dangerous leaving Religious Liberty at their Marcy.[23]

[21] William Wirt, *Sketches of the Life and Character of Patrick Henry* (Philadelphia, 1818), 272.

[22] Joseph Spencer to James Madison, February 28, 1788, *Documentary History of the Constitution*, IV, 525.

[23] *Ibid.*, IV, 526-28.

The Virginia dissenters had won a long struggle with the recently enacted bill establishing religious freedom and were in no mood to accept what they considered half measures from the proposed Constitution.

Edmund Randolph stood at the crossroads as convention time neared. He had refused to sign the Constitution at Philadelphia, but he was writing and talking like a good Federalist. The Antifederalists thought that Randolph bore watching but that he was probably still faithful to their cause. Actually, the Federalists had lured Randolph into their camp months before. As it became obvious that the Antifederalists would base their opposition on the need for amendments, Randolph voiced grave suspicions of their motives. He maintained that they were yelling for previous amendments as a cover for their real motive. A higher game was being played by the "Amendmentites," whom Randolph feared "more and more, daily; not knowing how far the scheme of those, who externally patronize them, may internally extend."[24] By June 4 the convention was under way and Randolph took his stand. He candidly supported the Federalists, an action which surprised many delegates and confirmed the suspicions of others.

Randolph's defection meant that Henry and Mason now shared leadership of the opposition, committed to carry the fight for amendments. Henry spoke first on behalf of alterations, and his remarks were but a prelude to the constant barrage which was maintained for the next three weeks. Was a tame relinquishment of all the liberty guaranteed by a bill of rights worthy of free men? On the contrary, Henry said, submission to a consolidated government without these guarantees was a betrayal of the spirit of the Revolution.[25] "Perhaps an invincible attachment to the dearest rights of man may, in these refined, enlightened days, be deemed old-fashioned," Henry declared, but if that were the case, he preferred being

[24] Edmund Randolph to James Madison, April 17, 1788, Conway, *Life of Randolph*, 102.
[25] Elliot, ed., *Debates*, III, 44-45.

"an old-fashioned fellow" to surrendering his liberty! The people in the adopting states had been "egregiously misled," even tricked into ratifying the Constitution, Henry added, but unless it was previously amended, Virginia could not accept the new plan.[26]

Randolph answered Henry with the startling charge that the Virginia Declaration of Rights frequently cited by Henry to defend his attack on the Constitution was not really valid. The Declaration of Rights "is not a part of our [state] Constitution," Randolph said, "it has never secured us against any danger; it has been repeatedly disregarded and violated."[27] This was indeed a remarkable statement from a public man in the state which had adopted the first bill of rights in the new nation. Moreover, Randolph placed the blame for one of the violations on Henry's shoulders, claiming that the wartime governor had himself called for the attainder of Josiah Philips in 1778.

Henry's memory must have been faulty, for he did not challenge the accuracy of the charge, but rather defended the attainder of 1778 as an act justified "by the laws of nature and of nations."[28] The Philips case involved a renegade tory who adopted guerrilla tactics during the early years of the war and operated from a base in the Dismal Swamp. Actually, Thomas Jefferson had drafted the attainder when Henry was governor, but when Philips was finally apprehended the attainder was not used and he was indicted "at Common law as a felon and robber."[29] (When he heard of Randoph's convention speech many years later, Jefferson charitably allowed that Randolph's zeal led him to lose sight "of the rigorous accuracies of fact.")[30] Of course, nothing in the Virginia Declaration of Rights prohibited an act of attainder if the legislature

[26] *Ibid.*, 63.
[27] *Ibid.*, 70.
[28] *Ibid.*, 140.
[29] Thomas Jefferson to William Wirt, August 14, 1814, Boyd, ed., *Jefferson Papers*, II, 191.
[30] Thomas Jefferson to Girardin, March 12, 1815, *ibid.*

chose to use that device. Henry shrugged off Randolph's garbled charge and continually returned to the subject of a bill of rights as an indispensable condition of ratification.

Shortly after the convention began Mason had dispatched a letter to General Lamb in New York. Mason had displayed Lamb's earlier letter to several other opponents of the Constitution who were also sitting in the convention. They had agreed on their opposition to the Constitution unless "previous amendments" were adopted. The Virginians were inclined to use the Massachusetts recommendations as a basis for their own amendments.[31] Meanwhile, Eleazer Oswald was seen on the streets of Richmond, and Madison suspected the Philadelphia publisher had brought news and advice from Antifederalists elsewhere. Madison's suspicions were correct. Henry wrote Lamb acknowledging a gift of Federal Republican literature from Oswald and added that Mason had agreed to act as chairman of the local Federal Republican Society. "He is [in] every way fit; and we have concluded to send you by Col. Oswald a copy of the Bill of Rights, and of the particular amendments we intend to propose in our convention," Henry wrote.[32] William Grayson and Richard Henry Lee, who was not a delegate to the convention, were also apprised of the Antifederalist plans.

The Federalists countered the measures of the opposition by seeking an early ratification. Madison accused Henry and his friends of an attempt "to spin out the Session in order to receive overtures" from the New York convention, or simply to tire the delegates into an adjournment without ever permitting a vote on the ratification issue.[33] If true, Henry could hardly be blamed for attempting to advance his own cause by political tactics. If, however, the further charge that Henry

[31] George Mason to John Lamb, June 9, 1788, Rowland, *Life of Mason,* II, 234-35.
[32] Patrick Henry to John Lamb, June 9, 1788, Leake, *Life of Lamb,* 307.
[33] James Madison to Alexander Hamilton, June 16, 1788, *Documentary History of the Constitution,* IV, 705.

cared but little for a bill of rights and actually worked for curbs on the power of the national government is true, he may deserve to be remembered as a hypocrite.[34] The evidence in the convention records indicates, however, Henry's constant attention to the bill of rights issue from the opening day until the final session. Mason naturally favored a bill of rights, but he did not hammer the point as Henry did. Henry spoke often and long, one speech lasting seven hours. On the convention floor he capitalized on the current knowledge of Jefferson's first thoughts on the Constitution, that four states ought to withhold ratification to assure the enactment of a bill of rights.[35] The amendments Jefferson favored "go to that despised thing, called a *bill of rights*, and all the rights which are dear to human nature," Henry said, and if Virginia adopted the Constitution there would be no state of sufficient importance left to secure amendments by rejecting the plan.

When Henry talked of a necessity for securing freedom of religion, his words piqued Madison. The point was a delicate one with Madison, who had worked for freedom of conscience in the Virginia Declaration of Rights in 1776 and had not ceased his labor until the bill establishing religious freedom had become law. He followed Henry to ask, "Is a bill of rights a security for religion?" Madison well knew that it had taken a bitter legislative fight extending over a decade to implement the religious article in the Virginia declaration. "If there were a majority of one sect, a bill of rights would be a poor protection for liberty," he said. The best assurance for religious freedom, Madison concluded, was the "multiplicity of sects which pervades America . . . for where there is such a variety of sects, there cannot be a majority of any one sect to oppress and persecute the rest."[36]

[34] See Irving Brant, *James Madison, Father of the Constitution* (Indianapolis, 1950), 205.

[35] Elliot, ed., *Debates*, III, 314-15. Jefferson's revised thoughts, embracing the "Massachusetts plan," were not known in America until later in the summer of 1788.

[36] *Ibid.*, 330.

In spite of the sound logic advanced by the Federalists, the warmest friends of the Constitution now perceived that from a tactical standpoint the failure to adopt a bill of rights at the Federal Convention had weakened their whole cause. As William Duer had pointed out, the Antifederalists found it difficult to agree on which amendments were necessary.[37] Only a bill of rights seemed to meet their universal approbation. Even Washington, as remote from the public pulse as he was at his Mount Vernon retreat, conceded that amendments would have to be made.[38] Thus the leading Federalists at Richmond decided, as had their colleagues in Boston a few months earlier, to accept amendments as a concession to the opposition. When the convention moved into its final week, Madison wrote Hamilton:

The plan meditated by the friends of the Constitution is to preface the ratification with some plain & general truths that can not affect the validity of the Act: & to subjoin a recommendation which may hold up amendments as objects to be pursued in the constitutional mode. These expedients are rendered prudent by the nice balance of numbers, and the scruples entertained by some who are in general well affected. Whether they will secure us a majority, I dare not positively to declare.[39]

Madison also informed Rufus King that the Federalists would support a bill of rights and other minor amendments rather than risk the adjournment which he believed the opposition was seeking. "It has been judged prudent . . . to maintain so exemplary a fairness on our part, (and even in some points to give way to unreasonable pretensions) as will withhold every pretext for so rash a step," he wrote.[40] The Federalists had to be firm in their opposition to alterations regarding direct taxes,

[37] William Duer to James Madison, June 23, 1788, *Documentary History of the Constitution*, IV, 748.

[38] George Washington to General John Armstrong, April 25, 1788, Fitzpatrick, ed., *Writings of Washington*, XXIX, 465.

[39] James Madison to Alexander Hamilton, June 22, 1788, *Documentary History of the Constitution*, IV, 746.

[40] James Madison to Rufus King, June 22, 1788, King, *Life and Correspondence of Rufus King*, I, 337.

navigation acts, and the methods of controlling elections; but a decision to give in on the demand for a bill of rights caused no harm and promised a great deal of good will, harmony, and votes. The combined advantages appealed irresistibly.

Henry's defiant attitude in the convention may have spurred the Federalists into their plan of positive action. During a heated discussion over a guarantee for jury trials in the vicinity of the alleged offense, Henry had used language calculated to shock everyone within hearing distance. Arbitrary men might "call any thing rebellion, and deprive you of a fair trial by an impartial jury of your neighbors," he said. "Old as I am, it is probable I may yet have the appellation of *rebel*," he continued, and he hoped to see the threat of "congressional oppression crushed in embryo."[41]

Judge Pendleton arose to explain that trial by jury in criminal cases was expressly preserved in the Constitution, but Henry's words had probably disquieted the minds of some delegates. To calm their apprehension, young John Marshall came forward to give his opinion on this topic. He asked the delegates to consider the Virginia Declaration of Rights. That document called for trial by jury, but Marshall cited several instances where this charge was not followed. These examples proved, Marshall said, that the "bill of rights is merely recommendatory." If this were not the case, he continued, many convenient laws would be clearly unconstitutional.

What does the government before you say? Does it exclude the legislature from giving a trial by jury in civil cases? If it does not forbid its exclusion, it is on the same footing on which your state government stands now. The legislature of Virginia does not give a trial by jury where it is not necessary, but gives it wherever it is thought expedient. The federal legislature will do so too, as it is formed on the same principles.[42]

With some justice it might be said that Marshall's finest train-

[41] Elliot, ed., *Debates*, III, 545-46.
[42] *Ibid.*, 561.

ing for his later years on the nation's highest bench came during this Richmond convention.

Marshall's argument notwithstanding, Henry's attack was damaging the Federalist cause. The inflexible stand of an earlier day was no longer politically expedient. A breach in the Federalist front was announced by George Wythe on June 24, when he called for amendments which would mend the alleged defects in the Constitution after ratification. He specifically mentioned freedom of the press and religion, and a guarantee of trial by jury. Wythe appealed to Henry to accept the amendments in a spirit of compromise and to join him in working for adoption.

The Federalists' willingness to grant concessions, however, merely put Henry on his guard. He still was convinced, he said, that nine-tenths of the people were opposed to ratification. "Subsequent amendments will not do for men of this cast," Henry said, but "if you agree to previous amendments, you shall have union, firm and solid."[43] As his trump card, Henry then placed before the convention a resolution calling on the delegates to refer a declaration of rights and other amendment proposals "to the other states in the confederacy, for their consideration, previous to ratification." Madison then expressed his willingness to meet the Antifederalists on a middle ground. Those amendments which Henry favored and which were reasonable Madison would recommend for subsequent adoption "not because they are necessary, but because they can produce no possible danger, and may gratify some gentlemen's wishes." But previous amendments, he said, would never get his consent.[44]

With the amendment question still hanging in the balance, Henry assured the convention that he had no plan to divide the Union or launch a secession movement, as some had feared, even if he should find himself in the minority. "My head, my hand, and my heart, shall be at liberty to retrieve the loss

[43] *Ibid.*, 592.   [44] *Ibid.*, 622.

of liberty, and remove the defects of the system in a constitutional way," he asserted. On the next day, the important question of previous amendments, including a bill of rights, came to a vote. The measure failed by a vote of 88 to 80. This defeat for the Antifederalists was quickly followed by balloting on ratification, which was approved 89 to 79.

Thus was the Constitution assured a trial by the Federalist triumph of June 25, 1788. To soothe the Antifederalists a committee was chosen to report on proposed amendments, and assignments were given to both Henry and Mason. This committee adopted a bill of rights which followed closely the Virginia Declaration of Rights, along with twenty other proposals that covered many of the changes on which Henry, Mason, and their colleague, William Grayson, had insisted.[45] The proposed forty amendments were prefaced with a statement enjoining the Virginia delegation in the new Congress to exert its energy and influence to obtain the ratification of these proposals. Before the convention adjourned, copies of the Virginia amendments were ordered for distribution to the governors and legislature of every state.

Ratification by Virginia gave new heart to the Federalists in New York. Clinton and his friends had relied on stout resistance from the Virginia Antifederalists and on the aid of Governor Randolph. They were both disappointed and disgusted with what they regarded as duplicity on Randolph's part. Richard Henry Lee was discouraged by the results of the convention, but still found some consolation in the amendments. Bad as they were, Lee wrote General Lamb, these amendments might help obtain the alterations necessary to prevent the abuses bound to occur after the Constitution had been approved.[46] Word of the Virginia ratification came when Colonel W. S. Livingston rode into Poughkeepsie with the unexpected news, for many Federalists had been prepared

[45] Ibid., 657-61.
[46] Richard Henry Lee to General John Lamb, June, 27, 1788, Ballagh, ed., Letters of Lee, II, 475.

for a different outcome. With a kind of sportsmanship rarely found in later political encounters, the Antifederalists went off to the taverns with their jubilant opponents. John Jay reported that the Virginia action was celebrated at the boarding tables of both factions, "and the two parties mingled at each table, and the toasts (of which each had copies) were communicated by the sound of drum and accompanied by the discharge of cannon."[47] All this despite that fact that a call either for a second convention or for previous amendments from Virginia would have furnished the Clinton group with an excuse to halt the ratifying process.

The news from Virginia must have upset the leading New York Antifederalists who had been preparing a plan of action designed to snarl ratification for over six months. Since the preceding fall the Antifederalist press had contributed its share of pamphlets to the cause. The *New York Journal* faithfully reprinted the latest arguments advanced by the Clinton faction. In November, 1787, one harbinger of the future indicated that the contest might end in compromise. Since both parties were well-intentioned, the writer suggested that "if a bill of rights could be agreed upon, it would probably solve the problem."[48] A satirical letter from "Roderick Razor" in the *New York Daily Advertiser* promised that the writer could speak "about standing armies and juries without trial and the extinguishing the liberty of speaking and printing, and excise, and all them things, as well as my betters; whose betters I expect one of these days to be."[49] The *Journal* countered with a letter from "One of the Nobility" who claimed that the political creed of every Federalist included:

(1) Infallibility of the Convention.
(2) Ignorance of the people.

[47] John Jay to Mrs. Jay, July 5, 1788, Johnston, ed., *Jay Correspondence*, III, 347-48.
[48] *New York Journal*, November 21, 1787, quoted in Clarence E. Miner, *The Ratification of the Federal Constitution by the State of New York* (New York, 1921), 69.
[49] *New York Daily Advertiser*, December 11, 1787, quoted in *ibid.*, 72.

(3) Non-essentiality of securing the rights of man.
(4) Superiority of aristocratic government.
(5) Cowardice of Americans, hence a standing army.
(6) Lack of necessity for freedom of press and trial by jury.[50]

Such was the psychology of party politics in New York on the eve of ratification.

Meanwhile, Lee's "Letters of a Federal Farmer" had been sent to every important population center in the state by the Federal Republican committee. An advertisement for the pamphlet which appeared in the *New York Journal* prior to the Poughkeepsie convention stated there were "very few dispassionate men, who do not wish to see amendments made to this system." The substance of the letters, the advertisement continued, was to demonstrate the need for amendments and to advance arguments in support of them. However, a shift in tactics had occurred. "It is a matter of small importance, whether these amendments precede or succeed the adoption of the constitution, so that they be made."[51] Melancton Smith, one of Clinton's lieutenants, also produced a pamphlet calling for amendments. Smith argued for previous amendments but did not specifically call for a bill of rights, although he ridiculed the Federalist contention that freedom of the press and trial by jury were secured because of the silence of the Constitution on those points.[52] "But it is contended, adopt it first, and then amend it," Smith wrote. "I ask, why not amend, and then adopt it?"[53]

Still unhappy with the Constitution he had refused to help frame, Robert Yates attempted to explain away the lack of a bill of rights in the New York constitution after Federalists had cited the document as proof of their own arguments. If the state legislature could not touch those precious liberties, why fear the silence of a federal constitution? This reasoning

[50] *New York Journal*, December 12, 1787, quoted in *ibid.*, 73.
[51] *New York Journal*, June 13, 1788.
[52] Ford, ed., *Pamphlets on the Constitution*, 113-14.
[53] *Ibid.*, 93.

would not apply to the new Constitution, Yates contended, because "the state governments are considered in it as mere dependencies, existing solely by its toleration, and possessing powers of which they may be deprived whenever the general government is disposed so to do."[54] This was a rebuttal to John Jay's remark that fears for the rights of mankind were groundless because "silence and blank paper neither grant nor take away anything."[55] Without a written statement, there would be no limit to the oppression of the general government, Yates concluded.

When the convention opened on June 17 a postponement of final ratification seemed essential to many Antifederalists. They maintained close contact with their Richmond allies and probably believed that Virginia would not cut the ground out from under their plan of attack.[56] The state officeholders, led by Governor Clinton, had a vested interest in the status quo under the Confederation which permitted the collection of a lucrative impost that went straight to the New York treasury.[57] Although the anti-Clinton forces were in the minority, their numbers included men who were only lukewarm to the Constitution but who were burning with a desire to wreck Clinton. John Jay, Alexander Hamilton, and Robert Livingston had been elected as delegates from New York City, which was strongly Federalist. The skill of their leadership was to determine the fate of ratification by New York.

For two weeks taxation was the main topic of discussion in the convention. While economic interests claimed the attention of the chief protagonists, Antifederalist Thomas Tredwell threw in his objection—the failure to secure liberty of the press, liberty of conscience, and the other rights demanded by the people. "It is ardently to be wished, sir, that these and other invaluable rights of freemen had been as cautiously

[54] Ford, ed., *Essays on the Constitution*, 299-300.
[55] Ford, ed., *Pamphlets on the Constitution*, 76.
[56] Miner, *Ratification in New York*, 97.
[57] *Ibid.*, 13-14.

secured as some of the paltry local interests of some of the individual states," Tredwell said. As with "the lawyers and Pharisees of old," too much attention had been directed to forms, he declared, and not enough to the more important subjects of justice. The spirit of 1776 was violated by proposing a constitution which did not safeguard the rights of the people. There was no bill of rights, no restriction of federal powers. And, Tredwell said, "a government is like a mad horse, which, notwithstanding all the curb you can put upon him, will sometimes run away with his rider." Just as a man would deserve a broken neck if he rode an unbridled horse, so should the people deserve oppression if they did not insist on limitations upon this proposed government. He concluded that to adopt the Constitution in its present form was to destroy liberty.[58]

While the debate appeared to be shifting to a discussion of civil liberty, Livingston brought news of the Virginia ratification from Richmond that gladdened the hearts of Hamilton and his friends. Jay was exhilarated. "That Event has disappointed the Expectations of Opposition here, which nevertheless continues pertinacious," Jay wrote. "The Unanimity of the southern District," he added, "operates powerfully on the Minds of the opposite Party."[59] There had been some discussion of amendments dealing with standing armies and the writ of habeas corpus, but the startling word from Virginia forced the Antifederalists into a position that would not allow half measures. Clinton called for conditional amendments on a large scale. Smith actually introduced the idea of ratification "on condition," which would give New York the right to withdraw from the compact if the desired amendments were not ratified within a specified time. Instead of headlong retreat, it was a sly bit of hedging that worried Hamilton.

At the moment, however, it appeared to some Federalists

[58] Elliot, ed., *Debates*, II, 398-406.
[59] John Jay to George Washington, July 4, 1788, *Documentary History of the Constitution*, IV, 766-67.

that the Clinton faction was running for cover. On July 8, Jay wrote Washington that a bill of rights had been offered by the Antifederalists to be incorporated in the ratification. "The Ground of *Rejection* therefore seems to be entirely deserted." Some of the Clinton party wanted previous amendments, Jay added. However, he suspected that the majority would be satisfied with conditional amendments, "in other words they are for ratifying the Constitution on Condition that certain amendments take place within a given Time—These circumstance afford Room for Hope."[60] Hamilton was not so sure. After he had taken time to digest the reports from Virginia, and had perceived what Clinton hoped to achieve at Poughkeepsie, Hamilton began to doubt whether a ratification burdened with amendments was worthwhile. If either previous amendments or a conditional ratification were approved, he still expected certain declarations, such as a bill of rights, to be carried along with the general scheme. The Federalists would go along with these as far as they could "without invalidating the act, and will concur in rational recommendations."[61] Beyond that point, the issue of events would rest with the Clintonians.

John Lansing brought the Antifederalist plan for a bill of rights to the convention floor where it was introduced as a necessary preface to the Constitution. When Hamilton and his coterie insisted that all the amendments should be adopted either as recommendations or explanations for the new Congress, the Antifederalists balked. Judge John Hobart, a Federalist, then moved for an adjournment which would give both sides an opportunity to reconsider the impasse, but Lansing and the Antifederalists pressed for a vote now. The Federalists were outvoted, 40 to 22—a seemingly clear indication that they had lost the advantage gained by the Virginia ratification.

[60] John Jay to George Washington, July 8, 1788, *ibid.*, 767.
[61] Alexander Hamilton to James Madison, July 8, 1788, *ibid.*, 768.

In desperation, Hamilton decided to risk a debate on the amendments, particularly on the bill of rights.[62] Then Madison's reply to his letter on conditional amendments arrived. Eagerly, Hamilton took the floor to read Madison's opinion on the issue that threatened to derail their convention. The same idea had been advanced at Richmond, Madison wrote, where it was considered worse than rejection. If New York adopted the Constitution with conditional amendments, the practical effect would be that she had not ratified the Constitution at all. "Compacts must be reciprocal. . . . An adoption for a limited time would be as defective as an adoption of some of the articles only," Madison declared. "In short any *condition* whatever must viciate the ratification."[63]

The Antifederalist ranks were split on July 23 when Samuel Jones proposed that the idea of conditional amendments be dropped. Jones asked that the phrase "on condition" which Smith had introduced be altered, and that instead New York should ratify "in full confidence" that other states would accept the New York amendments.[64] Smith then voted against his own resolution, while the perturbed Clinton sided with a minority that lost, 31 votes to 29. Still hoping to place a stumbling-block in the path of ratification, the Clinton men then asked "that there should be reserved to the state of New York a right to withdraw herself *from the Union* after a certain number of years, unless the amendments proposed should previously be submitted to a general convention." This motion was rejected, and it was now clear that the Antifederalists were in confusion.

The Federalists realized that some concession was necessary, however, and they agreed to the preparation of a circular letter which would be sent out to the states suggesting another

---

[62] Nathan Schachner, *Alexander Hamilton* (New York, 1946), 224.

[63] James Madison to Alexander Hamilton, July, 1788, *Documentary History of the Constitution*, IV, 803.

[64] Elliot, ed., *Debates*, II, 412. See also E. Wilder Spaulding, *His Excellency George Clinton* (New York, 1938), 181.

federal convention. Next day, the Constitution itself, with a recommended bill of rights attached, was ratified to cement the Union solidly in place. Only Rhode Island and North Carolina had failed to ratify. Even staunch Antifederalists conceded the probable concurrence of the two "holdouts."

The circular letter, which John Jay innocently helped frame, bore the seeds of dissension. It called attention to the amendments proposed by the other states, but did not go into the specific nature of the amendments which might be sought at a second convention. Washington declared that it was calculated to "set every thing afloat again."[65] Madison reported that the letter was seized by opponents everywhere "as the signal for united exertions in pursuit of *early* amendments."[66] Mason considered the circular letter the last hope of the Antifederalists. The master of Gunston Hall believed that the New York amendments were modelled after those he had helped draft in the Virginia convention, and said that if a convention were held the following spring there was still hope for "proper & safe Amendments."[67]

Many historians have long regarded Hamilton's final summation of the Federalist reply to the bill of rights clamor in *Federalist* LXXXIV as the most effective answer to the delicate question. Actually, Hamilton struck at the Antifederalist charges in both *Federalist* LXXXIII and LXXXIV, but these went into public print while the last important state was winding up the business of ratification. The Poughkeepsie convention had adjourned when the final installment of *Federalist* LXXXIV came from the New York press on August 12. Thus his reasoning came too late to be of any practical political value. Furthermore, his position was based on essentially the

[65] George Washington to Benjamin Lincoln, August 28, 1788, Fitzpatrick, ed., *Writings of Washington*, XXX, 63.
[66] James Madison to George Washington, August 24, 1788, *Documentary History of the Constitution*, V, 29.
[67] George Mason to John Mason, September 2, 1788, Mason Papers, Library of Congress.

same contentions James Wilson had made publicly almost a year earlier:

> I go further, and affirm that bills of rights, in the sense and to the extent in which they are contended for, are not only unnecessary in the proposed Constitution, but would even be dangerous. They would contain various exceptions to powers not granted; and, on this very account, would afford a colorable pretext to claim more than were granted. For why declare that things shall not be done which there is no power to do? Why, for instance, should it be said that the liberty of the press shall not be restrained, when no power is given by which restrictions may be imposed?[68]

By the time this argument reached the reading public, it was simply like a musket round fired after the battle had been won.

As the New York convention moved toward adjournment, North Carolina delegates were assembling at Hillsboro to consider ratification. Antifederalists in New York and Virginia had heard confident reports from their Carolina friends, who assured them that there would be no ratification by the delegates who had a variety of reasons to fear a strong central government. However, the outcome of the North Carolina contest was hardly of first importance, for eleven states were already committed to support the Constitution. The results must have startled some Federalists, however, for within a fortnight after their convention first met, the North Carolina delegates were headed homeward after virtually rejecting the Constitution by an impressive one hundred-vote majority.

Local issues again played a decisive role in the vote on ratification at this first North Carolina convention. Wealthy and able Willie Jones, the Eton-educated planter and devoted follower of Jefferson, exerted all of his power and influence against ratification. In many ways comparable to Patrick Henry, Jones was also a master politician, as his work during the Revolution had demonstrated. He was endowed with peculiar powers of persuasion over the agrarian classes which constituted the main fabric of the North Carolina electorate. Al-

[68] *The Federalist* . . . (Philadelphia, 1880), 631.

lied with Jones were Timothy Bloodworth, Thomas Person, and James Coor—men who lacked his background but joined him on equal terms in the political arena. These men were particularly anxious about the status of the state-issued paper money, and as is usually the case in political alliances, the self-interest of the leaders was involved. Perhaps in North Carolina more than in any other state except Rhode Island, the question of ratifying the Constitution was entwined with the local issue of "cheap money *versus* sound money."

Attachment to paper money alone, however, did not account for the rude way the Constitution was handled by the North Carolina convention. Early in December, 1787, Coor and Person had tried to persuade the state senate to permit the people to submit a list of objections and proposed alterations to the Constitution "in case they do not agree that the said proposed constitution shall become binding on the people of this State."[69] Had their suggestion been accepted it might have mitigated the intense feeling against the Constitution which eventually worked into the halls of the convention. In mid-December an Antifederalist declared in *Martin's North Carolina Gazette* that the people would never submit to any form of government not giving definite assurances "that sacred rights should not be violated."[70] Nor were the friends of the Constitution silent. James Iredell, the noted Federalist lawyer, answered Mason's "Objections" with a pamphlet based on the much quoted reasoning of James Wilson. A bill of rights was unnecessary because it would be both nugatory and ridiculous in a constitution of expressed powers. "As well might a Judge when he condemns a man to be hanged, give strong injunctions to the Sheriff that he should not be beheaded," Iredell explained.[71]

[69] Saunders and Clark, eds., *N. C. State Records*, XX, 372.

[70] *Martin's North Carolina Gazette*, December 19, 1787, quoted in Louise Irby Trenholme, *The Ratification of the Federal Constitution in North Carolina* (New York, 1932), 130.

[71] Griffith J. McRee, *Life and Correspondence of James Iredell* (New York, 1858), II, 187.

The suspicious attitude of certain frontier groups, already noted in Pennsylvania and Virginia, pervaded the western areas in North Carolina. The Baptists and Presbyterians particularly wanted assurances that freedom of religion would be guaranteed—for Protestants, anyway. In April, a report from New Bern indicated that a majority of the delegates to the convention were elected after making solemn promises that they would work for "the preservation of the civil and religious rights and liberties of their fellow citizens . . . [which] would be the ruling principle of their conduct."[72] As the opening date for the convention neared, the Antifederalist press insisted that a second federal convention should be called to mend the deficiencies of the proposed Constitution and "more effectually secure the liberties of the people."[73] Timothy Bloodworth assured General Lamb that the sentiments of the New York Antifederalists "perfectly coincide with our ideas" on the subject of requiring amendments to correct errors in the Constitution. "Permit us to observe that, we deem it expedient that the necessary amendments should originate with you," Bloodworth added. He asked Lamb to forward the proposed amendments, which were expected to meet with the approbation of the North Carolina Antifederalists who were "actuated by similar motives, the Love of Liberty and an attachment to Republican principles exclusive of sinister views."[74]

Apparently assured by a "head count" that the Antifederalists had sufficient voting strength to reject the Constitution, Willie Jones strode into the convention and almost immediately asked for a vote on ratification. Most of the members already knew how they intended to vote, he said, and much public money would be saved by an immediate vote. This

[72] Item dated April 2, in *Pennsylvania Gazette*, May 7, 1788.
[73] *Edenton Intelligencer*, June 4, 1788, quoted in Trenholme, *Ratification in North Carolina*, 144.
[74] Timothy Bloodworth to General John Lamb, July 1, 1788, William K. Boyd., ed., "Notes, Letters and Documents Concerning North Carolina and the Federal Constitution," Trinity College Historical Society, *Papers*, 14 (1922), 78-79.

maneuver was parried by the Federalists, but their counter-
blows only delayed the result made inevitable by local interests and the suspicious attitude of the delegates. As the
debate moved along, Bloodworth spoke for the majority when
he said, "I hope the representatives of North Carolina will
never swallow the Constitution till it is amended."[75] Samuel
Spencer wanted a bill of rights even "though it might not be
of any other service, it would at least satisfy the minds of the
people."[76] Spencer also said that a declaration of rights could
keep the states from being swallowed by a national government.
Iredell and Richard Dobbs Spaight attempted to answer the
objections over the failure to include a bill of rights, but as
Bloodworth said, their arguments "went in at one ear, and
out at the other."[77]

In many respects the North Carolina convention was an
abbreviated version of the Virginia convention, although the
final votes differed. The parallel interests of the two states
were demonstrated by the rehashed arguments with a Virginia
"ring." The discussion of practical problems was more typical
of the ratifying conventions than any debate over the bill of
rights issue. The arguments pro and con on a bill of rights
had become stereotyped, too, so that Delegate Henry Abbot's
complaint over the failure to permit religious tests might have
been an echo from the floor of the Massachusetts or New
Hampshire conventions. Such utterances only stress the unanimity of feeling in the young nation and reveal the common
attachments of a people which could overcome the sectional
differences apparent even at this early period. As Patrick
Henry had mentioned the earliest views expressed by Jefferson on a holdout plan to secure a bill of rights, so did Willie
Jones now cite the noted Virginian as authority for rejection
by North Carolina.[78] Jones was confident that a second convention would be called. "For my part," he said, "I would

[75] Elliot, ed., *Debates*, IV, 56.   [76] *Ibid.*, 138.
[77] *Ibid.*, 144.   [78] *Ibid.*, 226.

rather be eighteen years out of the Union than adopt it in its present form."

Finally, the Federalists conceded that they were out-numbered. Perhaps a compromise would swing enough Anti-federalists to their side, they reasoned, so they came out for ratification based on recommendations for later amendments. This artifice availed them nothing, for in a test vote the pro-posal to ratify and "at the same time recommend" was de-feated, 184 to 84. Then Jones led the convention in adopting a resolution which showed that North Carolina was in a state of friendly suspension from the Union, feeling that it was improper to either ratify or reject the Constitution.

The curious action of the convention did not silence the debate, which had often become personal and acrimonious. Bitterly disappointed by the failure to ratify, "A Citizen and Soldier" addressed a word of caution to the people of Eden-ton. Perhaps the Constitution did need amendments, the writer admitted, but it would be a mistake to think of calling on its enemies for those alterations. To do so would be as foolish as to "submit their locks and keys to the file of an artist who had attempted to rob them, or trust their lives with a physician who thirsted to drink their blood."[79] Jones and Person were accused of spreading word that North Carolina should stay out of the Union "for five or six years at least."[80] Jones also was charged with warning the people that ratifica-tion would mean debts had to be paid at once, the real reason (so Federalists claimed) why the vote had been so overwhelm-ingly negative. George Sterling blamed Jones for halting ratification, and charged that Jones's program was to execrate

the Saviors of our Country, the Federal Convention, for a pack of Scoundrels, go to the Convention full of d-mns & G-d d-mns, blow up an idle Fandango about Bills of Rights & Amendments, & what

[79] Hugh T. Lefler, ed., *A Plea for Federal Union, North Carolina, 1788* (Charlottesville, 1947), 52.
[80] William R. Davie to James Iredell, September 8, 1788, McRee, *Life of Iredell*, II, 239.

is still more infamous, throw us altogether out of the Union. Was this a time to smoak a pipe, & suck the paw like a surly Bear, when your house was on fire?[81]

Antifederalist action offset Federalist declamation. Clinton's circular letter was well received by the North Carolina assembly, which voted for the appointment of five delegates to the proposed second federal convention. Person, Bloodworth, and three other Antifederalists were chosen.[82] Willie Jones assured the people that their state could get into the Union any time she applied. They proposed to "let the dust settle," to see whether the Federalist claim that amendments would be proposed at the outset of the new Congress were true. Thus North Carolina stood outside the Union as the great experiment took shape, and her only partner in dissent was Rhode Island.

The passive majority in Rhode Island shared common ground with the North Carolina Antifederalists. They would not be hurried into the Union. Not until January of 1790 were delegates chosen for a ratifying convention. Meanwhile, her citizens debated the merits of the Constitution and were influenced by "a fear of heavy direct taxes on land and polls," the paper money issue, and allegations that each citizen's personal liberty was at stake.[83] Apparently they were happy with their local arrangements, where no bill of rights protected them; but extremely distrustful of potential federal power.

Thus, while Americans awaited the advent of the new government, scattered activity in various parts of the country afforded ample proof that opposition to the Constitution had not died. In Western Pennsylvania a county committee of correspondence was established by the citizens of Greensburg who wanted to encourage further demands for a bill of rights.[84]

[81] George Sterling to G. Nicol, December 14, 1788, quoted in Trenholme, *Ratification in North Carolina*, 202.

[82] *Ibid.*, 205.

[83] Hillman Metcalf Bishop, "Why Rhode Island Opposed the Federal Constitution," *Rhode Island History*, 8 (1949), 94-95.

[84] Ferguson, *Early Western Pennsylvania Politics*, 98.

A convention had been called for September 3 at Harrisburg to consider amendment proposals, but Federalists attributed the call for the convention to embittered state politicians. A circular letter in Bucks County declared that citizens should use their "utmost endeavors in a pacific way to procure such alterations in the Federal Constitution as may be necessary to secure the rights and liberties of ourselves and posterity."[85] Delegates from thirteen counties gathered for the Harrisburg convention and adopted twelve amendments. One asked for a guarantee of the sanctity of the state bills of rights, and others called for checks on a standing army and on federal control of the militia.[86] In the same month, Eleazer Oswald made his unsuccessful plea to the Pennsylvania General Assembly asking for the impeachment of the Supreme Court judges who had sentenced him to a month in jail. Oswald contended that his arrest and trial violated the state declaration of rights. He remained convinced that the whole plan to prosecute him had been conceived by a faction "whose sentiments upon the new constitution have not in every respect coincided with mine."[87]

Late in October the New York Antifederalists met at Fraunces Tavern to organize a group dedicated to the calling of a second convention. Led by General Lamb and other hold-overs from the Federal Republican Committee, this circle of Clinton's friends organized sentiment in New York state for amendments and eventually nominated Clinton for the vice presidency.[88] Rhode Island Antifederalists sent a favorable response to the New York circular letter. Other indications of support came from Virginia and North Carolina.[89]

But in the other states the proposal was received with definite coolness. In Connecticut the circular letter was read in a chilly atmosphere. Not one Antifederalist had "hardiness

[85] Thomas, *Political Tendencies in Early Pennsylvania,* 155.
[86] McMaster and Stone, eds., *Pennsylvania and the Federal Constitution* 562-63.
[87] *Pennsylvania Reports,* 1 Dallas 319.
[88] Spaulding, *New York in the Critical Period,* 269-70.
[89] *Pennsylvania Gazette,* December 3, 10, 1788.

enough to call up the consideration of that Letter, or to mention one word of its subject."[90] The Pennsylvania legislature greeted an invitation to the proposed second convention with the reply that the harmony of the Union depended upon the willingness of the states to let the Constitution "proceed undisturbed in its operation by premature amendments."[91] This judgment was in accord with Madison's view. "Let the enemies to the System wait untill some experience shall have taken place, and the business will be conducted with more light as well as with less heat," he counseled.[92]

During the period when the transition to a new form of government was taking place Americans had time to reflect on the momentous events which had recently absorbed their attention. Nearly all agreed that Washington's known role in drafting the Constitution, his support of it, and the presumption that he would be the first president had assured the Constitution a trial. Practical politicians saw too that the issue had been resolved by a dangerously close margin in the key states.[93] That Washington's stature was sufficient to overcome the objections raised by the omission of a bill of rights is doubtful. With Washington in line as the first president, however, and with the adoption of a federal bill of rights conceded by all but the most hardened Federalists, a fair test for the new government seemed assured.

[90] Jonathan Trumbull to George Washington, October 28, 1788, *Documentary History of the Constitution*, V, 101.

[91] Smith, "Movement Towards a Second Convention," in Jameson, ed., *Essays on Constitutional History*, 110.

[92] James Madison to Edmund Pendleton, October 20, 1788, *Documentary History of the Constitution*, V, 94.

[93] Nelson B. Lasson, *The History and Development of the Fourth Amendment* ... (Baltimore, 1937), 103-05.

CHAPTER IX

THE CAMPAIGN PLEDGE FULFILLED

IN THE MONTHS before the newly elected Congress assembled there were ugly whispers that the Federalist hierarchy had no intention of permitting amendments to encumber their "energetic government." Wait and see, the diehard Antifederalists warned, for history shows few examples of men surrendering the powers that they have recently gained. Patrick Henry labored for James Madison's defeat as a candidate for the Senate, voicing doubts about the sincerity of his promise to work for amendments. Edmund Randolph was afraid any delay in adopting amendments would strengthen the majority which opposed them and make the friends of amendments liable to treatment as heretics. "I confess to you without reserve that I feel great distrust of some of those who will certainly be influential agents in the government." A united front was needed, and even one amendment, if adopted without dissension, would "bear down all malcontents."[1]

From his vantage point at the Continental Congress in New York Madison saw that the call for a new convention was a powder keg which might blow away all the good work achieved since the spring of 1787. He consoled himself with the thought that there were many opponents of the convention, even in the Antifederalist ranks, who preferred to use the fifth article of the Constitution to introduce "those supplemental safeguards to liberty ag[ain]st which no objections

[1] Charles Lee to George Washington, October 29, 1788, *Documentary History of the Constitution*, V, 103; Edmund Randolph to James Madison, September 3, 1788, Conway, *Life of Randolph*, 118.

can be raised."[2] Henry fanned the flames of suspicion in Virginia by asking the House of Delegates to call upon Congress for another convention. The Virginia lawmakers approved Henry's request and declared another assembly necessary because civil liberties, "if not cancelled, were rendered insecure under the Constitution."[3] The number of amendments proposed, the deluge of newspaper essays, and the sharp pamphlet warfare doubtless confused Federalists and Antifederalists alike. Some citizens conceded that party zeal had carried both sides to extreme measures of vituperation. Others shared St. John de Crèvecoeur's feeling that the first Congress would have its hands full.

What a cool & exploring sagacity will be wanted in the discussion & acceptation of those numberless amendments, which a few of the States insist upon, in order to please every body, & yet to discriminate the useful from the needless &c.[4]

How Congress would handle the problem of amendments when it assembled in March, 1789, was to some extent dependent upon the outcome of the state elections. Staunch Federalists were capturing most of the ballots. Soon Washington was beckoned from Mount Vernon by a unanimous call. Madison, now an open friend of amendments designed to protect individual rights, trailed both Richard Henry Lee and William Grayson in the balloting for the Virginia senators. Lee declared that his attachment to the cause of civil liberty was forcing him back into public life.[5] He was an Antifederalist, but he lacked Henry's enthusiasm for another federal convention. The word from Pennsylvania was that the Antifederalists had suddenly warmed to the Constitution. "They are now very federal," a correspondent assured Washington;

[2] James Madison to Thomas Jefferson, September 21, 1788, Gaillard Hunt, ed., *The Writings of James Madison* (New York, 1900-10), V, 264.
[3] *Ibid.*, V, 295 n.
[4] St. John de Crèvecoeur to Thomas Jefferson, October 20, 1788, *Documentary History of the Constitution*, V, 93.
[5] Richard Henry Lee to John Jones, October 15, 1788, Ballagh, ed., *Letters of Lee*, II, 479.

"They want Amendments & they must get into the Seats of Government to bring them about—or what is better—to share the Loaves and Fishes."[6] The freshest advice from Massachusetts, Connecticut, and South Carolina indicated that there would be no sudden attempt to rush amendments through the Congress without adequate counsel and consideration.

Madison appeared to be the natural leader for the Federalists whose campaign promises had included a bill of rights. But at the moment Madison's chance for a seat in the new Congress was slim. He had been defeated in the Senate race by Henry's manipulations. Not only had the Senate seat been denied to him but a neat bit of gerrymandering had been used in an attempt to keep him out of the House of Representatives as well. James Monroe, himself a man of parts with a popular following, was advanced to oppose Madison on the Antifederalist ticket. In addition to the ordinary worries of the congressional campaign and the press of business in the Continental Congress Madison had persistent reports from Virginia that his enemies in the state were misrepresenting his position.

Beset with these distractions, Madison still found time to clarify his position on a bill of rights. Writing to Jefferson, he claimed that many good men regarded a declaration of rights as out of place in the Constitution. "My own opinion has always been in favor of a bill of rights;" he continued, "provided it be so framed as not to imply powers not meant to be included in the enumeration."[7] He had not considered the omission of a bill of rights an error and had not "been anxious to supply it even by *subsequent* amendment." Madison declared that he did not share Wilson's belief that the federal government was prevented from interfering with the rights of citizens because it was a government of enumerated powers. On the other hand, he suspected that a declaration of rights might contain the seeds of harm because "some of the most

[6] Richard Peters to George Washington, September 17, 1788, *Documentary History of the Constitution*, V, 65.
[7] James Madison to Thomas Jefferson, October 17, 1788, *ibid.*, 86-91.

essential rights could not be obtained in the requisite latitude."
For example, the tacit assumption by Congress of religious
freedom was preferable to a bill of rights provision which
conceivably could be narrowly defined. The limited powers
of the federal government and the watchfulness of the state
governments also would provide a security for the rights of
the people far better than an ordinary bill of rights.

Madison then proceeded to examine the sources of oppression in a government. He was dubious of the genuine
value of the state bills of rights. Experience proved "the inefficacy of a bill of rights on those occasions when its controul
is most needed." The legislative majority in every state had
violated these "parchment barriers" whenever it served their
interest to do so, as his experience with the law establishing
religious freedom in Virginia had demonstrated. The real
power in this Republic would lie with the majority, and the
danger to private right was "*chiefly* to be apprehended . . .
from acts in which the Government is the mere instrument
of the major number of the constituents."

After considerable study and reasoning from these premises, Madison saw then only two desirable ends to be gained
by passing a bill of rights. A bill of rights might supply a
standard of free government which would create a national
tradition to "counteract the impulses of interest and passion."
There was also the possibility that the arbitrary acts of the
government, rather than oppressive majorities, might invade
the citizens' rights. In this case "a bill of rights will be a
good ground for an appeal to the sense of the community."
Madison clearly thought that sound standards set up by a
bill of rights were more likely to produce beneficial results
than the potentialities of the document as a check on the misused
powers of government, for if public opinion were swayed by a
bill of rights there was little chance that the popular will
would tolerate despotism. But should the danger of arbitrary

government exist at all, "it is prudent to guard ag[ain]st it, especially when the precaution can do no injury."

Assuming a bill of rights to be proper, Madison contended that the document should be worded to avoid setting up principles, such as a prohibition of a standing army, that might have to be violated in periods of crisis. He preferred a few general principles gleaned from the state bills of rights to a long catalog of specific guarantees for personal rights. Essentially conservative in his opinions, Madison thought there was another solution to the problem. "The best security ag[ain]st these evils is to remove the pretext for them," he said.

Jefferson experienced none of the misgiving which bothered his friend. In addition to his other earlier reasons for a bill of rights he now saw the necessity for compromise. He expected that the bill of rights would "draw over so great a proportion of the minorities, as to leave little danger in the opposition of the residue" of the Constitution.[8] The minorities in most of the ratifying states were composed of able men, "so much so as to render it prudent, were it not otherwise reasonable, to make some sacrifices to them." Madison himself became more impressed with the practical results which a compromise could effect. If the first Congress followed the trend of the times, Madison wrote, it would offer "every desireable safeguard for popular rights" as appeasement to the Antifederalists. Gracious acceptance of these amendments would separate "the well meaning from the designing opponents, fix on the latter their true character, and give to the Government its due popularity and stability."[9]

Madison had no illusions about the intentions of Clinton, Henry, and the other leaders of a movement for a second convention. "Amendments" to Madison meant a bill of rights. To Clinton and Henry the word "amendments" also connoted

---

[8] Thomas Jefferson to George Washington, November [December] 4, 1788, *ibid.*, 129.
[9] James Madison to Thomas Jefferson, December 8, 1788, *ibid.*, 131-32.

a weakening of the federal system in favor of the states on such all-important questions as direct taxation and the treaty-making power. "The universal cry is for amendments, & the Federals are obliged to join in it," Henry wrote Lee, "I firmly believe the American union depends on the success of amendments."[10] The Federalists in the Virginia House of Delegates had tried to remove the threat in the Henry resolution calling for a second convention by offering a substitute measure which recommended that the state legislatures ratify a bill of rights and the other Virginia recommendations by the methods prescribed in the Constitution. Until the states had ratified these amendments, Congress ought to conform its laws "to the true spirit of the said bill of rights."[11] This Federalist substitute was rejected. Rebuffs from the other states soon indicated the futility of the convention movement, however, thus forcing advocates of a second convention to await the action, or inaction (as the Antifederalists suspected), of the first Congress.

In the district where Madison was contesting with Monroe for an opportunity to serve in the forthcoming Congress, the voters apparently conceived "amendments" to mean a declaration of rights. A whispering campaign circulated rumors that Madison was perfectly satisfied with the Constitution, and saw no need for a single amendment. Henry had made the same accusation in the House of Delegates, and now the word was being spread, backed by the prestige of Henry's name.

Madison returned to the district for a hurried tour designed to contradict publicly the anti-amendment label. In a letter to a campaign worker, he wrote:

it is my sincere opinion that the Constitution ought to be revised, and that the first Congress meeting under it, ought to prepare and recommend to the States for ratification, the most satisfactory provisions for

[10] Patrick Henry to Richard Henry Lee, November 15, 1788, William Wirt Henry, *Life, Correspondence and Speeches of Patrick Henry* (New York, 1891), II, 429-30.
[11] *Ibid.*, 417-18.

all essential rights, particularly the rights of Conscience in the fullest latitude, the freedom of the press, trials by jury, security against general warrants &c.

There were several other alterations Madison thought worth considering. He made plain his belief that Congress, and not another federal convention, was the proper agency for recommending the amendments to the states.[12] The intense interest in the congressional campaigns led a Richmond correspondent to observe that "Every Person seems to be more engaged either for, or against the new Government, than in their own private concerns." Madison's stand won over influential churchmen, including Baptist John Leland; and his exertions enabled him to defeat Monroe despite the Antifederalist rumors and the gerrymander.[13]

While the newly elected Congress was gathering in New York, Jefferson penned his reflections on Madison's candid letter concerning a bill of rights. Jefferson generally agreed with all Madison had put down, and as an argument in favor of a declaration he added "the legal check which it puts into the hands of the judiciary." Madison had failed to mention the Supreme Court as a branch of the government which could use a bill of rights with great effect, but the potentialities of the high court as a protector of a citizen's rights had not escaped Jefferson.[14] A bill of rights "is like all other human blessings alloyed with some inconveniences," Jefferson admitted, but its good far outweighed its evil. When he had designed a constitution for Virginia in the early days of the Revolution he had not included one, which was probably a mistake; but he now realized that in a constitution "which leaves some precious articles unnoticed, and raises implications against others, a declaration of rights becomes necessary by way of

[12] James Madison to George Eve, January 2, 1789, *Documentary History of the Constitution*, V, 141-43.

[13] A. Donald to Thomas Jefferson, January 16, 1789, *ibid.*, 146; Butterfield, "Elder John Leland," *loc. cit.*, 193.

[14] Thomas Jefferson to James Madison, March 15, 1789, *Documentary History of the Constitution*, V, 161-63.

supplement." Not all human rights could be protected, but "half a loaf is better than no bread. if we cannot secure all our rights, let us secure what we can." State bills of rights were no longer sufficient because they were now agents of the general government. Madison had claimed that experience showed the inefficacy of a bill of rights. This was true, Jefferson said, "but tho it is not absolutely efficacious under all circumstances, it is of great potency always, and rarely inefficacious." Weighing the good and bad, he decided, the balance heavily favored a bill of rights. It could cramp a government in performing certain functions, but this evil would be temporary, and capable of revision. To Jefferson, the dangers which lurked in the failure to have a bill of rights would be "permanent, afflicting & irreparable . . . in constant progression from bad to worse." A few days earlier, Jefferson had decided that the Antifederalists had strayed farther from the path of good government than their opponents.[15] Before the month ended, however, Jefferson acknowledged a debt to the Antifederalists. "There has been just opposition enough to produce probably further guards to liberty without touching the energy of the government," he surmised, "and this will bring over the bulk of the opposition to the side of the new government."[16]

Although the new Congress was scheduled to meet on March 4, numerous delays postponed an official opening for the House of Representatives until April 1. The Senate did not have a quorum until April 6. Both houses adopted their rules, then the Senate promptly got tangled on the question of a proper title for the president. In the House, where all money bills had to originate under the Constitution, attention was immediately diverted to the levying of duties on imports. Definitely committed to work for immediate amendments,

[15] Thomas Jefferson to Francis Hopkinson, March 13, 1789, *ibid.*, 159. Jefferson said he was neither a Federalist nor an Antifederalist. "If I could not go to heaven but with a party, I would not go there at all," he declared.
[16] Thomas Jefferson to Admiral J. Paul Jones, March 23, 1789, *ibid.*, 167.

Madison was not disturbed by the outward signs that this Federalist congress might backslide on campaign promises and play into the hands of its opponents. He assured correspondents at home that although amendments had not been mentioned yet, he knew there would be "no great difficulty in obtaining reasonable ones."[17] To Randolph he wrote that the Federalists would support such amendments "as I am known to have espoused . . . though with some, the concurrence will proceed from a spirit of conciliation rather than conviction."[18]

The order of business in Congress was interrupted for the inauguration of President Washington. In his first message Washington alluded to the demand for amendments to the Constitution but cautiously declared that he would make no specific recommendations for the alterations. Instead, he gave Congress full responsibility for this important topic. Washington did, however, advise Congress to make no radical changes which would weaken the powers of the government. He was solicitous of "the characteristic rights of freemen," and declared that "a regard for the public harmony will sufficiently influence your deliberations on the question" of how personal rights could be "impregnably fortified" while an energetic government was maintained.[19]

When the House then resumed its debate on import duties, Madison announced his intention of introducing the subject of amendments on May 25. His decision to make a public announcement on amendments perhaps was prompted by the wide notice given to the reported debates in the newspapers, where no mention of amendments had been seen. On the following day, Congressman Theodorick Bland of Virginia presented the Henry resolution from the Virginia legislature. Congress sidestepped the issue of a new federal convention raised in the resolution by shelving it, ostensibly to await

[17] James Madison to Edmund Pendleton, April 8, 1789, *ibid.*, 170.
[18] James Madison to Edmund Randolph, April 12, 1789, *ibid.*, 170-71.
[19] Fitzpatrick, ed., *Writings of Washington*, XXX, 295.

further resolutions from other states.[20] A similar request from the New York Assembly was presented on the next day, but both were forgotten when Madison's amendment proposals were finally introduced. Judge Iredell learned that Madison's action had "excited general expectation, though it appears to be the general opinion of people out of doors that nothing will be done."[21] The vital revenue bill continued to occupy the attention of the House, however, and it was not possible for Madison to bring the amendments up for debate until two weeks after the date he had originally announced. By this time he had decided that a bill of rights could be incorporated into the main body of the original Constitution rather than be attached as a series of amendments.[22]

While Madison was concerned with the form of the bill of rights he intended to propose, Hugh Williamson wrote from North Carolina that the Antifederalists there were hoping Congress would not act on the vital issue. "To the best of my Belief the true antis in the State do not wish to hear that Congress have adopted many of the modifications or alterations proposed by this State & Virg[ini]a."[23] Richard Henry Lee advised Henry of Madison's announcement and expressed his doubts about the worth of what Madison might propose. "I apprehend that his ideas, and those of our convention, on this subject, are not similar," Lee wrote.[24] With the aid of Grayson, Lee expected to alter Madison's proposals when they reached the Senate "so as to effect, if possible, the wishes of

[20] *The Debates and Proceedings in the Congress of the United States* (Washington, 1834-56), 1 Cong., 1 Sess., I, 248-51. (Hereafter cited as *Annals of Congress*.)

[21] T. Lowther to James Iredell, May 9, 1789, McRee, *Life of Iredell*, II, 259.

[22] James Madison to Thomas Jefferson, May 27, 1789, Hunt, ed., *Writings of Madison*, V, 372 n.

[23] Hugh Williamson to James Madison, May 24, 1789, quoted in Elizabeth G. McPherson, ed., "Unpublished Letters from North Carolinians to James Madison and James Monroe," *North Carolina Historical Review*, 14 (1937), 162-63.

[24] Richard Henry Lee to Patrick Henry, May 28, 1789, Ballagh, ed., *Letters of Lee*, II, 487.

our legislature." Lee feared that many of the Virginia recommendations would not succeed, "but my hopes are strong that such as may effectually secure civil liberty will not be refused."

Nevertheless, Madison's appearance as a champion of amendments considerably weakened the Antifederalist attack. Benjamin Hawkins told him that the opponents of the Constitution had spread gossip to the effect that the Federalists would never agree to amendments. Now, the North Carolinian wrote, "your motion on that great and delicate subject directly contradicts it."[25] The Antifederalists were swearing that they would never forgive "Bland, Grayson and their other friend [Lee] for suffering any business however important to be done in Congress prior to the subject of amendment, and moreover for suffering this important prophecy by their tardiness to be contradicted." Hawkins followed this report with advice which indicated his anxiety over the amendments. If major stumbling blocks fell in their way, Hawkins wished that "the subject could be postponed 'till after the meeting of our [state] Convention."[26]

Despite the failure of the House to settle the import question, Madison believed the amendment issue could wait no longer. More than three months after the date when Congress was scheduled to begin its session, he asked the House to resolve itself into a Committee of the Whole to consider amendments "as contemplated in the fifth article of the Constitution."[27] Instead of rushing to support his proposals, Madison's fellow congressmen seemed to be in no hurry to take up the topic which had so recently stirred the Republic. Many agreed with Aedanus Burke that amendments to the Constitution were necessary, "but this was not the proper time to bring them forward." Let us wait until the government is organized, he said, and not risk disrupting the harmony which now prevailed

[25] Benjamin Hawkins to James Madison, June 1, 1789, *Documentary History of the Constitution*, V, 175.
[26] Hawkins to Madison, June [July] 3, 1789, Madison Papers, Library of Congress.
[27] *Annals of Congress*, 1 Cong., 1 Sess., I, 424ff.

in the House. Madison answered that he had postponed the issue twice and that he considered further delay impolitic. He added that if the subject of amendments were postponed time after time, "it may occasion suspicions, which, though not well founded, may tend to inflame or prejudice the public mind against our decisions." It was his duty to place the proposition before the House, he said. "I do not expect it will be decided immediately; but if some step is taken in the business, it will give [the public] reason to believe that we may come to a final result."

Roger Sherman, who had opposed a bill of rights in the Federal Convention, followed Madison. His state, Connecticut, wanted no amendments. What the people everywhere wanted was a stable government. Sherman said he was ready to see amendments introduced as a matter of form, but not as an interruption of the really important business at hand. A halt in the organization of the government to discuss amendments, Sherman predicted, "will alarm the fears of twenty of our constituents where it will please one." William L. Smith of South Carolina assured Madison he "had done his duty" by offering amendments, "and if he did not succeed, he was not to blame."

Madison did not consider his duty so lightly discharged, however. Even one day's debate on the subject would relieve many apprehensions and convince the public that the Federalists were ready to "evince that spirit of deference and concession for which they have hitherto been distinguished." Many who had opposed the Constitution were ready to support the new government. Their only price was an explicit declaration of the great rights of mankind. There had been numerous reasons for the opposition to the Constitution, Madison continued,

but I believe that the great mass of the people who opposed it, disliked it because it did not contain effectual provisions against the encroachments on particular rights, and those safeguards which they have been long accustomed to have interposed between them and the magistrate who exercises the sovereign power.

As long as a great number of citizens thought these securities necessary it would be an injustice to ignore their desires. These safeguards could be added to the Constitution without endangering the worthwhile features of the new government.

Madison then read to the House his plan of amendment. His proposals covered all of the ten articles which eventually formed the federal Bill of Rights. Even his phraseology was preserved in the final draft in numerous cases. Several other provisions were added by the congressional committees to take care of the criticism directed at the apportionment of representatives, congressional salaries, and the possible overlapping of executive, legislative, and judicial powers. But the bulk of the changes were aimed at securing the civil liberties of citizens, and Madison presentēd them in a form that would merely enlarge the Constitution to eight articles. In drafting the proposals, Madison had leaned heavily on the Virginia Declaration of Rights, but he had also incorporated additional features adopted by the ratifying conventions. He followed a reading of the amendments with a lengthy speech which embodied the arguments presented to Jefferson in earlier correspondence.[28] After canvassing the whole field of objections to a bill of rights, he declared that a specific declaration of rights would be worth while because it offered "tranquillity of the public mind, and the stability of the Government." Madison alluded to Jefferson's striking observation that the "independent tribunals of justice will consider themselves in a peculiar manner the guardians of those rights . . . [and] resist every encroachment upon rights expressly stipulated . . . by the declaration of rights."[29]

Madison concluded that these changes could not "endanger the beauty of the Government in any one important feature, even in the eyes of its most sanguine admirers." The alterations would go far toward making "the constitution better in

[28] Madison's manuscript outline is reprinted in Hunt, ed., *Writings of Madison*, V, 389-90.
[29] *Annals of Congress*, 1 Cong., 1 Sess., I, 435-36.

the opinion of those who are opposed to it, without weakening its frame or abridging its usefulness, in the judgment of those who are attached to it, [and] we act the part of wise and liberal men who make such alterations as shall produce that effect." He then withdrew his previous motion for discussion by the Committee of the Whole and moved that a committee be appointed to consider and report on his proposals.

Few congressmen seemed as certain as Madison of the urgency of amending the Constitution. James Jackson and Elbridge Gerry thought premature alterations would suspend the organization of the general government. Gerry, only recently come from the ranks which demanded a bill of rights, now feared a second convention but thought that a full and free public discussion should precede action by the Congress. Even General Thomas Sumter, recent leader of the South Carolina Antifederalists, was willing to postpone action on the amendments. John Page had already suggested that the propositions be printed, if only to show the people that something was being done about the amendments they wished. Several congressmen thought the public would consider the plan to refer the amendments to a special committee an attempt to pigeonhole the alterations. Finally, after Madison changed his proposals to resolutions, which could be adopted by the House, the matter was referred to the Committee of the Whole for a later session.

Both North Carolina and Rhode Island had figured in these discussions, for Congress was anxious to complete the ratification process and to proceed with a feeling of unanimity which was lacking in the present assemblage. While the failure to introduce amendments had boosted Antifederalist hopes in North Carolina, William R. Davie now spoke of Madison's leadership in obtaining amendments with warm delight. Davie assured Madison that the recommendations North Carolina had forwarded with its rejection were misleading. "That farrago of amendments borrowed from Virginia is by no means to be considered as the sense of this country;" Davie contended, "they were proposed amidst the violence and confusion of party heat . . . and adopted by the opposition without one moment's consideration." Davie had been collecting the objections of his neighbors, who seemed to be more concerned about trial by jury and freedom of conscience than any other points. Instead of a general bill of rights they seemed to prefer "some general negative confining Congress to the exercise of the powers particularly granted, with some express negative restriction in some important cases."[80] Madison's proposals were already formulated when he received this letter, but his amendments covered all North Carolina requested. If the Federalist reports from North Carolina were true, congressional approval of the amendments would assure speedy ratification by a second North Carolina convention.

Reactions to Madison's amendments were mixed. Young Fisher Ames of Massachusetts called them "the fruit of much labor and research." Ames reported that Madison had "hunted up all grievances and complaints of newspapers, all the articles of conventions, and the small talk of their debates," in compiling his propositions.[31] He was inclined to think that Madison had tried to cover too much ground but added that "it may do some good towards quieting men, who attend to sounds only, and may get the mover some popularity, which he wishes." William Grayson sent word of Madison's proposals to Henry, objecting to the great overemphasis on personal liberty and slight attention for the judiciary, direct taxation, and other issues.[32] The whole object, Grayson wrote, was

unquestionably to break the spirit of the Antifederalist party by divisions. . . . In this system however of *divide* & *impera,* they are opposed by a very heavy column, from the little States, who being in possession

[30] William R. Davie to James Madison, June 10, 1789, *Documentary History of the Constitution,* V, 176-77.

[31] Fisher Ames to Thomas Dwight, June 11, 1789, Seth Ames, ed., *The Works of Fisher Ames* (Boston, 1854), I, 52-53.

[32] William Grayson to Patrick Henry, June 12, 1789, Henry, *Life of Henry,* III, 391.

of rights they had no pretensions to in justice, are afraid of touching a subject which may bring into investigation or controversy their fortunate situation. . . .

Tench Coxe dispatched a laudatory letter which noted that the most ardent and irritable Federalists were pleased by the amendments, while the Antifederalists were "stript of every rational, and most of the popular arguments they have heretofore used."[33] It would be a mistake to court the favor of the opposition with "improper concessions" said "Light-Horse Harry" Lee, adding that he would disarm the dissenters by conceding reasonable amendments. Lee thought the plan now before the House of Representatives would accomplish "this great good."[34] From North Carolina Madison received assurances that unless Congress agreed to amendments in line with those he had proposed, a second state ratifying convention would repudiate the Constitution.[35]

Madison's proposed amendments were widely publicized. Four days after his House speech, the amendments were printed in the *New York Daily Advertiser*. Other newspapers quickly followed suit. The ubiquitous Thomas Lloyd published them in his *Congressional Register,* a weekly report of the House debates.[36] News of the proposals thus was spread across the Republic in a comparatively short time, but the journalistic reception of the Madison plan was on the whole one of caution. The *Pennsylvania Gazette,* still wary of a second convention, took a stand against calling together "fifteen hundred reformers in the present fluctuation of sentiments. . . . If we must at all amend, I pray for merely amusing amendments, a little frothy garnish."[37] Madison stuffed a letter

[33] Tench Coxe to James Madison, June 18, 1789, *Documentary History of the Constitution,* V, 178.
[34] Henry Lee to George Washington, July 1, 1789, *ibid.,* 180-81.
[35] Hugh Williamson to James Madison, July 2, 1789, quoted in McPherson, ed., "Unpublished Letters," *North Carolina Historical Review,* 14 (1937), 167.
[36] Vincent L. Eaton, "The First Publication of the Bill of Rights," *New Colophon,* 2, part 7 (September, 1949), 280.
[37] *Pennsylvania Gazette,* July 15, 1789.

to Jefferson with the newspaper clippings, adding an explanatory note of his own. The proposals represented only those amendments Madison considered most likely to be adopted by both the Congress and the states. "If I am not mistaken they will if passed, be satisfactory to majority of those who have opposed the Constitution," he added.[38]

Madison's willingness to become the legislative champion of amendments indicated that he, though young in years, was an experienced hand at practical politics. He candidly confessed to Pendleton that his proposals were limited to issues which would excite the least exertions of the opposition. "Nothing of a controvertible nature ought to be hazarded by those who are sincere in wishing for the approbation of 2/3 of each House, and 3/4 of the State Legislatures," he explained.[39] Among the most zealous Federalists there was an undercurrent of opinion decidedly unfavorable to amendments, principally on the ground that hastily enacted alterations would demolish the effectiveness of the Constitution. Madison was caught between this faction and his own campaign pledge, which, if fulfilled, would allay not only the doubts of many of his constituents, but a large portion of citizens throughout the Republic. To a man of Madison's talents and temperament the situation offered an ideal opportunity. He played off Scylla against Charybdis instead of trying to go between them. He had to apologize to his home constituents because more could not be gained. To the anti-amendment group in the House he was forced to defend the lengths he had gone in safeguarding the personal rights of citizens. To his neighbors and his colleagues Madison counseled the need for compromise. His task called for political tight-rope walking, and he performed the feat with the skill of a veteran.

On July 21, six weeks after his first discussion of amend-

[38] James Madison to Thomas Jefferson, June 13, 1789, quoted in Frank Monaghan, ed., *Heritage of Freedom* (Princeton, 1947), 63.

[39] James Madison to Edmund Pendleton, June 21, 1789, Hunt, ed., *Writings of Madison*, V, 406 n.

ments, Madison reintroduced the subject to the House. He declared that it was time to discuss the amendments in the Committee of the Whole. The House voted instead to send his proposals, along with the recommendations from the states, to a special committee composed of John Vining of Delaware, chairman, Madison, and Roger Sherman, a consistent opponent of a federal bill of rights.[40] This committee lost no time in framing a report, which was presented to the House a week later, where it was tabled. After some further delays, the House agreed to consider the committee report, although there were continual outcries that more important business was pressing. Madison replied that the Congress was pledged as a matter of good faith to pass on the proposed amendments and that further delay could only excite the suspicions of the people. Representative John Page emphasized the character of the bill of rights as a political concession. He reminded his colleagues that numerous patriotic gentlemen, whose support had made ratification possible, expected these amendments.

The amendment question was debated for over a week in the Committee of the Whole. Madison still favored alterations in the main text of the Constitution rather than a separate list of amendments. Other congressmen agreed with Roger Sherman, who moved for separate amendments and declared that Madison's proposal placed contradictory articles side by side.[41] James Jackson of Georgia argued that the Constitution as ratified should be left untouched, otherwise it would "be patched up, from time to time, with various stuffs resembling Joseph's coat of many colors." The majority sided with Madison, however, and supported Thomas Hartley when he said that "the time of the House was too precious to be squandered away in discussing mere matter of form." Sherman's motion

---

[40] *Annals of Congress*, 1 Cong., 1 Sess., I, 665. A brief account of the progress of the federal Bill of Rights through both the House of Representatives and the Senate is found in Anon., *History of Congress* (Philadelphia, 1843), 152-73.

[41] *Annals of Congress*, 1 Cong., 1 Sess., I, 708ff. The actual vote favoring separate amendments came later.

for separate amendments was defeated on August 13. Six days later Sherman renewed his motion to add the amendments "by way of supplement." The official record states that

> Hereupon ensued a debate similar to what took place in the Committee of the whole . . . but, on the question, Mr. SHERMAN'S motion was carried by two-thirds of the House: in consequence it was agreed to.

The contents of the Madison proposals were thoroughly examined in the House when it sat as a Committee of the Whole. A simple statement about the nature of government, offered as an additional clause to the preamble, threatened to involve the House in a wearisome debate over abstractions. Proposals for apportioning representation and fixing the pay of legislators were subjects of sharp controversy. On the other hand, the guarantees of individual rights in matters of speech, religion, petitions, and a free press provoked less discussion although they formed the nucleus of the amendments. The same attacks familiar since 1787 were repeated by opponents of a bill of rights. Protection for individual liberties was unnecessary, trivial, absurd, harmless, vital, or urgent, depending upon the mood and manner of the speaker. Madison himself became impatient when the discussion seemed trailing toward a dead end and attempted to restrict the debate to a few plain, simple proposals which he thought the people had a right to expect from Congress.

Even when the discussion followed the committee report it sometimes went to extremes, as in Samuel Livermore's remarks on the "cruel and unusual punishments" clause. Livermore thought it was occasionally necessary to cut off the ears of a criminal, and asked if it will be necessary to prevent "these punishments because they are cruel?" Madison considered the proposed section which would prevent states from infringing the rights of conscience, free speech, a free press, and trial by jury "the most valuable on the whole list."[42] If it were neces-

[42] Ibid., 755.

sary to restrain the national government, he said, it was equally important to place checks on the state governments. Representative Thomas Tucker of South Carolina argued that the states had already been excessively weakened, but his colleagues would not agree to strike the passage from the report. Burke and Tucker remained true to their Antifederalist leanings and attempted to add amendments restricting the power of Congress over elections and forbidding direct taxes, but their proposals were defeated. Certain amendments recommended by the various state conventions had been omitted from the report, a fact which was expected to irritate those states for "having misplaced their confidence in the General Government." But the weary representatives sustained the judgment of the committee. Not all of the criticism was destructive, however. Even Sherman was capable of offering constructive suggestions for the plan he had called superfluous, if not dangerous.[43] The committee report survived the debate and on August 24 it was forwarded to the Senate as seventeen proposed amendments to the Constitution.[44]

Meanwhile, the public continued to show considerable interest in a bill of rights. The Reverend John Leland, as the spokesman for a group of Virginia Baptists, wrote President Washington that their committee had "voted unanimously that the Constitution does not make sufficient provision for the secure enjoyment of religious liberty." Leland added that it was some consolation to know "that if religious liberty is rather insecure in the Constitution, the Administration will certainly prevent all oppression; for a Washington will preside." Washington assured the Baptists that he had no fears concerning the constitutional status of religious liberty. To merit their continued approbation he promised that if any challenge appeared "no one would be more zealous than my-

[43] *Ibid.*, 768.
[44] See *Documentary History of the Constitution*, V, 193-97.

self to establish effectual barriers against the horrors of spiritual tyranny, and every species of religious persecution."[45]

The voices of doubt were not stilled, however. Madison heard that a minister, who had visited Virginia during the summer, had been constantly queried on the "propriety & safety of the New Constitution, especially in regard to the rights of conscience on which head they appeared much alarmed . . . [but] they appeared to be satisfied after he had gone through the subject."[46] Madison realized that try as he might he could not please everyone. He learned that Antifederalists in Philadelphia were dissatisfied with his proposals. Richard Peters assured him that "as long as they have one unreasonable Wish ungratified the Clamour will be the same."[47]

Madison was well aware that his handiwork was not above criticism. He explained to Randolph that pushing the proposed amendments through the House had been difficult enough since some congressmen were out to defeat any "plan short of their wishes, but likely to satisfy a great part of their companions in opposition throughout the Union."[48] Even if he had wanted to include every amendment recommended by the Virginia convention, Madison said, "I should have acted from prudence the very part to which I have been led by choice." But there was one unexpected source of commendation for Madison. George Mason declared that he had received the news of the proposed amendments with great satisfaction. He added, "With two or three further Amendments . . . I could cheerfuly put my Hand and Heart to the New Government."[49]

Even before the Senate began debate on the amendments, Senator Pierce Butler of South Carolina called them "*milk-*

[45] John Leland to George Washington, August 8, 1789, quoted in Robert B. C. Howell, *The Early Baptists of Virginia* (Philadelphia, 1857), 226-27; Fitzpatrick, ed., *Writings of Washington*, XXX, 321 n.
[46] James Manning to James Madison, August 29, 1789, *Documentary History of the Constitution*, V, 201-02.
[47] Richard Peters to James Madison, August 24, 1789, *ibid.*, 193.
[48] James Madison to Edmund Randolph, August 21, 1789, *ibid.*, 191-92.
[49] George Mason to Samuel Griffin [1789], quoted in Helen Hill, *George Mason, Constitutionalist* (Cambridge, Mass., 1938), 242.

and-water amendments." Butler told Judge Iredell that if North Carolina withheld ratification while awaiting worthwhile amendments then she would be out of the Union for some time. Butler thought personal liberty "already well secured" and suggested that Madison himself had only introduced the amendments "to keep his promise with his constituents."[50] When the amendments were taken to the Senate on the day following House approval an attempt was made to postpone their consideration until the next session of Congress. Fortunately Senator William Maclay of Pennsylvania kept a diary which permits the historian to look behind the locked doors of the Senate chamber. Maclay noted that the amendments were "treated contemptuously" by Senators Ralph Izard, John Langdon, and Robert Morris. Izard of South Carolina moved for postponement into the next session. Langdon seconded this proposal, "and Mr. Morris got up and spoke angrily but not well" against hasty approval of the amendments.[51] Maclay was not in sympathy with a move to delay the adoption of a bill of rights. "I could not help observing the six year-class [of Senators] hung together on this business, or the most of them," he noted in his diary. Izard's motion was defeated despite the insistence of its backers that a little experience might prove whether the amendments were necessary, a suggestion which disgusted Senator Richard Henry Lee. Lee said he was not completely satisfied with the proposals, but he considered it fatuous to speak of the need for experience before seeking amendments. "As if experience were not necessary to prove the propriety of those great principles of Civil liberty which the wisdom of the Ages has found to be necessary barriers against the encroachments of power in the hand of frail Man!" Lee claimed that he had to fight to preserve the legislative life of the amendments, as he was convinced "that if we

[50] Pierce Butler to James Iredell, August 11, 1789, McRee, *Life of Iredell*, II, 265.
[51] Edgar S. Maclay, ed., *Journal of William Maclay* (New York, 1890), 131.

212 THE BIRTH OF THE BILL OF RIGHTS, 1776-1791

cannot gain the whole loaf, we shall at least have some bread."[52] Finally, the Senate agreed to take up the subject of amendments on August 31. The actual discussion was further delayed until September 2.

Since the Senate debates were at this time not open to the public, the twenty-two members were able to discuss the amendments more freely than the members of the House of Representatives. With a majority of the senators convinced that some amendments must go forth from Congress, the group set about the task of editing the House version. They slashed out wordiness with a free hand. The third and fourth articles were fused to read:

Congress shall make no law establishing articles of faith, or a mode of worship, or prohibiting the free exercise of religion, or abridging the freedom of speech, or the press, or the right of people peaceably to assemble, and petition to the government for the redress of grievances.

This version was proposed as the third amendment. Three more House articles alluding to trial by jury and court procedure were dropped after their meaning had been incorporated into other sections. The Senate rejected that amendment which Madison said he prized above all the others, the one that prohibited the states from infringing on personal rights. The proposal to bind elected representatives to the instructions of their constituents, which had failed in the House, was supported only by Lee and Grayson. An effort to prohibit the levying of direct taxes also was rejected, while the suggestion that the clause on religious tests be amended to read "no other religious tests" was defeated as it had been in the House. Generally speaking, the Senate followed the House in refusing to add the suggestions from the Tucker-Burke faction. Lee and Grayson probably were responsible for the wholesale introduction of what represented a compendium of the Virginia recommendations not already accepted. These additions were

[52] Richard Henry Lee to Charles Lee, August 28, 1789, Ballagh, ed., *Letters of Lee*, II, 499.

not accepted, but their introduction kept the Virginians in compliance with the instructions of the ratifying convention.

After the Senate had completed its revision of the seventeen House proposals, twelve amendments remained. These revised articles of amendment then were sent back to the House of Representatives for concurrence.

While the Senate was deliberating upon the amendments, Jefferson in Paris had given them his attention. He alluded to the proposals as a "declaration of rights," and indicated that he liked it "as far as it goes; but I should have been for going further."[53] Jefferson preferred more precise wording in some of the articles. He still opposed the granting of government monopolies and feared a standing army, particularly one composed of foreign mercenaries. These things he would guard against and was confident that they eventually would be prohibited by the Constitution.

Another reaction to Madison's proposals came when the Rhode Island General Assembly sent word to Washington and Congress that the amendments had "already afforded some relief and satisfaction to the minds of the People of this State" and expressed a desire to join the other states "under a constitution and form of government so well poised as neither to need alteration or be liable thereto by a majority only of nine States out of thirteen."[54]

The amendments were not universally acclaimed despite the efforts made to conciliate all factions. Patrick Henry was said to have preferred a single amendment on direct taxes to all the amendments approved in Congress.[55] The trend of the Senate debate disappointed Richard Henry Lee, who declared that his colleagues had "mutilated and enfeebled" the amendments. "It is too much the fashion now to look at the rights of the People, as a Miser inspects a Security, to find a

[53] Thomas Jefferson to James Madison, August 28, 1789, *Documentary History of the Constitution*, V, 198-99.
[54] John Collins to George Washington, September [?], 1789, *ibid.*, 207-08.
[55] David Stuart to George Washington, September 12, 1789, *ibid.*, 205.

flaw," he complained.[56] Lee assured Henry that he had worked diligently on behalf of the Virginia convention recommendations. "We might as well have attempted to move Mount Atlas upon our shoulders" as to get Senate approval for the proposals, he said. Lee added, in lamenting the failure of the Antifederalist strategy, that "the idea of subsequent amendments, was little better than putting oneself to death first, in expectation that the doctor, who wished our destruction, would afterwards restore us to life."[57] Overlooking the fact that personal rights were an integral part of the congressional amendments, Lee spoke of the failure to adopt essential features that would check the tendency toward a consolidated government. It was the rights of the states, and not the rights of individual citizens, which now bothered Lee. He conceded that some valuable rights were set forth in the amendments, "but the power to violate them to all intents and purposes remains unchanged."

When the House took up the proposed changes in the amendments on September 19, it was obvious that only a conference could resolve the differences created by the Senate revision. Madison, Sherman, and Vining were chosen to work out the details of a further compromise with the Senate. Oliver Ellsworth, Charles Carroll, and William Paterson were named as the Senate conferees. The conference committee rapidly smoothed over the rough spots objected to by their colleagues. One snag in the discussion was a change in the third article which prohibited Congress from making a law "establishing articles of faith." This was altered to "an establishment of religion."[58] A preamble was drafted to explain that the amendments were being submitted to the states in answer to the expressed desire of certain ratifying conventions "that further declaratory and restrictive clauses should be added." By

---

[56] Richard Henry Lee to Francis Lightfoot Lee, September 13, 1789, Ballagh, ed., *Letters of Lee*, II, 500.

[57] Richard Henry Lee to Patrick Henry, September 14, 1789, *ibid.*, 501-03.

[58] Anon., *History of Congress*, 171.

September 25, both houses had approved the twelve amendments which emerged from the joint conference. These were forwarded to the President for transmission to the states. The twelve proposals included provisions for safeguarding the personal rights of citizens, a statement on the powers reserved for the states, and two articles calling for apportionment of legislators and fixing the pay of congressmen.[59]

Lee and Grayson lost no time in dispatching the proposed amendments to the Virginia legislature with a covering letter apologizing for the quality of the enclosed proposals. The record would show that they had worked for the "radical amendments proposed by the [Virginia] Convention," but that they had been overwhelmed.[60] Grayson assured Henry that the Senate had mutilated the proposals originally sent up from the House. The results were disastrous. "They are good for nothing, and I believe, as many others do, that they will do more harm than benefit."[61]

Henry concurred wholeheartedly with the senators and attempted to postpone consideration of the amendments until the next session of the House of Delegates. His motion was voted down, but the Antifederalist activity caused discussion of the amendments to continue over many months. Although Virginia was one of the first states to consider ratification of the amendments, her legislature was the last (of the necessary eleven) to approve them. Confident the other states would not balk, Madison believed that an unfavorable public reaction would cause the Virginia legislators to regret their dilatory tactics.[62]

Passage of the "bill of rights" amendments removed a

[59] See Appendix B.

[60] Richard Henry Lee and William Grayson to the Speaker of the House of Representatives, September 28, 1789, *Documentary History of the Constitution*, V, 217-18. A similar letter to the governor is printed in *ibid.*, 216-17.

[61] William Grayson to Patrick Henry, September 29, 1789, Henry, *Life of Henry*, III, 406.

[62] See Edmund Randolph to George Washington, November 26, 1789, *Documentary History of the Constitution*, V, 216; James Madison to George Washington, January 4, 1790, *ibid.*, 230-31; Rowland, *Life of Mason*, II, 319-23.

major obstacle to ratification of the Constitution in North Carolina. Richard Dobbs Spaight, who complained that he had not
enjoyed a single day of perfect health since the abortive Hillsboro convention, was seemingly restored to full vigor when
the Fayetteville convention approved ratification on November 21.[63] The twelve amendments sent out by Congress had
dispelled some of the doubts harbored by delegates, but the
hardiest Antifederalists did not give in easily. They admitted
that the amendments, when adopted, would "embrace in some
measure . . . the object that this State had in view by a Bill
of Rights, and many of the amendments proposed by the
last Convention," but they were not completely satisfied. Free
elections, a prohibition against direct taxes, a guarantee that
there would be no interference with paper money already in
circulation, and a prohibition on standing armies—all were demanded in further amendments. The Federalist majority later
accepted these proposals in the form of further recommendatory amendments. This Federalist action was a gesture of good
will and a concession to the defeated "Antis."

Before Jefferson returned from his post in France and as
Secretary of State received official notification of the entrance
of North Carolina into the Union, New Jersey had already
ratified the amendments. A short time later he accepted their
ratification by the Maryland legislature. "The opposition to
our new constitution has almost totally disappeared," he wrote
Lafayette.[64] North Carolina followed Maryland in the ratifying process, and New Hampshire, South Carolina, Delaware,
Pennsylvania, and New York followed suit. There were sufficient objections to the first and second articles, however, to
portend their defeat. The first amendment which the states
rejected had called for a fixed schedule that apportioned seats
in the House of Representatives on a ratio which apparently

[63] Richard Dobbs Spaight to James Iredell, November 26, 1789, McRee,
Life of Iredell, II, 273; Clark, ed., *N. C. State Records*, XXII, 45-52.
    [64] Thomas Jefferson to the Marquis de la Fayette, April 2, 1790, *Documen-
tary History of the Constitution*, V, 240.

seemed disadvantageous. The second rejected amendment prohibited senators and representatives from altering their salaries "until an election of Representatives shall have intervened." Obviously, neither dealt with personal rights.

The Rhode Island convention narrowly voted for ratification late in May. Moving swiftly the Rhode Island General Assembly then approved the amendments in June, 1790. Over a year passed before further state action. Then Vermont became the tenth state to ratify, having been admitted into the Republic on March 4, 1791. The admission of Vermont brought to eleven the number of ratifications necessary, under the three-fourths rule, to give effect to the amendments. Ratification of the amendments by Vermont on November 3 still left four states unreported. Almost unnoticed, the Virginia legislature ratified the first ten amendments to the Constitution on December 15, 1791. Thus Virginia, the first state to provide legal safeguards for personal liberty, was the last of the necessary eleven states to ratify the Federal Bill of Rights.[65]

Both the state and the federal bills of rights formed a legal canopy for the personal liberty of every citizen. Freedom of the press, religious freedom, free speech, and the other rights protected by the first ten amendments of the Constitution had a direct relation to events in the colonies prior to the Revolution. The revolt which loosened the bonds of restraint sped the process of enacting these guarantees into fundamental laws, and the various state declarations of rights resulted. Like all man-made laws, these bills of rights did not prevent some injustices. Nevertheless, they clearly demonstrated that the American Revolution had a broad ideological base and that it was not only a military, political, and social upheaval—but also a legal rebellion.

Throughout the Revolution and during the Confederation

[65] As a token gesture celebrating the 150th anniversary of ratification of the Federal Bill of Rights in 1941 the three states which had never approved the amendments—Connecticut, Georgia, and Massachusetts—formally ratified the measures.

era the state bills of rights were looked to by citizens for protection of their personal liberties. The demand for a bill of
rights during the ratification period was later interpreted by
Justice Story as "a matter of very exaggerated declamation and
party zeal, for the mere purpose of defeating the Constitution."[66] A more dispassionate view now indicates that a broad
base of public opinion forced the adoption of the Bill of Rights
upon those political leaders who knew the value of compromise.
Jefferson, Madison, and other public men who urged the acceptance of a bill of rights when adoption of the Constitution
was still in doubt foresaw the salutary effects of a federal Bill
of Rights as a bench mark in the American experience in self-
government. The Bill of Rights also served notice to all the
world that national independence, without personal liberty,
was an empty prize.

[66] Joseph Story, *Commentaries on the Constitution of the United States*
(Boston, 1873), II, 602.

CHAPTER X

SINCE 1791

J EFFERSON MUST have had some feeling of personal satisfaction when he was able to announce officially the ratification of the first ten amendments. He favored the Bill of Rights, since it fitted in with his idea expressed during the Revolution that "the spirit of the times may alter, will alter . . . [and thus] the time for fixing every essential right on a legal basis is while our rulers are honest, and ourselves united. From the conclusion of this war we shall be going down hill."[1] Adding the Bill of Rights to the Constitution was a step which convinced many men that the Republic was not, after all, headed down hill.

A summary of the course of American civil liberty since 1791 to determine whether we have gone forward would call for many volumes. Much of the fabric of the original Constitution has been stretched out of shape, or made to appear ill-fitting, and the Bill of Rights has been put to tests which Jefferson could not have foreseen. But we can imagine, for example, that the reasons for a Fifth Amendment would appear as sound to Madison, Jefferson, or Mason today—despite the advent of wire-tapping techniques and make-your-own-rules legislative investigating committees—as the reasons presented in 1776 or 1789. The rise of corporations, the income tax, and geographical considerations, to mention a few items, have caused many phrases in the original Constitution to be turned "inside out." But the dignity of the human personality remains the same, whether the right involved be that of blocking the door to a redcoat soldier or holding a private telephone

[1] Thomas Jefferson, *Notes on the State of Virginia*, Peden, ed. (Chapel Hill, 1955), 161.

conversation. Each volume in a history of American civil liberty would have to take the measure of Jefferson's prediction and decide whether or not our essential rights have been placed in a vehicle that is going down hill. It may be worth while, therefore, in a history of this struggle for a bill of rights, to review somewhat hastily the subsequent vicissitudes of personal freedom.

Seven years after Jefferson had certified the Bill of Rights as officially ratified Congress passed legislation which had the outward goal of preserving the safety of the Republic. To preserve our state and save our liberties, so the reasoning of the majority ran, we must restrict certain liberties during a period of crisis. Used first as an explanation for the Alien and Sedition Acts, this type of logic became familiar to Americans and still persists. Legislators seem to judge each crisis to be a little more pressing, more urgent, and potentially more catastrophic than the last affair. The pattern is altogether too clear and too familiar. The Alien and Sedition Acts form Exhibit A.

Ostensibly these acts were designed to block pro-French activity during the "cold war" then in progress between France and the United States. Actually, the laws were partisan in purpose, aimed at stifling all opposition to the Federalist party. "It is too much to expect that all party divisions will be done away as long as there are rival States and rival individuals; all we can reasonably hope is, and this we may confidently expect, that no State or individual, to gratify its ambition, will enlist under foreign banners," President Adams wrote.[2] That a Republican might have been pro-French, anti-British, and still a good American was inconceivable to men of Adams' stamp. The Federalists undoubtedly believed that any measure which would contribute to the downfall of the opposition was vital and expedient, for the Republican leader was Jefferson—"an *atheist* in Religion and a *fanatic* in politics"—and the party

---

[2] Adams to the Inhabitants of the County of Middlesex, Virginia, [July, 1798?], Adams, ed., *Works of Adams*, IX, 214-15.

itself was "a composition indeed of very incongruous materials but all tending to mischief—some of them to the overthrow of the Government by depriving it of its due energies, others of them to a Revolution after the manner of Buonaparte." Thus spake Alexander Hamilton, who was Mr. Federalist himself.[3]

Naturally, the Republicans considered themselves the true exponents of American liberty, hence the Alien and Sedition Acts drew the wrath of the public men, back-country farmers, and others in the party rank and file. In the Kentucky and Virginia Resolutions Jefferson and Madison plainly branded the acts as contrary to the Bill of Rights. The Sedition Act was used by prosecuting attorneys to jail a variety of citizens, ranging from a drunken vagrant to a member of Congress, the criterion for arrest being outspoken criticism of President Adams' administration. The Alien Friends Act "established the concept of guilt by suspicion for the period of its operation."[4] As it happened, the act was not enforced, but it hung over the heads of many alien visitors and apparently caused the exodus of many Frenchmen.

The practice of challenging the constitutionality of acts of Congress before the courts had not yet developed, and hence the validity of these laws under the Bill of Rights was never tested there. Probably the preponderance of arch-Federalists on the high court accounts for the Republican decision to side-step the bench.[5] As expressed in the Kentucky and Virginia Resolutions, Jefferson's idea (shared with Madison) was that a state might nullify an unconstitutional law. Such a doctrine proved unnecessary, however, as the acts expired between June 25, 1800, and March 3, 1801.

[3] Alexander Hamilton to John Jay, May 7, 1800, Johnston, ed., *Jay Papers*, IV, 271.
[4] James Morton Smith, "The Enforcement of the Alien Friends Act," *Mississippi Valley Historical Review*, 41 (1954), 86.
[5] John C. Miller, *Crisis in Freedom* (Boston, 1951), 138-39. See also James Morton Smith, "The Alien and Sedition Laws: Study in the Development of American Civil Liberties" (Ph.D. dissertation, Cornell University, 1951).

Personal rights in the years between Jefferson's first administration and the Civil War were often suppressed as the abolitionists tried to spread their radical gospel and the proslavery men sought to preserve the status quo. Before the slavery dispute had gained momentum the Supreme Court made a ruling in the case of Barron *v.* Baltimore in 1833, in which Chief Justice John Marshall affirmed what survivors of the Constitutional Convention and the ratification debates already knew: the federal Bill of Rights prohibited encroachments by the national government only and the ten amendments "contain no expression indicating an intention to apply them to the state governments."[6] Thus northern agitators and abolitionist newspapers were suppressed in the South, while slavery adherents and their ideas gained practically no hearing in the North, and both the state officials and local public opinion seemed combined in an effort to squelch dissent. Raising a cry for free speech or a free press, even though most states had a bill of rights, would have been a vain appeal. Lost in the din was Jefferson's calm advice to partisans of an earlier day "that the minority possess their equal rights, which equal law must protect, and to violate would be oppression."[7] As a result, martyrdom was the lot of such men as the Reverend Elijah Lovejoy, abolitionist editor who was murdered by a mob at Alton, Illinois, in 1837.

Nor was freedom of religion preserved inviolate during this stormy period in our history. It was a fruitful time for zealous visionaries who believed they had discovered great religious truths and who went about converting others. Many of these bands suffered persecution, but none paid more for their convictions than the Mormons. The faithful of the Church of Jesus Christ of the Latter-day Saints were harassed from place to place until their leader and founder, Joseph

[6] 7 Peters 249.
[7] Jefferson's First Inaugural Address, March 4, 1801, Henry S. Commager, ed., *Documents of American History* (2nd edn., New York, 1940), I, 187.

Smith, was killed at Carthage, Illinois, in 1844, and they sought refuge beyond the boundaries of the United States.

After the trying years of declamation and denunciation over the slavery and sectional controversies, civil war brought renewed threats to civil liberties. Lincoln personally suspended the writ of habeas corpus. Suspected traitors or outspoken critics of the war policy were arrested without warrants, held in jails without charge, and released without trial. Editors opposed or lukewarm toward the war were fair bait for federal marshals or unruly crowds who wrecked newspaper plants. College campuses were not immune to the fever to stamp out dissent. At the commencement held by Cornell College in Iowa in 1863 a near riot took place when several students arrived wearing "Copperhead" badges—symbols of strong anti-Lincoln feeling. "One girl about 18 years old who had on a copperhead pin was assaulted by the loyal women present and a severe scuffle ensued, during which the girl aforesaid had her wearing apparel badly used up," a newspaper reported.[8] In these circumstances, a plea for the respect of individual rights was regarded as grounds for suspected treason.

Slavery was the issue that excited the most people, however. It was the status of the Negro that had stirred up the country from crisis to crisis and finally forced a civil war upon its people. Long before Appomattox it was obvious that the days of Negro serfdom were numbered. The problem confronting the North was: how should freedom for Negroes be made legal and binding? Amending the Constitution promised the most speedy and effective means. Between 1865 and 1870, therefore, the Thirteenth, Fourteenth, and Fifteenth amendments were ratified. They were designed to grant the Negro full citizenship with the right of suffrage, but the "privileges and immunities of citizens" mentioned in the Fourteenth Amendment were narrowly interpreted by the Supreme Court in the Slaughter House cases of 1873. Here the substantive

[8] *Iowa State Register*, Des Moines, July 8, 1863.

and procedural rights which form the heart of the Bill of Rights were not regarded by the high court as within the scope of a citizen's privileges and immunities. The court refused to construe the "privileges and immunities" clause as a means of erasing the distinction between state and national citizenship.[9] In effect, this left the states the authority to decide which citizens were first-class and which were not, and the result was a North-South demarcation for the Negroes' rights.

Ironically, Negroes were not involved in the Slaughter House cases or many other early court tests of the Fourteenth Amendment. In 1882 smooth-talking Roscoe Conkling went some distance toward convincing the court that framers of that amendment had been thinking of corporations as well as of persons.[10] In accepting this reasoning the Supreme Court gave the growing corporate enterprises a distinctive status, for industry and commerce were now able to come before the courts and claim protection under the "due process" clause.

Meanwhile, the status of the Negro remained in doubt until the monumental case of Plessy v. Ferguson, decided in 1896, when the Supreme Court put its stamp of approval on the concept of "separate but equal" facilities for whites and colored people. State-sanctioned segregation thus had the sugar-coating of one of the most powerful agencies of the federal government. The constricted interpretation of individual rights in the Slaughter House cases was buttressed by decisions in 1900 and 1908; for as late as 1907 Justice Harlan found himself in a minority when he suggested that free speech and a free press were rights protected by the "due process" clause of the Fourteenth Amendment.

Hemmed in by the verbiage of court decisions, civil rights suffered another jolt when the nation went to war in 1917.

[9] 16 Wallace 77-79.
[10] Carl B. Swisher, *American Constitutional Development* (Cambridge, Mass., 1943), 404-05. See also Andrew C. McLaughlin, "The Court, the Corporation, and Conkling," *American Historical Review*, 46 (1940), 56-57. However, McLaughlin says Conkling had assists other than his own eloquence.

A sedition act was passed by Congress and enforced "with a high degree of ruthlessness."[11] A wave of anti-German sentiment reached violent proportions. German-speaking preachers in some communities were forced to kiss publicly the flag. Many leaders of the Socialist Party, some with a German background, were jailed and denied their constitutional guarantees. As an outgrowth of these conditions, however, came one of the first moves that eventually gave the Bill of Rights some of the "teeth" its framers thought it had in 1791. In the decision on a case arising from the Espionage Act of 1917 Justice Holmes said that the proper test of the limits of such matters as free speech and a free press was to determine whether "the words used are used in such circumstances and are of such a nature as to create a clear and present danger that they will bring about the substantive evils that Congress has a right to prevent. It is a question of proximity and degree."[12] This formula was not accepted by the court as good law until 1940, but the ground for its eventual approval was staked out in 1919.[13]

A second move for implementing the Bill of Rights came early in the 1920's when the Supreme Court began to broaden the concepts of the privileges and immunities of citizenship covered by the Fourteenth Amendment. Then in the important case of Gitlow v. New York the high court declared that "we may and do assume that freedom of speech and of the press— which are protected by the First Amendment from abridgment by Congress—are among the fundamental personal rights and 'liberties' protected by the due process clause of the Fourteenth Amendment from impairment by the States."[14] Subsequent decisions brought all of the freedoms mentioned in the First Amendment under the protective cloak of the Fourteenth, and

[11] Swisher, *American Constitutional Development*, 97.
[12] Schenck *v.* United States, 249 U. S. 52.
[13] Edward S. Corwin, *The Constitution and What It Means Today* (11th edn., Princeton, 1954), 196-98.
[14] 268 U. S. 666.

these civil liberties were "at last effectively nationalized against state infringement."[15]

This did not mean, however, that all of the personal rights mentioned in the first ten amendments had moved into the states' realm of responsibility through the Fourteenth Amendment. Outside the First Amendment are the numerous procedural rights, and in 1937 the Supreme Court appeared to place these apart from those rights which are "of the very essence of a scheme of ordered liberty."[16] Only the First Amendment fitted this pattern. In a dissenting opinion given by Justice Black in 1947 this classification was attacked, with a warning to Black's colleagues: "To hold that this Court can determine what, if any, provisions of the Bill of Rights will be enforced, and if so to what degree, is to frustrate the great design of a written Constitution."[17] Although Justice Black and others have found in the historical background of the Fourteenth Amendment evidence that justifies the position that the first eight amendments were regarded as encompassing the privileges and immunities of citizenship, this view had not been accepted by a majority of the Supreme Court in early 1955.[18]

Generally speaking, the years following World War I have marked the greatest development of civil rights through legal protection—more specifically, Supreme Court decisions. There have been some other encouraging signs. Lynching, not confined to the southern states but most frequently practiced there, began to die out. The appearance of the Ku Klux Klan in many communities during the decade following World War I indicated that not every American was dedicated to the ideal of liberty and justice for all, but a wave of public revulsion

[15] Robert E. Cushman, *Leading Constitutional Decisions* (9th edn., New York, 1950), 113.

[16] Palko *v.* Connecticut, 302 U. S. 325.

[17] Adamson *v.* California, 332 U. S. 89.

[18] See Charles Fairman and Stanley Morrison, "Does the Fourteenth Amendment Incorporate the Bill of Rights? The Original Understanding [and] The Judicial Interpretation," *Stanford Law Review*, 2 (1949), 5-173.

soon caused the Klan to wither into ineffectiveness. During the period when federal agents sought to enforce the Eighteenth (Prohibition) Amendment, the Fourth and Fifth amendments became a refuge for bootleggers who contended that evidence used against them was sometimes obtained without search warrants and then used as incriminating material in courts.[19] Later decisions, made after the Eighteenth Amendment had been repealed, afforded federal agents more latitude in their pursuit of criminals.

The coming of World War II served to remind citizens that in times of crisis freedom sometimes becomes a tenuous thing. Shortly after the disaster at Pearl Harbor thousands of American citizens of Japanese descent were forced from their western homes and herded into relocation camps. Their civil rights were disregarded on the grounds that the public safety was involved. Wartime experience did help to break down the long-standing color barrier against Negroes, however. Segregation by state law had been struck a hard blow in a Supreme Court decision of 1938 that took a dim view of the "separate but equal" concept in state-supported higher education. Decisions in 1948 and 1950 went further in shattering the possibilities of segregation in public schools, and in disposing of a group of cases in 1954 Chief Justice Warren announced that segregation in grade and high schools was unconstitutional. In a unanimous voice the justices declared that to separate Negro children "from others of similar age and qualifications solely because of their race generates a feeling of inferiority as to their status in a community that may affect their hearts and minds in a way unlikely ever to be undone."[20] Not all state officials or citizens were ready to accept this decision, however, and its implementation appeared to be no easy task.

A problem of perhaps equal importance that grew some-

[19] Corwin, *The Constitution and What It Means Today*, 204-05.
[20] Brown v. Board of Education, 347 U. S. 494.

what grotesquely following World War II was the matter of internal security. With the growing power of the Soviet Union abroad, evidence came to light that certain Americans had betrayed their country because of an attachment to a foreign power or Marxian idealism. Riding the crest of a general wave of public indignation were certain elements bent on exploiting the situation. One manifestation was the use of a term which blended elements of the Bill of Rights into a metaphor mixed with Marxist tinges—the so-called "Fifth-Amendment communists"—persons who used the amendment's provisions to avoid self-incrimination. Of them Dean Erwin N. Griswold has said:

People have often been branded as Fifth-Amendment communists— from which the less thinking portions of the general public conclude at once that it has been established that they are conspiratorial treasonous communists, when there may be no evidence that they are communists at all. Their claim of privilege may in fact be largely a reflection on the kind of hearing to which they have been subjected, and thus in reality something which should bear heavily against those who are branding them as Fifth-Amendment communists.[21]

The growing power of the legislative investigating committee as a quasi-judicial body brought the problem into sharp focus. A chronicler of the times will some day note whether or not those who would chip away at the permanent values of the Bill of Rights in a moment of temporary excitement had triumphed.

The presumption, at least, is that they will not. The plain good sense of the American people has so far vindicated the hopes of the Revolutionary generation. To be sure, there were fewer public men inclined to speak out for strict observance of the Bill of Rights after World War II, and none made a clarion plea for freedom of expression as Jefferson did in 1801 when he said:

If there be any among us who would wish to dissolve this Union or to change its republican form, let them stand undisturbed as monu-

---

[21] Erwin N. Griswold, *The Fifth Amendment Today* (Cambridge, Mass., 1955), 69.

ments of the safety with which error of opinion may be tolerated where reason is left free to combat it.[22]

But the maxims of Justice Holmes and Judge Learned Hand have been a voice of conscience during certain American events of the mid-1950's.

At the middle of the twentieth century it was clear, as it had been in 1791, that the surest sanctuary of freedom for the citizen still was not in the Constitution or the Bill of Rights, but in the minds of the people. The simple language of the Bill of Rights expressed ideas which were universals to Madison, Jefferson, Mason, and their contemporaries. Not all of those ideas have weathered well. Gradually, the need to insure citizens the right to bear arms or the prohibition on quartering troops have become obsolete. But the provisions for freedom of speech, freedom of the press, freedom of religion, and the right of assembly have lost none of their vitality. Indeed, the judicial interpretations of the First Amendment have been so flexible that methods of expression undreamed of by the framers of the various bills of rights have been protected from infringement. As Gouverneur Morris and Jefferson foresaw, the courts have become the arm of government which protects citizens from the caprice of public opinion and the whimsical workings of legislatures. What they did not foresee was complete rejection of the eighteenth-century notion that government was at best a necessary evil which must be curbed to safeguard individual freedom. In the twentieth century the concept seems to be that government can be a positive force for good when it is dedicated to preserving the citizen's rights in a complex society which demands numerous governmental services.

Various external pressures and the changing character of the nation itself have doubtless caused the generations of Americans since the Revolution to modify the eighteenth-century

[22] First Inaugural Address, Commager, ed., *Documents of American History*, I, 187.

conception of the rights which the citizen possesses as inherent natural rights. Perhaps individual liberty has become a secondary concern, subordinate to the paramount issue of safety of the nation. It is quite likely that the great men of the Revolution would be extremely uncomfortable in such a climate of opinion, since they had risked their lives for the principle that individual freedom was the sine qua non of good government. However, they foresaw change, believing that in the Bill of Rights great standards of personal freedom had been established. Their hope was that an enlightened and responsible citizenry could uphold the enduring values of the Bill of Rights regardless of the circumstances.

Appendix A

THE VIRGINIA DECLARATION OF RIGHTS
(Adopted June 12, 1776)[1]

A DECLARATION *of* RIGHTS *made by the representatives of the good people of* Virginia, *assembled in full and free Convention; which rights do pertain to them, and their posterity, as the basis and foundation of government.*

1. That all men are by nature equally free and independent, and have certain inherent rights, of which, when they enter into a state of society, they cannot, by any compact, deprive or divest their posterity; namely, the enjoyment of life and liberty, with the means of acquiring and possessing property, and pursuing and obtaining happiness and safety.

2. That all power is vested in, and consequently derived from, the people; that magistrates are their trustees and servants, and at all times amenable to them.

3. That government is, or ought to be, instituted for the common benefit, protection, and security, of the people, nation, or community, of all the various modes and forms of government that is best, which is capable of producing the greatest degree of happiness and safety, and is most effectually secured against the danger of mal-administration; and that whenever any government shall be found inadequate or contrary to these purposes, a majority of the community hath an indubitable, unalienable, and indefeasible right, to reform, alter, or abolish it, in such manner as shall be judged most conducive to the publick weal.

4. That no man, or set of men, are entitled to exclusive or separate emoluments or privileges from the community, but in consideration of publick services; which, not being descendible, neither ought the offices of magistrate, legislator, or judge, to be hereditary.

5. That the legislative and executive powers of the state should be separate and distinct from the judiciary; and, that the members of the two first may be restrained from oppression, by feeling and participating

[1] *Ordinances Passed at General Convention . . . of Virginia, . . . in the City of Williamsburg, on Monday the 6th of May, Anno Dom: 1776* (Williamsburg, [1776]), 100-03.

the burthens of the people, they should, at fixed periods, be reduced to a private station, return into that body from which they were originally taken, and the vacancies be supplied by frequent, certain, and regular elections, in which all, or any part of the former members, to be again eligible, or ineligible, as the laws shall direct.

6. That elections of members to serve as representatives of the people, in assembly, ought to be free; and that all men, having sufficient evidence of permanent common interest with, and attachment to, the community, have the right of suffrage, and cannot be taxed or deprived of their property for publick uses without their own consent, or that of their representatives so elected, nor bound by any law to which they have not, in like manner, assented for the publick good.

7. That all power of suspending laws, or the execution of laws, by any authority without consent of the representatives of the people, is injurious to their rights, and ought not to be exercised.

8. That in all capital or criminal prosecutions a man hath a right to demand the cause and nature of his accusation, to be confronted with the accusers and witnesses, to call for evidence in his favour, and to a speedy trial by an impartial jury of his vicinage, without whose unanimous consent he cannot be found guilty, nor can he be compelled to give evidence against himself; that no man be deprived of his liberty except by the law of the land, or the judgment of his peers.

9. That excessive bail ought not to be required, nor excessive fines imposed, nor cruel and unusual punishments inflicted.

10. That general warrants, whereby any officer or messenger may be commanded to search suspected places without evidence of a fact committed, or to seize any person or persons not named, or whose offence is not particularly described and supported by evidence, are grevious and oppressive, and ought not to be granted.

11. That in controversies respecting property, and in suits between man and man, the ancient trial by jury is preferable to any other, and ought to be held sacred.

12. That the freedom of the press is one of the great bulwarks of liberty, and can never be restrained but by despotick governments.

13. That a well regulated militia, composed of the body of the people, trained to arms, is the proper, natural, and safe defence of a free state; that standing armies, in time of peace, should be avoided, as dangerous to liberty; and that, in all cases, the military should be under strict subordination to, and governed by, the civil power.

14. That the people have a right to uniform government; and therefore, that no government separate from, or independent of, the

government of *Virginia,* ought to be erected or established within the limits thereof.

15. That no free government, or the blessings of liberty, can be preserved to any people but by a firm adherence to justice, moderation, temperance, frugality, and virtue, and by frequent recurrence to fundamental principles.

16. That religion, or the duty which we owe to our CREATOR, and the manner of discharging it, can be directed only by reason and conviction, not by force or violence; and therefore all men are equally entitled to the free exercise of religion, according to the dictates of conscience; and that it is the mutual duty of all to practise Christian forbearance, love, and charity, towards each other.

Appendix B

THE FEDERAL BILL OF RIGHTS[1]

(Proclaimed December 15, 1791)[2]

ARTICLE I

Congress shall make no law respecting an establishment of religion, or prohibiting the free exercise thereof; or abridging the freedom of speech, or of the press; or the right of the people peaceably to assemble, and to petition the Government for a redress of grievance.

ARTICLE II

A well-regulated Militia being necessary to the security of a free

---

[1] The Bill of Rights consists of III through XII of the amendments sent to the states by the First Congress. The rejected articles were:

Article I

After the first enumeration required by the first Article of the Constitution, there shall be one Representative for every thirty thousand, until the number shall amount to one hundred, after which, the proportion shall be so regulated by Congress, that there shall be not less than one hundred Representatives, nor less than one representative for every forty thousand persons, until the number of Representatives shall amount to two hundred, after which the proportion shall be so regulated by Congress, that there shall not be less than two hundred representatives, nor more than one Representative for every fifty thousand persons.

Article II

No law, varying the compensation for the services of the Senators and Representatives, shall take effect, until an election of Representatives shall have intervened.

[2] *Documentary History of the Constitution,* II, 321-24.

State, the right of the people to keep and bear Arms shall not be infringed.

ARTICLE III

No soldier shall, in time of peace be quartered in any house, without the consent of the Owner, nor in time of war, but in a manner to be prescribed by law.

ARTICLE IV

The right of the people to be secure in their persons, houses, papers, and effects, against unreasonable searches and seizures, shall not be violated, and no Warrants shall issue, but upon probable cause, supported by Oath or affirmation, and particularly describing the place to be searched, and the person or things to be seized.

ARTICLE V

No person shall be held to answer for a capital, or otherwise infamous crime, unless on a presentment or indictment of a Grand Jury, except in cases arising in the land or naval forces, or in the Militia, when in actual service in time of War or public danger; nor shall any person be subject for the same offense to be twice put in jeopardy of life or limb; nor shall be compelled in any criminal case to be a witness against himself, nor be deprived of life, liberty, or property, without due process of law; nor shall private property be taken for public use, without just compensation.

ARTICLE VI

In all criminal prosecutions, the accused shall enjoy the right to a speedy and public trial, by an impartial jury of the State and district wherein the crime shall have been committed, which district shall have been previously ascertained by law, and to be informed of the nature and cause of the accusation; to be confronted with the witness against him; to have compulsory process for obtaining witnesses in his favor, and to have the Assistance of Counsel for his defense.

ARTICLE VII

In Suits at common law, where the value in controversy shall exceed twenty dollars, the right of trial by jury shall be preserved, and no fact tried by a jury, shall be otherwise re-examined in any Court of the United States, than according to the rules of the common law.

ARTICLE VIII

Excessive bail shall not be required, nor excessive fines imposed, nor cruel and unusual punishments inflicted.

ARTICLE IX

The enumeration in the Constitution, of certain rights, shall not be construed to deny or disparage others retained by the people.

ARTICLE X

The powers not delegated to the United States by the Constitution, nor prohibited by it to the States, are reserved to the States respectively, or to the people.

INDEX